Meaning,
Basic Self-Knowledge,
and Mind

CSLI Lecture Notes
Number 132

Meaning,
Basic Self-Knowledge,
and Mind

Essays on Tyler Burge

edited by
María J. Frápolli
Esther Romero

CSLI
PUBLICATIONS

Center for the Study of
Language and Information
Stanford, California

Library of Congress Cataloging-in-Publication Data

Meaning, basic self-knowledge, and mind : essays on Tyler Burge /
edited by María J. Frápolli and Esther Romero.
p.   cm. – (CSLI lecture notes ; no. 132)
Includes bibliographical references and index.

ISBN 1-57586-347-2 (alk. paper)
ISBN 1-57586-346-4 (pbk. : alk. paper)

1. Burge, Tyler.
I. Frápolli, María J., 1960–
II. Romero, Esther.
III. Series.
B945.B7684M42   2003
191–dc21   2003005222

∞ The acid-free paper used in this book meets the minimum requirements of the American National Standard for Information Sciences—Permanence of Paper for Printed Library Materials, ANSI Z39.48-1984.

CSLI was founded in 1983 by researchers from Stanford University, SRI International, and Xerox PARC to further the research and development of integrated theories of language, information, and computation. CSLI headquarters and CSLI Publications are located on the campus of Stanford University.

CSLI Publications reports new developments in the study of language, information, and computation. In addition to lecture notes, our publications include monographs, working papers, revised dissertations, and conference proceedings. Our aim is to make new results, ideas, and approaches available as quickly as possible. Please visit our web site at
http://cslipublications.stanford.edu/
for comments on this and other titles, as well as for changes and corrections by the author and publisher.

Contents

v

Contributors

MARTIN DAVIES: Australian National University, Research School of Social Sciences, Canberra ACT 0200 (Australia)
martin.davies@anu.edu.au

STEVEN DAVIS: Philosophy Department, Simon Fraser University, BURNABY, B.C. V5A 1S6, (U.S.A.)
sdavis@sfu.ca

MARÍA JOSÉ FRÁPOLLI SANZ: Departamento de Filosofía, Universidad de Granada, 18011 Granada, (SPAIN)
frapolli@ugr.es

CHRISTOPHER GAUKER: Department of Philosophy, University of Cincinnati, P. O. Box 210374, Cincinnati, OH 45221-0374, (U.S.A.)
christopher.gauker@uc.edu

ANTONI GOMILA BENEJAM: Departamento de Historia y Filosofía de la Ciencia, la Educación y el Lenguaje, Universidad de Las Islas Baleares, Carretera de Valldemossa, Km. 7.5, 07071 Palma de Mallorca, (Spain)
vdpsagb0@uib.es

TOBIES GRIMALTÓS: Departament de Metafísica i Teoria del Coneixement, Universitat de València, Avda. Blasco Ibáñez, 21, 46010 València, (Spain)
Tobies.Grimaltos@uv.es

MANUEL LIZ: Facultad de Filosofía, Universidad de la Laguna, Santa Cruz de Tenerife, (Spain)
manuliz@ull.es

CARLOS MOYA: Departamento de Metafísica y Teoría del Conocimiento, Universidad de Valencia, 46080 Valencia, (Spain)
Carlos.Moya@uv.es

DANIEL QUESADA: Universitat Autònoma de Barcelona, Edif.B, Departamento de Filosofía, Bellaterra, 08193 Barcelona, (Spain)
daniel.quesada@uab.es

JORGE RODRÍGUEZ MARQUEZE: Departamento de Filosofía, Universidad de Oviedo, Campus de Humanidades, 33011 Oviedo, (Spain)
jorge@pinon.ccu.uniovi.es

ESTHER ROMERO GONZÁLEZ: Departamento de Filosofía, Universidad de Granada, 18011 Granada , (Spain)
eromero@ugr.es

STUART SILVERS: Clemson University, North Carolina, (U.S.A.)
sstuart@clemson.edu

Preface and Acknowledgments

The papers included in this volume have been written in honor of Tyler Burge. Most of them were presented at the *VIII Seminario Interuniversitario de Filosofía y Ciencia Cognitiva: Primera Persona, Otras Mentes e Interlocución* which took place at the Department of Philosophy in the University of Granada (Spain), during 23-25 May 1996. There are also three papers, those written by Christopher Gauker, Martin Davies and Steven Davis, which have been requested as an invitation to participate in this project.

According to the title of the Seminar, the papers deal with Burge's externalism and its implications to the philosophy of language and of mind, and with the epistemological problems derived from anti-individualism and the first person. We have organized the papers into three sections. Section I, "Meaning", includes the contributions whose main topic fall into questions related with meanings, terms and linguistic communication. Section II, "Basic Self-knowledge", includes the works dealing with the epistemological difficulties raised by anti-individualism, together with our intuitions about the privileged access that everybody has to the content of some of his/her mental states. Section III, "Mind", gathers together the contributions on the status of concepts, the nature of the mental, and the implications of Burge's positions to the central questions in the philosophy of mind. Finally, we include the replies that Tyler Burge has elaborated for each paper.

The *VIII Seminario Interuniversitario de Filosofía y Ciencia Cognitiva* has been possible thanks to the financial support of the *General Management of Research* of Granada University. We are also grateful to the Department of Philosophy and to our colleagues of the Field of Logic and Philosophy of Science for their generous help. Among them, we would like to mention Juan J. Acero, former teacher and present colleague and friend, for his steady support and advice. We are in debt to Francesc Camós and Neftalí Villanueva for their invaluable help in preparing the manuscript, without which this volume would not have seen the light. Our gratitude also goes to Dikran Karagueuzian and the rest of editors of CSLI have proved their competence and patience during the process of publication of the volume. And, especially, we are deeply indebted to Professor Tyler Burge for his kindness during his stay among us, and his generosity and help at any moment. To all of them, people and institutions, our acknowledgement.

María J. Frápolli and Esther Romero

1

Social Externalism and Linguistic Communication

CHRISTOPHER GAUKER

1 Introduction

Many philosophers and linguists would characterize the process of linguistic communication as follows: When a speaker has a belief with a certain content and intends a hearer to recognize that he or she has a belief with that content, the speaker searches for words that, in light of semantic conventions and the context of utterance, will enable the hearer to recognize that speaker has that belief. Upon finding words that the speaker thinks will have that result, the speaker speaks those words and, if communication is successful, the hearer infers that the speaker has a belief with the content in question. Call this conception of communication the *expressive theory of communication.*

The viability of the expressive theory of communication will depend on whether we can make good sense of the pertinent concept of *content.* One way to refute the expressive theory would be to show that we couldn't understand the pertinent notion of content apart from an independent understanding of linguistic communication. My purpose in this paper is to argue that Tyler Burge's social externalism leads to just such a refutation of the expressive theory of communication. Roughly, if the very content of a person's thought is relative to the way words are used in his or her linguistic community, then we cannot turn around and ex-

Meaning, Basic Self-Knowledge and Mind: Essays on Tyler Burge.
María J. Frápolli and Esther Romero (eds.).
Copyright © 2003, CSLI Publications.

plain the way words are used by saying that the function of words is to convey the contents of thoughts.

Here I will not undertake a defense of Burge's social externalism, although I will explain what I think it means. (For my defense of it, see my 1987, 1991 and 1994, ch. 3.) My purpose is just to explain why social externalism really does require the rejection of the expressive theory of communication. For various reasons, one might imagine that the incompatibility is merely apparent—that it will disappear if only we are careful to draw certain distinctions. I will argue that no, the incompatibility is very real. I will close with a question for Prof. Burge, who does not seem to agree that his most famous idea has this important consequence.

2 The expressive theory

To begin, I should explain in more detail what I mean by *the expressive theory of communication* and the role that the concept of content is supposed to play in it. In brief, the expressive theory states that the primary function of language is to enable speakers to convey the contents of their beliefs to hearers. An expressivist would think that the exercise of this primary function may be illustrated by examples such as this: If I believe that there is poison ivy in the backyard and I believe that you do not know that, and I believe it would be useful for you to know that, then I might say "There is poison ivy in the backyard", intending that you will at least infer that I believe there is poison ivy in the backyard and expecting perhaps also that you will go on to infer that there is poison ivy in the backyard from the fact that I believe it.

An expressivist does not have to hold that speakers intend to convey the content of their thoughts to hearers every time they speak, or even that this is the case more often than not. Of course there are also commands, requests, questions, lies, jokes and poems. The point is only that the semantic rules of language are primarily designed to allow this conveying of content to happen. (Here I use the term *semantic rule* in a broad sense to include what some would call *pragmatic rules*.) I am content to define expressivism as the thesis that the primary function of language is to convey the contents of beliefs, because this is how many philosophers and linguists would explain specifically the *informative uses* of language, and I think that these philosophers and linguists would also maintain that the informative uses are those that above all give shape to language. However, I could just as well define expressivism as merely the thesis that the *informative* uses of language are those in which the speaker intends to convey the content of his or her thought to a hearer, because I think that Burge's social externalism entails the rejection of even this much. The most dubious aspect of the expressive theory is not its claim that the informative use is primary but the claim that intentions to convey a content normally underlie the informative uses.

Expressivism, as I propose to define it, holds that the end result of successfully conveying the content of a belief is that the hearer recognizes that the speaker has a belief having that content. Alternatively, the end result of successfully conveying a content might be taken to be that the hearer actually forms a belief with the content in question. The former definition is intended to capture those episodes of speech in which the speaker does not succeed in actually persuading the hearer and also those episodes in which the content the speaker intends to convey is the content of a belief that the hearer already possesses. Whichever way the expressivist defines the end result of successfully conveying a content, the expressivist must allow that speakers often fail to achieve this result.

The process by which this end result is achieved is supposed to be one in which the speaker chooses words on the basis of the semantic rules of the language in light of the situation that the interlocutors are actually in and in which the hearer recognizes the content of the speaker's belief on the basis of the words spoken, the situation and the semantic rules. These semantic rules are rules that in some way guide the speaker's choice of words, and thus they go beyond a mere assignment of literal meaning to the sentences of the language. They may make reference not only to the content the speaker wishes to convey and the conventional meanings of words but also to certain parameters constituting the context of utterance. For instance, in choosing to speak sentences containing quantifiers, such as "all" or "some", and in interpreting such sentences, we must take into account the *domain of discourse*. The values of these other parameters, constituting the context of utterance, may be constrained by further semantic rules in light of the character of the situation in which the conversation takes place. (It is these rules that are sometimes dubbed *pragmatic*.) The rules that constrain their values will often fail to pick out a definite value, and to this extent speaker and hearer may be left to their own creative devices.

Given that the speaker intends the hearer to recognize that the speaker has a thought with a certain content, the speaker's objective has to be to choose words in such a way that in light of the conventional meanings of the words spoken, the external situation and the presumption that the speaker is conforming to the semantic rules of the language, the hearer can recognize that the speaker has a thought with that content. If the speaker chooses well, then insofar as the hearer shares with the speaker an understanding of the semantic rules and an acquaintance with the external situation, the hearer may indeed be able to do this. If the speaker makes a poor choice, there will be a disparity (or only an accidental congruence) between the content that the speaker intended the hearer to recognize as the content he or she intended to convey and the content that the hearer comes to think of as the content the speaker intended to convey.

The concept of content is crucial to the expressive theory of communication. Without it the expressive theory would come to little more than this: Something happens in the mind of the speaker, which causes the speaker to make some sounds; the hearer hears these sounds and then something happens in the mind of the hearer. Such a vacuous theory would not be worth mentioning except that those who would defend the expressive theory against my refutation often wind up defending nothing more than this. If we want to explain linguistic communication in terms of what happens in the minds of interlocutors, then we have to specify the relation between what happens in the mind of the speaker and what is supposed to happen (when the primary function of language is successfully exercised) in the mind of the hearer. The expressivist describes that relation in terms of *content*. The content of the belief that the speaker intends the hearer to attribute to him or her has to be *the same* as the content of the belief that the hearer attributes to the speaker as a result of the speaker's act of speech.

Likewise, the expressive theory of communication is distorted if we lose track of the fact that the pertinent notion of content is supposed to be one that plays specifically this role as what speaker and hearer share when the primary function of language is successfully exercised. This is easy to do since in fact there are several other notions of content at play in the philosophical literature. One of these is the *epistemological* notion of content. Here the content of a belief is identified in terms of the contents of the beliefs, perceptions and circumstances that justify it and the beliefs and actions that it in turn justifies. Another, closely related notion is the *folk psychological* notion of content. Here the content of a thought is supposed to be identified in terms of its causal/explanatory relations to perceptions, actions and other thoughts. Beyond these, there are various *semantic* notions of content. For instance, there is the notion of content as what intertranslatable sentences from different languages have in common. This concept of content, in the guise of *literal meaning*, may play a role in the expressive theory of communication, but it is not the same as the concept of content as that which is conveyed. Also, if we want to explain how the truth value of a sentence is a function of the reference of its several components, we might want to introduce a notion of content such that we can say that the referents of "that"-clauses, such as "that Ortcutt is a spy" in "Ralph believes that Ortcutt is a spy", are the normal contents of the sentences that follow the word "that". For each of these notions of content there will be a corresponding notion of *concepts*. Basically, a concept is a component, or aspect, of a content, which stands to the whole content as a word or phrase stands to a sentence.

The confusion of the expressivist's proprietary notion of content with these others can have the result that essentially vacuous claims are put forward as if they actually meant something. It sometimes happens that a theorist displays in various ways commitment to the expressivist framework (for instance, in the conception of semantic rules that he or she espouses) but then declares that it is not to be expected, even in cases of successful communication, that the content of the belief that speaker intends to convey will match the content of the belief that the hearer ends up attributing to the speaker (e. g., Bezuidenhout 1997). Such theories are not contradictory, because the concept of content thus employed can derive content from its engagement in issues other than the nature of linguistic communication. While not contradictory, such a theory of communication is liable to be vacuous unless the theorist can explain what relation has to obtain between the content that the speaker intends to convey and the content that the hearer attributes to the speaker other than to say that they must be similar in some way. But if the theorist can tell us what relation has to obtain between the content that the speaker intends to convey and the content that the hearer attributes to the speaker in order for communication to be successful, then we can use that relation to define a kind of content that must be the *same* between speaker and hearer when communication is successful: Two thoughts will have *the very same content* in the proprietary sense if and only if their contents in the nonproprietary sense bear that relation to one another. (This sameness will be an equivalence relation provided the theory provides for the assumption that if A communicates something to B then B can communicate the same back to A and can communicate the same to a third party C.)

It should be evident, then, that the expressive theory of communication requires a serious theory of the nature of thought content. That does not mean that one is not justified in adopting an expressivist theory of communication without first developing a viable theory of content.   It does mean that if we can show that something stands in the way of developing such a theory of content, then that is a good reason to reject the expressive theory.

3   The content of social externalism

What I get out of Burge's 1979 paper, "Individualism and the Mental", is the following conclusion, which I call *social externalism*:   The very content of a person's thought is relative to the way words are used in the surrounding linguistic community.   In Burge's own formulation it is the claim that the content of a person's thought is attributable in part to the character of the person's social environment quite apart from the ways in which that social environment might have affected the person's internal physical states (1979, 79).   In this section, I want to say just enough about the reasons to believe this to bring out the fact that the notion of content at issue is the notion of content in terms of which the expressivist would explain linguistic communication, and to show that the pertinent variable really is the way words are used.

First, I should point out in advance that the upshot of my argument in this paper will be that social externalism, formulated as a thesis about mental content, is strictly speaking false, because the mental content it posits does not exist.   This is not to say that there is nothing right about it.   The commitment to mental content could be removed by reformulating social externalism as a thesis about the proper interpretation of a person's words.   For two reasons I formulate it here as a thesis about mental content.   First, my reductio on expressivism will require the assumption that if there were such a thing as content in the expressivist's proprietary sense, then social externalism would be true of it.   Second, the arguments for social externalism formulated as anything other than a thesis about content (e.g., as a thesis about the proper interpretation of words) would inevitably have to pass through the formulation as a thesis about content, because the opponent we have to argue against is inevitably someone who believes in content in the expressivist's sense.   So for the remainder of this section I will play along with the expressive theory of communication with respect to its postulation of mental content.

What persuades me that Burge's social externalism is true (under the assumption that there is such a thing as content in the pertinent sense) is that we must suppose it to be true in order to understand the possibility of linguistic communication in a community exhibiting a division of epistemic labor.   In such a community, every member stands ready to acknowledge that he or she may be mistaken in judging that a given object, event, or state of affairs is an instance of a given type if that type is a type regarding which other members of the community qualify as experts. Still, in such a community, those who are nonexperts in a certain area have to be permitted to use the vocabulary of the experts. For instance, they have to be able to use it in taking instruction from the experts and in collaborating with the experts. Moreover, when they use it, it will normally have to be understood as meaning the same thing that it means when the experts use it. If we adopt the expressive theory of communication, this means that those who use it will normally have to be understood as intending to convey the same content that the experts would intend to convey by means of it.

For instance, imagine Gus, who has a problem with his car. Sometimes when he presses on the accelerator the car feels a little bit sluggish, especially when going up hills. He takes his car to his auto mechanic, suspecting this might be a symptom of something more serious. The laconic mechanic simply tells him that he should try using "high octane gasoline". Gus asks no questions, but the next time he needs gas, he drives up to the full service island at the filling station and says to the attendant, "My car needs high octane gasoline; so fill 'er up with that". As a matter of fact, Gus suffers from misconceptions about high-octane gasoline. He does not know that the octane rating is a measure of the degree to which the gasoline resists engine knocking. He thinks high-octane gasoline is more powerful gasoline that will make any car accelerate faster. Still, what he is asking for is high-octane gasoline, and that is exactly what the attendant should put in his fuel tank. In other words, the content of Gus's belief about his car (considered as what he intends to conveys in words) literally contains the concept *high-octane gasoline*. It would be a mistake to say that the concept that his belief contains is really just *extra powerful gasoline*. If that is what he has in mind and the attendant is not ignorant of this, then the attendant's reply to his request should be simply, "We don't have any". Typically the attendant would not have such insight into Gus's mind, but we should not have to suppose that the beneficial effects of the division of epistemic labor depend on such ignorance.

Thus, we find that in order to render intelligible the division of epistemic labor within the context of the expressive theory of communication, we have to suppose that the contents of the thoughts that people intend to convey by means of words stemming from regions of discourse in which they are not experts are determined not only by what they themselves know but also by the discourse of the experts. There are various places to try to wriggle out of this conclusion. Elsewhere (1991;

1994, ch. 3), I have put my foot down on all of those that I am aware of. It might be said that Gus, in saying "My car needs high octane gasoline", is merely paraphrasing his mechanic's words; but that is not right, since the division of epistemic labor must allow for a certain amount of creativity in the nonexpert's use of a term. Or one might try to define various concepts of content in such a way that which content a person has in mind will depend only what is going on within that person's own head; but then it will turn out that those kinds of content cannot plausibly be what is conveyed in linguistic communication. I will not take up these issues here. Again, the reason I am going this far into the argument for social externalism is just that I want to emphasize that the notion of content at issue is precisely that which the expressivist supposes is conveyed in linguistic communication. That is evident from the fact that the question has been what the content of people's thoughts must be if the conveying of thoughts by means of language is to support a division of epistemic labor.

The way in which content is relative to the way words are used in the surrounding community can be dramatized by imagining alternative possible worlds. Imagine a world much like our world but in which what fuel experts call "high octane gasoline" is not (or not just) gasoline that resists knocking, but is actually gasoline that makes cars (in general) accelerate faster. We do not have a word in English for that kind of gasoline, but we can make one up. Call it "high schmoctane gasoline". Imagine that such a world contains a person who, with respect to his internal physical structure, is exactly like Gus. We will call him "Russ", although people in his world call him "Gus". If we confine our attention to things going on at and beneath the surfaces of their bodies, then we will find no physical difference between Gus and Russ at all. So the differences between their worlds have not *made* any difference to what has gone on inside their bodies. Just as we should interpret Gus as literally asking for high-octane gasoline, we should interpret Russ as literally asking for high schmoctane gasoline. More precisely, the content of Gus's thought contains the concept *high-octane gasoline*, while the content of Russ's thought contains the concept *high schmoctane gasoline*. But the relevant difference between their worlds is just that the relevant experts in Gus's community use the expression "high octane gasoline" in one way, and the relevant experts in Russ's community use the expression "high octane gasoline" in a different way. So we should conclude that thought content is relative to the way words are used in the surrounding linguistic community.

In view of present purposes, it is important to make sure that the source of the difference between the contents of Gus's and Russ's thoughts really is the way words are used and not something else. There are indeed several differences between Gus's and Russ's worlds. The thoughts of the manufacturers of gasoline in Gus's world differ in content from the thoughts of the manufacturers of gasoline in Russ's world. Further, there are different substances in the gas tanks beneath the asphalt at the filling stations. Nonetheless, as I will now explain, the contents of Gus's and Russ's thoughts are relative to the *way words are used* and not to these other things.

As for the differences between the contents of the thoughts of the relevant experts, we cannot attribute the difference between the contents of Gus's and Russ's thought to these, because the content of these experts' thoughts is likewise relative. It is an oversimplification to suppose that in a society exhibiting a division of epistemic labor there will be for each kind of thing an expert who knows all of the essential properties of that kind. Just as the content of the thought that a nonexpert expresses by means of a word depends on the uses that the experts make of that word, so too the content that a given expert expresses by means of a word depends on the uses that the other experts make of it. (For present purposes "expert" does not mean someone empowered to semantically legislate, but only someone who *knows better*.) There may be thought contents the possession of which is not relative to anything in the social constitution of a thinker's environment (I doubt it, but for present purposes I need not deny it), but those thought contents that depend on the experts' uses of terms are not of that kind, not even when they are the contents of the thoughts of an expert. So if we said that the content of the thought that a nonexpert conveys by means of a term is relative to the experts' thought contents, then we would have to say that the experts' thought contents were relative to other experts' thought contents in the same way. We would not have identified anything that can be characterized independently that we could say thought content is relative to. For purposes of developing a fundamental theory of thought content, then, it is necessary to formulate the relativization as a relativization to the way the local experts use the term.

As for the differences in distribution of chemical kinds, that cannot be not what Gus's and Russ's thought contents are relative to, because we could tell the story differently, so that there were no such differences. (Suppose that in both worlds both high octane and high schmoctane gasoline are available at normal gas stations. A virtue of Burge's original "arthritis" example was that the pertinent counterfactual did not suggest a different distribution of the pertinent pathologies between the actual and counterfactual situations.) However the objection might be deepened in a manner that meets this response by drawing on a certain common conception of the meaning of natural kind terms. Many philosophers, following Kripke and Putnam, suppose that the history of a term is relevant to its meaning. A term is introduced into the language via some kind of effect that the thing denoted has on those speakers who introduce it, and this process of introduction, as well as subsequent history, differentiates the meaning of the term from the meanings of other terms that have different histories. (In the simplest case, we might imagine that a speaker baptizes a substance with a term, declaring, "I hereby dub thee 'high octane gasoline'!") It might be argued that if the content of the thought that Gus expresses with "high octane gasoline" is different from the content of the thought that Russ expresses with those words, then what makes the difference is not the difference in expert usage between their worlds but the different histories of the expression in their worlds. (Steven Davis (1997) has made precisely this proposal in connection with a different example.)

There are indeed some reasons to be persuaded by this. First, it is tempting to think of a natural kind term as the proper name for a stuff or a condition (such as a disease), and it does seem that history plays a part in the reference of proper names. Thus, if in world 1 the name "Gödel" derives from the name of a man who proved the incompleteness of arithmetic and in world 2 it derives from someone else (not Gödel in fact) who is falsely credited with proving the incompleteness of arithmetic, then even if current dispositions with respect to the name "Gödel" are the same in the two worlds, we might wish to say that the name "Gödel" has a different meaning in the two worlds. Second, we wish to allow that formally contrary opinions about natural kinds may have a common subject matter. Thus Newton and Einstein were both talking about *mass*, though Newton said it was conserved and Einstein denied it. Only thus is it possible to construe changes in opinion as discoveries concerning kinds that people were previously acquainted with. Nonetheless, I do not think that in the cases that concern us the difference in content between two thinkers can be entirely traced to a difference in the histories of their terms in such a way as to exclude the relevance of difference in current usage.

The way for me to show this is to clarify what I mean by *the way words are used*. We want to define this broadly enough to include much more than the actual course of events in the world (including all of the linguistic events). We do not need to include all that might be said in world histories that are essentially impossible. However, we will wish to include those possible world histories in which people rather like ourselves, speaking a language that we would recognize as the language in question, react to events that are plausible eventualities in the world as we know it. If the way words are used is defined in this way, and not more narrowly, then I think no one will suggest that the history of a natural kind term makes a difference to its meaning without making a difference to the way words are used.

Imagine two worlds that contain exactly the same natural kinds. Suppose also that the two worlds have arrived at exactly the same arrangements of matter, albeit as a result of different histories. The people in world 1 use the word "gold" in just the way the people in world 2 use it. Moreover, there is no discovery that the people in world 1 might make that the people in world 2 might not make as well; and hence there is no usage contingent upon such a discovery in world 1 that is not equally a prospect in world 2. However at an earlier stage in the histories of these worlds, the usage of the word "gold" in world 1 differed from the usage of "gold" in world 2 in such a way that the actual extension of "gold" in world 1 was broader than the actual extension of "gold" in world 2. I do not think this difference entails that at the later stage the word "gold" means anything different in world 1 from what it means in world 2. For instance, I do not think that it would be true to say in the language of the people in world 1 at the later stage that their forebears would have been mistaken in calling, say, platinum "gold" unless it is likewise true to say in the language of the people of world 2 that their forebears would have been mistaken to call platinum "gold". What leads people to think that the actual constitution of the local environment is a component of meaning above and beyond actual usage is that they define current usage narrowly, in such a way that it does not incorporate the ways words will be used as a result of the discoveries that might ultimately be made about the actual constitution of the local environment.

4 Concessions on both sides

The objection to expressivism must not be formulated as simply the claim that content *depends* on language. The expressivist can certainly allow that in many ways the contents to be conveyed in language in turn *depend* on language. Nor can the antithesis to expressivism be formulated as simply the claim that words do not express thoughts. The antiexpressivist can certainly allow that in some sense words express thoughts.

4.1 What the expressivist can allow

The expressivist can allow that thought content depends on language in at least all of the following ways:

• What we think is largely what other people tell us.

• Some of the things that there are to think about are themselves linguistic entities. For example, thoughts about words depend on language. So do thoughts about books.

• Some of the things that there are to think about, though not themselves linguistic entities, have a nature intimately bound up with language. An example would be Wednesdays. So a thought about a Wednesday appointment would be a thought that depended on language. Another example might be civil laws.

• There may be some thoughts that it would be very difficult for a person to hold in mind without the help of a linguistic image (a visual image of writing or an auditory image of sounds). An example might be thoughts of differential equations. Likewise, certain inferences might be difficult if we could not use linguistic expressions as representatives for the thoughts that they express.

• Children, and even adults, may acquire certain concepts only as a result of trying to understand the contents of the beliefs that others intend to convey in words. For instance, the only reason a child acquires the concept *chair*, as opposed to other similar concepts, such as *seat* or *furniture-that-people-sit-on*, may be that this is the concept that others apparently intend to convey by means of the word "chair".

• Another aspect of the process of concept acquisition may be experimentation in the use of words. For instance, a person who is uncertain what concept pertaining to people is supposed to be conveyed by the term "geek" might try using it in a sentence or two and seeing if hearers act as though they understand.

• Insofar as language facilitates science as a collective activity and science invents concepts corresponding to the natural kinds that it discovers, language facilitates the conceptualization of natural kinds.

The expressivist may maintain that people use words in the way they do because the primary function of language is to enable speakers to convey the content of their beliefs to hearers and yet, without introducing any circularity, may allow that in all of these ways the contents of people's thoughts depend on language. In each case, language is cited as a factor in explaining how thoughts with a certain content are formed or how there can be a certain sort of thing to think about. In none of these cases, is language cited as a factor in our account of what the thought's having a certain content actually consists in. In each case, we can allow that what thoughts a person thinks depends on language in the manner described while denying that a thought's having a certain content is in part a matter of words being used in a certain way in the surrounding linguistic community.

The threat to expressivism is only that we will have to appeal to the way words are used in explaining what it is for a person's thought to have the sort of content that the expressivist wishes to appeal to in explaining how words are used. Some of the dependencies listed above may ultimately be problematic for the expressivist insofar as contemplation of them may lead us to recognize the dependency of the very nature of content on the way words are used in the surrounding linguistic community. For instance, we might realize that whether a person is really thinking about Wednesdays or Schmednesdays depends on how words are used in the surrounding linguistic community. But then the problem is that we cannot explain what it is for a thought to have a certain content apart from the way words are used in the surrounding linguistic community; it is not that Wednesdays are entities in some sense constituted by language.

4.2 What the antiexpressivist can allow

The antiexpressivist need not deny that people sometimes choose their words with the specific intent of instilling a certain mental state in another. What the antiexpressivist denies is only that the primary function of informative uses of language is to enable speakers to convey the content of their thoughts to hearers. This is not the same thing because an act of instilling a mental state may not be conceived as a matter of the speaker's choosing words in order to enable the hearer to recognize the content of his or her thought and, more importantly, because the intention to instill a specific mental state may not at all be the normal case. Further, the antiexpressivist need not deny that people usually speak *on purpose*, although the antiexpressivist may doubt whether their usual purposes have much in common. For instance, a typical reason for speaking would be that the hearer needs to know what to do in case the motor will not start. Once they have a reason to speak, their reasons for saying the things they say may be little more than that those are the things that are relevant to the task at hand.

Moreover, the antiexpressivist need not deny the utility of talk of meaning. Certainly we sometimes have to ask people what they *mean*. We might even ask them to try to *express their thoughts* more clearly. If we overhear a bit of conversation, we may report that we are uncertain whether the speaker was *expressing* his or her own *thought* or was merely paraphrasing someone else. When communication between two people is ineffective, we may explain that the one party did not understand what the other one *meant*. In all these ways, our ordinary talk about language seems to endorse the expressive theory of communication. In view of this, to argue that the expressive theory is simply mistaken may seem to be a perverse contradiction of plainest common sense. On the contrary, one may very well reject the expressive theory of communication, considered as a fundamental theory of the nature of linguistic communication, without advocating a reform in our ordinary ways of talking about language. No doubt these ways of talking about language serve an important function in the conduct of conversations, and a theory of language must explain how they do their work. But it is not necessary to view them as offering key insights into the nature of language, insights that we can develop into a viable theory of how language really works.

Asking a person to explain what he or she means is a useful way to try to make progress in discussions where otherwise progress would come to a halt. In effect we are asking the person to try a different verbal strategy. If we report uncertainty over whether a speaker was expressing his or her own thought or instead merely paraphrasing someone else, we are in effect expressing uncertainty whether we should hold the speaker accountable for an assertion. When we explain that one person failed to do as another person intended because the first one did not understand what the second one meant, or what thought the second was trying to convey, we in effect identify the ways in which the conversation departed from the norms of discourse that ought to be followed if communication is to be successful.

Such glosses on "what we really mean" in talking of meaning will not suffice, of course, as an alternative to the expressivist's way of locating meaning in a substantive theory of communication. The way in which talk of meaning and expression plays a role in the conduct of conversations is something we have to try to comprehend in a precise theory of language. To do this, we will need to know what it means to adopt a verbal strategy. We will need to know what it amounts to hold a person accountable for an assertion. We will need to be able to specify the norms of discourse and the ways in which they affect interlocutors. We will need to have a definite conception of successful communication. But it is not just obvious that the expressive theory is the proper framework for explaining these things. (For some of the elements of an alternative, see my 1994 and 1998.)

When tossing about for the rudiments of a theory, it is a good idea to start with concepts one already understands. In a sense, as masters of ordinary language, we do understand the concepts of meaning and expression. We understand how to employ those concepts in the conduct of conversation. So the expressivist's idea that by concentrating on those concepts we might develop a viable theory of language is a very reasonable hunch. What social externalism shows, as we will see, is that this reasonable hunch does not pan out. It is a platitude that there is no sharp distinction between common sense and scientific theory. In the case of the theory of language, however, this platitude is misleading, for in the case of explaining the nature of language, common sense fails to yield a viable starting point for science.

5 The reductio

Suppose, for a reductio ad absurdum, that there is such a thing as content in the expressivist's proprietary sense. The expressivist holds that people use words they way they do because the primary function of language is to enable speakers to convey the contents of their beliefs to hearers. Burge's social externalism states that what is for a person's thought to have the content it has is explicable only in terms of the way words are used in the linguistic community. But that means that the expressivist's explanation of the way words are used leads in circles. So it is not a good explanation.

Let us trace one of these circles in detail. Why do people use the term "high octane gasoline" in the way they do? For instance, why does Gus say "high octane gasoline" when he drives up to the full service island after his brief discussion with his mechanic? According to the expressivist, the proximal explanation is that Gus has a belief containing the concept *high octane gasoline*, namely, his belief that his car needs high octane gasoline, and the words he speaks are the words that, in light of their meaning and the context, he thinks will enable the gas station attendant to recognize that he has a belief with such a content. But now, what is it for a belief to have such a content—to contain the concept *high-octane gasoline*? Well, there may be various things that have to be said in answer to this, but one thing that has to be said, assuming the truth of Burge's social externalism, is that other people in Gus's linguistic community use the term "high octane gasoline" in a certain way. Thus we find that in explaining why people use the term "high octane gasoline" in the way they do, we have to cite the fact that people use the term "high octane gasoline" in the way they do. That is circular.

I should emphasize that this is a reductio on the expressivist's explanation of language and not a straight refutation. A straight refutation would be a defense of some thesis that simply contradicted the expressivist theory of communication without acquiescing in any way in the expressivist's point of view. That is not the kind of argument we have here. Burge's externalism, as I have formulated it, is a thesis about thought content in just the expressivist's sense. Already in supposing that there is such a thing as content in this sense we are buying into the expressivist conception of linguistic communication. What we find is that, having assumed in this way that expressivism is true, we cannot maintain the expressivist's sort of explanation of the way words are used. If we reject expressivism, then of course we reject the expressivist's propriety notion of content. Since this is integral also to the thesis of social externalism, we must reject that as well, which, again, is not to say that there is nothing right about it, for instance, as a thesis about the proper interpretation of people's words.

I acknowledge that this argument is liable to seem unpersuasive to committed expressivists just because it involves so many slippery concepts, such as *explanation* and the *nature* of a thing, not to mention *content* and *the way words are used*. So now I want to address a variety of considerations to which someone might appeal in order to show that the prima facie reductio really is not sound.

5.1 Reformulation in terms of rules of use

If we simply say that words are used as they are because speakers intend to convey the contents of their thought and that speakers' thoughts have the contents they have because words are used in the way they are, then that does seem to be a circle. But maybe the circle could be broken if we differentiated more sharply between the uses of words. We might find that the uses of words to which a given content is relative never include the uses we wish to explain in terms of that content. In that case, there would be no circle, just a series of one-way dependencies.

Toward rebutting this, let me emphasize again that according to the expressivist there will be certain principles governing the use of words for purposes of conveying the contents of beliefs. These will be the rules of semantics as the expressivist conceives of them. Only by virtue of their sharing such rules will the speaker reasonably be able to expect that the hearer will be able to recognize the content of the speaker's belief on the basis of the speaker's choice of words. Precisely how such rules should be formulated would depend on how the structure of a sentence uttered should depend on the structure of the content to be conveyed. It would also depend on how the context of utterance is supposed to be exploited. However, for illustration we may suppose that one such rule would be just this:

> *The high-octane rule:* If the content to be conveyed contains the concept *high-octane gasoline*, then the speaker shall use the term "high octane gasoline".

This is really only a caricature of the sort of rule that the expressivist would wish to cite, but it captures the expressivist's main idea that the rules of semantics relate linguistic expressions to features of the content to be conveyed. The expressivist will have to suppose that the speaker and hearer in some sense have *knowledge* of such rules, but expressivists may differ amongst themselves over the kind of knowledge this has to be. When an expressivist sets out to explain in detail an act of speech that exhibits what the expressivist considers to be the primary function of language (an informative use), the expressivist will explain it as a result of the speaker's applying rules such as these.

When we say that the expressivist proposes to explain *the use of words*, we do not, in so saying, have to presuppose any particular classification of actual and potential utterances into *uses*. But relative to the explanations that the expressivist actually gives, there will be certain natural classifications. A *use* of a word will be the type of utterance governed by a semantic rule of the sort that, as I have just explained, the expressivist would cite in explanation of speech behavior. For each semantic rule mentioning a specific expression there is a corresponding use of that expression such that two utterances of the expression, whether actual or merely potential, will count as the same use if and only if that semantic rule governed both utterances. In arguing that the expressivist's theory of the use of words is circular, we may employ specifically this notion of the *use* of an expression. Burge's social externalism may be understood by the expressivist as the claim that the content of a speaker's thought is relative to the semantic rules governing the rest of that speaker's linguistic community. For example, the concept that Gus expresses by means of the expression "high octane gasoline" is *high-octane gasoline* just because in his community the use of the expression "high octane gasoline" is governed by the high-octane rule.

In light of this explanation of what is meant by the *use* of a word, the charge of circularity can be reformulated in terms of the expressivist's semantic rules, thus: The expressivist proposes to formulate certain rules of semantics adherence to which makes it possible for speakers to convey the contents of their beliefs to hearers. These rules are formulated in terms of the contents of the beliefs to be conveyed. But Burge's social externalism, as seen from the perspective of expressivism, shows that we cannot understand what it is for a person's thought to have a given content apart from the fact that the speech of members of the surrounding linguistic community is governed by just such rules. So the expressivist's semantic rules cannot be formulated in a manner that does not beg the question of what these rules really say.

Again, let us trace one of these circles in detail. In explaining why Gus speaks as he does, the expressivist proposes to cite Gus's adherence to something like the high-octane rule, which refers to the concept *high-octane gasoline*. But now, what are we to understand the high-octane rule to mean? That depends on what sort of thing a *concept* is (within the scope of the assumption that it is an aspect or a component of a content). Assuming that the high octane rule really is one of those that the expressivist would cite in identifying the uses of the expression "high octane gasoline" in Gus's community, the conclusion we may draw from Burge's social externalism is that in explaining what it is to have the concept *high octane gasoline* (again, an aspect or component of a content) we must have recourse to the fact that the high octane rule is a rule governing the speech of members of Gus's linguistic community. But this means we cannot get any grip at all on the meaning of the high-octane rule.

Suppose, for an analogy, that we wished to explain people's behavior by citing their knowledge of the rule "One should not commit fernombury". If we could explicate fernombury by saying that it is an act of preventing another person from using something that is that other's rightful possession, then we might be able to cite the rule in explaining why people refrain from certain actions. But suppose that what we can say is only that fernombury is the act of preventing a person from using his or her possessions in a community of people who adhere to a rule according to which one should not commit fernombury (so that where no such rule is in force an act of preventing someone from using his or her possessions is not fernombury). In that case we could have no grip at all on what the meaning of the rule really is.

In sum, the charge of circularity cannot be evaded by tracing more carefully the dependency of uses. That it cannot be can be demonstrated by reformulating the circularity charge as the charge that the expressivist cannot give a non-question-begging account of the principles by which speakers' choice of words is governed.

5.2 Particular vs. general explanations

I have acknowledged above that there is a legitimate place for talk of the expression of thought in words. That Gus used the term "high octane gasoline" to express a thought about high octane gasoline is something we might indeed wish to say. For example, if there were a question about whether Gus misspoke or was lying or was making a joke or was paraphrasing someone else, then we might want to say this as a way of affirming that he was speaking sincerely for himself. Accordingly, I ought not to object if someone wants to say the same thing in a somewhat more elaborate way by saying that Gus intended the gas station attendant to believe that he had a belief with a content containing the concept *high octane gasoline*. So likewise, it might be said, I ought not to object to generalizing from this particular explanation and concluding that people use words the way they do because they intend their hearers to recognize that they have beliefs having certain contents.

My answer to this is that there are kinds of explanation that we may legitimately offer in particular cases that cannot be generalized and that explanation in terms of expression of thought is one of these. For instance, we might explain why John bought a new stereo amplifier by saying that John is an audiophile. John's buying a certain new stereo amplifier is an instance of the following type: actions that express an interest in high-end audio equipment. We may explain the particular act by citing John's disposition toward the type. But the explanation we offer of this particular instance does not generalize to the whole type. It is not explanatory to say that John tends to do things that express an interest in high-end stereo equipment because he is an audiophile. My claim is that similarly our explanation that Gus spoke as he did because he intended to convey the content of a belief does not generalize to allow us to conclude that in general people speak as they do because they intend to convey the contents of their beliefs.

There is little more to being an audiophile than having a tendency to do things that express an interest in high-end audio equipment. Nonetheless, we can cite John's being an audiophile to explain his purchase of a new amplifier, because there may be occasions on which his interest in high-end audio equipment is not an expression of his audiophilia. For instance, he might want to buy an amplifier to replace the one that he smashed that belonged to a friend. By explaining that it was because of his audiophilia, we indicate that this occasion is not one of those. Similarly, there is little more to verbally conveying the content of a thought than using language in the assertive sort of way. Nonetheless, we can cite the conveying of thought content in explanation of why Gus said "My car needs high octane gasoline" because there may be occasions on which a person speaks in other than the ordinary assertive sort of way. For instance, he might have misspoken or been lying or telling a joke or paraphrasing someone else.

Precisely because there is little more to the claim that a person is an audiophile than the claim that he or she tends to do things that express an interest in high end audio equipment, it is not explanatory to say that in general John tends to do things that express an interest in high end audio equipment because he is an audiophile. Likewise, there is little more to the claim that a person used certain words to convey the content of his or her belief than the claim that he or she used words in the ordinary assertive sort of way, and so it is not explanatory to say that in general when a person uses words in the ordinary assertive sort of way it is because he or she wishes to convey the content of a belief that he or she has.

Two paragraphs back I said without qualification, "there is little more to verbally conveying the content of a thought than using language in the assertive sort of way". Since this is supposed to express an analytic connection, the point is that there is little more to *the claim* that words have been used to convey the content of a thought than *the claim* that words were used in the ordinary assertive sort of way. Obviously, this is not something I can expect the expressivist to agree with. For the expressivist, the theory of how words express the contents of thoughts is supposed to be a substantive theory of what is involved in using words in the ordinary assertive sort of way. But the objection I am answering does not purport to find a specific flaw in the reductio on expressivism but only to persuade us that it must be mistaken somewhere. So to answer it, it suffices to show that from the point of view of the proponent of the reductio there is reason to deny that the expressivist's reasoning here is sound.

Even so, it may not be obvious that even an opponent of expressivism ought to agree with what I have said about claims to the effect that words have been used to convey the content of a thought. In fact, I think that what I said is not exactly right. As I explained in section 4.2 above, the antiexpressivist will need an alternative framework for explaining the function of the whole panoply of ordinary ways of talking about language and meaning. From the point of view of such an alternative framework it will probably seem too simple just to say that claims to the effect that words express beliefs are claims to the effect that words are used in the ordinary assertive sort of way. But from the point of view of that alternative framework we will still want to deny that particular explanations in terms of the conveying of thought content can be generalized, and what I have said here illustrates the sort of basis we will have for that denial.

5.3 Descriptions vs. the thing described

Suppose someone asserts, "The cause of his death caused his death". Is that a vacuous assertion? Not necessarily. "The cause of his death" refers to some event c, "his death" refers to some event e, and what is asserted may be that c caused e. Since c might not have caused e, that assertion is not vacuous. It is not vacuous even though the concept *the cause of his death* cannot be understood apart from the concept *causes death*. Or suppose someone says, "He went for a walk because he decided to". Is that a vacuous explanation? Certainly it is not very helpful, but, again, the decision is one thing, the walking another; so the assertion that a causal relation obtains between them is not vacuous. It is not vacuous even though the concept of deciding to go for a walk cannot be understood apart from the concept of going for a walk.

In a similar manner one might hope to rescue explanations of speech in terms of content. Consider: "Gus said 'high octane gasoline' because the content of the thought that he wished to convey contained the concept *high octane gasoline*". Someone might think that what I am saying is that such explanations are vacuous because the concept of content (and, hence, the concept of concepts in the pertinent sense) cannot be analyzed apart from the concept of using words. In response, it might be said, the decision to convey a content is distinct from the act of speech, and so it is not vacuous to assert that the former caused the latter.

Recall that I do not dispute the legitimacy of particular explanations in terms of content. Saying on a particular occasion that Gus used the term "high octane gasoline" because the content of the thought he wished to convey contained the concept high-octane gasoline might distinguish this case from various others. What I question is the legitimacy of generalizing and saying that in general, or whenever people engage in informative uses of language, they aim to convey the contents of their thoughts. With this in mind, I think it should be clear that the analogy to "The cause of his death caused his death" does not help the expressivist. It would not be legitimate to try to generalize from such an explanation and to say that in general it is the causes of death that cause death.

The other example is more challenging. Would there be anything wrong, besides oversimplification, in generalizing and saying that in general people go for a walk because they have decided to go for a walk? That depends on what we can say about decisions to go for a walk as a general type. If decisions to go for a walk can be characterized as a distinctive type of neurological event, then I think the generalization is substantive. For in that case, decisions to go for a walk form a type that can in principle be grasped apart from the fact that decisions to go for a walk tend to lead to walks. In that case, the explanation is substantive even if we cannot already specify the pertinent neurological type and may perhaps be substantive even if we do not yet suspect that there is such a neurological type. But if decisions to go for a walk have nothing in common that distinguishes them from other things apart from being decisions to go for a walk, then I think the generalization is vacuous, for in that case we cannot grasp what it is for something to be a decision to go for a walk other than as something that tends to result in a person's going for a walk.

The expressivist's explanation of linguistic behavior is analogous to the claim that people go for walks because they have decided to in the case in which we cannot grasp what it is for something to be a decision to go for a walk other than as something that tends to result in a person's going for a walk. What Burge's social externalism shows is that we cannot grasp what it is for a thought to have a certain content apart from the uses of those words that are supposed to convey it. If we cannot grasp what it is for a thought to have a certain content apart from its being something that certain words have the function of conveying, then it is vacuous to say that people use those words to convey thoughts having that content. So Burge's social externalism entails that the expressivist's general explanations are vacuous.

5.4 Intention-based semantics

Expressivists may be divided into two camps. All agree that there must be something about the linguistic expressions that a speaker uses that enables the hearer to recognize the content of the speaker's belief. Speaker and hearer must share a semantic theory of some kind. But expressivists differ over the nature of this semantic theory. In one camp are those expressivists who believe in *intention-based semantics*. These expressivists explicate not only individual acts of speech but also general semantic rules in terms of speakers' intentions. In the other camp are those who think the semantic rules that speakers exploit in conveying the contents of their beliefs are grounded in something else.

The proponents of intention-based semantics include Grice (1968), Bennett (1975) and early Schiffer (1972). These expressivists believe that the semantic properties of words derive what from what speakers normally intend to do with them. Thus, they might say that what speakers know about the term "high octane gasoline" is that speakers will use it when the content that they intend the hearer to recognize their beliefs to have contains the concept *high-octane gasoline*. This sort of generalization about what speakers tend, or ought or "have it in their repertoire" to do, might be the only sort of semantic rule that interlocutors need.

Among those who take a different approach are David Lewis and Donald Davidson. Lewis (1975) defines a language as an abstract entity assigning meanings to sentences. Interlocutors conform to conventions whereby they speak only sentences whose meanings they believe and whereby they take others to believe what their sentences mean. Davidson (1990) explains the provenance of the semantics for a language in terms of a theory of radical interpretation rather than in terms of what speakers tend to intend. On his conception of radical interpretation, attribution of belief and desire go hand in hand with interpretation of the language, but the assignment of truth conditions to sentences is a force that independently shapes the overall interpretive project. Lewis and Davidson agree with Grice that interlocutors' primary use for their knowledge of semantics is to enable hearers to infer what the speakers intend and to enable speakers to predict what hearers will infer. But on their theories, at the heart of the method by which speakers do this is a semantic theory that does not have speakers' intentions as its subject matter.

One might suppose that what Burge's social externalism conflicts with is only intention-based semantics and not the expressive theory of communication generally. That is the charge that Ausonio Marras made against me in his review of my 1994 (Marras 1996). Burge himself may have encouraged this idea by targeting specifically intention-based semantics in his "Individualism and the Mental" (1979, 109). Again, in Burge's review of Grice 1989, it is only Grice's "reductive analysis" that Burge mentions as seeming to conflict with the fact that the content of a thought expressed in words depends on the public meaning of those words (Burge 1992b). My claim is that social expressivism conflicts with expressivism generally.

Recent history suggests a way of reconciling expressivism with Burge's social externalism provided only that our expressivism does not incorporate intention-based semantics. A familiar position, due above all to Wilfrid Sellars (1963/1956), is that language is conceptually prior to thought while thought is ontologically prior to language. Language is conceptually prior to thought in that overt speech is our conceptual model for thought. We think of thinking as like inner talking. Just as words are meaningful inasmuch as they play a certain role in our thinking and in our interactions with the world, so too thought is meaningful by virtue of its functional role. But thought is ontologically prior to language in that thought is the inner cause of overt speech. Indeed, we should think of thoughts as theoretical entities postulated for the sake of explaining speech and other behaviors.

This distinction between two kinds of priority suggests a strategy for reconciling social externalism with expressivism inasmuch as social externalism might be treated as a statement of conceptual priorities while expressivism is treated as a statement of causal priorities. What Burge's social externalism shows, it might be said, is just that the conceptual dependence of thought on language is very strong. The concepts that we take words to express are inextricably bound up with their overt use. Indeed, the meaningfulness of words is our model for the meaningfulness of thought in a manner that would render intention-based semantics circular. Nonetheless, it might be said, the conceptual dependence of thought on language is nothing against the causal dependence of language on thought.

Actually, this strategy for reconciling social externalism with expressivism is very contrary to Sellars's own philosophy. Sellars very explicitly rejected the expressivist's conception of the etiology of speech. He wrote:

> Although the theory postulates that overt discourse is the culmination of a process, which begins with 'inner discourse', this should not be taken to mean that overt discourse stands to 'inner discourse' *as voluntary movements stand to intentions and motives.* True, overt linguistic events *can* be produced as means to ends. But serious errors creep into the interpretation of both language and thought if one interprets the idea that overt linguistic episodes *express* thoughts, on the model of the use of an instrument. (1963/1956, 188, §58, italics in the original)

For Sellars, overt acts of speech can be said to *express* thoughts, but only in the sense that overt acts of speech offer glimpses of a larger *train* of thought the rest of which is hidden from view.

Furthermore, the strategy described does not make much sense. I do not see how language can be our model for thought if speaking is supposed to be the product of intendings such as the expressivist postulates. If we think of acts of speech as fundamentally actions performed for reasons and tightly model thinking on those actions, then we will have to think of thoughts as actions performed for reasons, which makes no sense. Perhaps while thinking of acts of speech as actions performed for reasons we might think of speech episodes as having other aspects and suppose that thought is modeled on speech only under these other guises (e.g., with respect to syntactic structure). But even then, if the meaningfulness of words is to be our model for the contentfulness of thoughts, we will require that words have a certain meaningfulness apart from their being actions performed for reasons, and in that case I do not know why we should have to think of them as fundamentally actions performed for reasons at all.

In any case, the target of my reductio is certainly not only intention-based semantics. My claim is that the expressivist cannot explain the uses of words without going in circles. These uses of words are the types of utterance identified by the semantic rules that will justify a speaker's choice of words. The reductio proceeds in the same fashion whether we think of those semantic rules as intention-based or not.

6 Language without expression

So pervasive is the expressive theory of communication that many will prefer to suppose that I have posed some kind of paradox rather than accede to my refutation of the expressive theory of communication. So now I will briefly address some of the primary motives for expressivism and indicate how they can be resisted. (For further exposition of the ideas in this section, see my 1994 and 1997.)

One of the most persistent sources for expressivist intuitions is the observation that animals and prelinguistic infants *think*. Thus even Burge thinks that he is conceding something to Grice when he writes, "Mental states do appear to predate language" (Burge 1992a, 22). Even I once wrote:

> One clearly unacceptable alternative [to the "instrumental" conception of language] is that a thought is itself a formula of the speaker's public language and speaking is just the *unveiling* of this formula. One problem is that on this account no creature that does not speak a language could be properly said to think. To attribute thoughts to animals and young children, we would have to suppose that they were prevented from speaking only by their inability to form articulate sounds, which is absurd. (Gauker 1987, pp. 48-49)

This idea, that Grice's expressive theory of communication is supported by the fact that thought is prior to language, exhibits the common assumption that thought is just one kind of thing. If we distinguish between different kinds of thinking, then we may see that the fact that one kind of thinking is independent of language is no support for the idea that language emerges as the expression of thought. In particular, we need to distinguish between *conceptual thought* and other kinds.

Say that a *basic* conceptual thought is a representation of a particular thing as belonging to a general category. I will suppose that it is clear enough what it means to say that two thoughts bear *inferential relations* to one another (although in fact this is in a lot of ways not clear). Then I define a *conceptual* thought recursively as either a basic conceptual thought or a thought that bears inferential relations to other conceptual thoughts. For instance, if someone thinks that *that* is a chair, then that is an episode of conceptual thinking. Such a thought represents an individual object as belonging to a general category, namely, chairs. If someone thinks that people can sit in chairs, then that is a conceptual thought by virtue of its inferential relations to thoughts such as the thought that *that* is a chair. If we imagine that a rich capacity for conceptual thought exists in children prior to their acquisition of language and that it existed in early hominids prior to the emergence of language, then it will indeed be hard to resist the idea that language is learned, and was originally invented, to facilitate the conveying of conceptual thought. Inevitably we will suppose that language originates in the attempt to find external signs of inner conceptualizations.

In fact, it is not obvious that conceptual thought is possible in creatures that possess no language. No doubt some kind of thinking underlies and leads to language, but it is not obvious that it has to be conceptual thought. Besides conceptual thought, there may be many other kinds of mental process that deserve to be called thought and that can be cited in explanation of problem solving. To take just one example, consider *imagistic* thinking. If I need to replace a washer in a faucet that I have never taken apart before, I can do it. I can take it apart, remember how the pieces went together, replace the old washer with a new one, and put it back together. It is not obvious that this requires me to represent the individual parts as belonging to general categories, although I may incidentally do so. In addition to such imagistic thinking there may be other mental processes that deserve to be called thinking that we cannot begin to get a grasp on by means of analogies to publicly observable things such as words and images but which we will be able to understand only in neurophysiological terms. The thinking that underlies the use of language may not be conceptual thought but one of these other kinds.

From this point of view, we might say the same sort of thing about our ordinary talk of beliefs and desires as I said above about our ordinary talk of meanings. As I explained, talk about meanings plays a useful role in the conduct of conversations, and our theory of language has to comprehend this kind of talk. Likewise, talk about what people believe and what they desire plays an important role in the conduct of conversations. Along with explaining how every other aspect of language does some work for us, our theory of language has to explain how that kind of talk does some work for us. But we do not have to take our ordinary talk of people's beliefs and desires as pointing to the basic entities in terms of which we should expect to construct a fundamental theory of human behavior.

Another persistent source of expressivist intuitions is the idea that only in terms of content can we formulate the norms of discourse. Sometimes, perhaps, we can read the content to be conveyed more or less directly off the form of words and the external circumstances of utterance. But in other cases, utterances may be ambiguous or incomplete in various ways, or the literal meaning of a speaker's words may not be directly pertinent to the aims of the conversation. In these cases, a hearer may need to consider what content the speaker may have intended to convey. The conception of linguistic communication as the conveying of content seems to demonstrate its theoretical utility in such cases.

In my opinion, this apparent virtue of expressivism is entirely illusory. The most articulate indication of what a person has in mind is what he or she says. When what a person says is not articulate enough for exact understanding, we will not often get a more exact understanding by inferring his or her thoughts from his or her nonverbal behavior on the basis of a general theory of human thought or a general theory of the thinking of that person in particular. Rather, we may make use of our own grasp of what it is appropriate to say in light of the external situation and the goals of the conversation. The way in which we make use of this is not to interpret, in the sense of ascribing a content, but rather to respond in a variety of other ways. The response that indicates understanding may be nonverbal, taking the form of compliance with a request, or it may be verbal, taking the form of a paraphrase or an answer or a pertinent objection. There is knowledge that we make use of in responding, but this is not knowledge of psychology but knowledge how to respond appropriately. Our knowledge of what is appropriate is not ineffable, though there may be few generalizations, and an explicit formulation of what is appropriate is seldom any part of the cause of the response that indicates understanding.

7 The content of Burge's thought

If we abandon the expressive theory of communication, then we will abandon along with it the expressivist's proprietary notion of content. Strangely, Tyler Burge himself shows no reluctance to theorize in terms of content. As I pointed out in section 2, there are many apparently different notions of content at play in the philosophical literature. Burge has employed many of these different concepts of content in his various writings. Sometimes the differences have been acknowledged, sometimes not. (For instance, in "Individualism and the Mental" (1979), he failed to distinguish clearly between content considered as the reference of "that"-clauses and content considered as what is conveyed in communication, and this failure became the source of much criticism of him; whereas in "Intellectual Norms and the Foundations of Mind" (1986b), his main objective was to distinguish between content as cognitive value and content as linguistic meaning.) It is not obvious that one could not have a legitimate use for some notion of content while altogether repudiating the expressive theory of communication. However I cannot in fact disentangle Burge's own conception of content from its roots in the expressive theory of communication. So it seems to me that Burge occupies an unstable position.

Initially, in 1979, I think Burge thought of his thesis concerning content as an explication of an item of ordinary understanding. His objective was "to better understand our common mentalistic notions" (1979, 87). Everyone who talks about people's thoughts, he might have said, must be acquainted with the concept of content, even if they do not call it that. In my opinion, his topic was never an item of ordinary understanding. Everybody understands that words have meaning and that it is often a problem to figure out what a person means. But as soon as we say such things as that in general thoughts have content or that to attribute a thought is to say that the person stands in a certain attitude toward a certain content, we have left the ordinary understanding behind and have introduced a theoretical framework that we must not simply take for granted. I think it is clear in Burge's attempt to identify a nonindividualistic conception of content in psychological theories of vision (Burge 1986a) that his topic is not merely an item of ordinary understanding. It is even clearer, as I will now explain, in his more recent investigation into a topic in epistemology, where a commitment to some form of expressivism seems especially strong.

In his 1993 paper, "Content Preservation", Burge elaborates a conception of people's epistemic entitlement to accept other people's verbal testimony. Empiricists have often supposed that people are entitled to accept other people's testimony only insofar as they have evidence, from within their own perceptual experience, that those other people are reliable sources. Against this, Burge defends what he calls the *acceptance principle*, which states that if an intelligible message is presented as true, then we have an apriori entitlement to accept it as true unless a reason not to do so presents itself. It is not the case that we are war-ranted in accepting other people's testimony as true only when we can make a good inference from a perception of words and collateral as-sumptions about the reliability of the speaker to the truth of the proposi-tion expressed.

Throughout his discussion, Burge characterizes linguistic communi-cation as a process in which a propositional content passes from one mind to another. "In interlocution", he writes, "perception of utter-ances makes possible the passage of propositional content from one mind to another" (481). Moreover, the concept of content plays a spe-cial role in his account of our entitlement to accept people's testimony. "It is not just the rationality of a source that marks an apriori prima fa-cie connection to truth", he writes. "The very content of an intelligible message presented as true does so as well" (471). Thus Burge proposes to use the notion of propositional content in a theoretical context in a way that I would have thought was precluded by his own social external-ism.

I can think of several things Burge might say to this. First, he might point out that he has not committed himself to specifically the expres-sivist theory of linguistic communication. Expressivism, as I have de-fined it, says that speakers speak with intentions regarding the contents of their own thoughts. It is true that Burge has not posited any such in-tentions. At the same time, it is not very easy to see how to treat com-munication as the transmission of content without ultimately positing such intentions. (We do not have to suppose that those intentions are conscious or the products of deliberation.) In any case, I have charac-terized expressivism as positing such intentions only to give it a definite shape, one that is recognizable in the literature. The idea that runs con-trary to Burge's social externalism is really only the basic idea that we may explain the way words are used as a process in which speakers convey the content of their thoughts to hearers. I do not understand how Burge can deploy the notion of propositional content as he does in "Content Preservation" without assuming at least that much of the ex-pressivist's theory and in that way putting himself into a position that I have argued is inconsistent.

Second, Burge might claim that his apparent reference to content is only a manner of speaking. Wherever he writes of content, he might say, we can reformulate his claims in terms of intelligibility and under-standing, which is the language that he himself uses in places. He does not say that we are apriori prima facie entitled to accept a *propositional content* as true if it is presented to us by another as true. He says, "We are apriori prima facie entitled to accept *something* that is prima facie *intelligible* and presented as true" (472, my emphasis). Or we might take his references to content as just a way of talking about interpretation (which is what he asks us to do in his 1986b, note 15). But at one crucial juncture I do not see how to make the substitutions. Burge explains as follows why the intelligibility of a message, as having a certain content, indicates "an apriori prima facie connection to truth":

> For content is constitutively dependent, in the first instance, on patterned connections to a subject matter, connections that insure in normal circumstances a baseline of true thought presentations. So presentations' having content must have an origin in getting things right. (471)

According to Burge, this is the principle of charity in reverse (487-88). The principle of charity, as made familiar by Davidson, says that in order to interpret a person's words or state of mind, we must presume the person to be largely a thinker of truths. Burge's observation is that an interpretation is often taken for granted and not a result of applying any such methodological principles at all. Nonetheless, the connection between interpretability and truth remains, so that interpretability may itself be construed as an indicator of truth. The trouble is, I do not see how to formulate the point without characterizing interpretation as the attribution of content. We cannot say merely that "intelligibility" or "interpretability" is an indicator of truth, because there are too many kinds of intelligibility. Automobiles and ecosystems are "intelligible" and "interpretable", but we do not consider them to be sources of testimony that we are entitled to accept. The pertinent notions of intelligibility and interpretability seem to be specifically those that involve the attribution of content.

Finally, Burge might take refuge in my concession that there is a legitimate place for talk of meaning and expression in the conduct of conversations. One of the primary uses for talk of meaning will be in setting discourse back on track when it has become unproductive. When two people have explained their ideas and shared their data, and have answered one another's objections to their views, then if they still cannot reach agreement, they might turn their attention to their language and ask one another what they "mean" by their terms and check to make sure they have understood what thoughts the other was trying to "express". More generally, the place for talk of meaning and content might be to establish or enforce the norms of productive discourse. Burge's own enterprise in "Content Preservation", he might say, is a normative enterprise of this kind. It is not his intention to stand outside the practice of language in order to explain how it works but, while participating in it, to improve it, by removing certain obstacles to understanding.

This response is implausible to me because I do not see that there are any serious obstacles that might be removed through the kind of epistemological discourse in which Burge is engaged. Solipsism might be a genuine mental disorder in some cases, but in those cases it will not be removed through Burge's defense of our a priori entitlement to testimony. If our discursive practices contained rhetorical vortices that sucked people in and trapped them in the assumption that they cannot believe what others say just because they have no reliable evidence that their testimony is reliable, then Burge's epistemological discourse within the practice might offer something to grab onto. But again I do not see that there is any real danger of this kind. The fact is, Burge is examining our epistemological practices from the outside with the intention of justifying the role that testimony seems to play in people's lives. From that point of view, Burge's thesis commits him to the expressivism that is inconsistent with his social externalism.

This is not the place to examine Burge's theory of testimony in detail, but in case anyone thinks that the ends justify the means, I would like to add that in my opinion his use of the notion of content has not yielded a viable theory of testimony. At crucial junctures Burge offers no more than a "conceptual connection" as justification for his claims. We are entitled to accept testimony because "prima facie intelligible propositional contents prima facie presented as true bear an apriori prima facie conceptual relation to a rational source of true presentations-as-true" (472). We are entitled to assume that speech in the declarative mood has assertive force because "the connection between declarative mood and presentations-as-true is conceptual" (482). In my opinion, this appeal to conceptual analysis is an unfair rhetorical strategy. In effect, Burge claims for himself an insight into the nature of things without telling us how this insight might be achieved. According to Burge's acceptance principle we are entitled to believe what we are told "unless there are stronger reasons not to do so" (467). The rub is, this will not entitle us to believe anything until we know what counts as a stronger reason not to do so. If we once discover that someone has spoken falsely, is that not reason enough to doubt everything everyone says forever after? Presumably not, but why not? Burge offers no answers to such questions. In practice such questions do not arise, but how is that an answer?

8 Conclusion

I have argued that Burge's social externalism together with the expressive theory of communication lead to absurdity. From this we might conclude that, strictly speaking, social externalism is false, since it too rests on the existence of the expressivist's proprietary concept of content. But the fault lies not with the arguments for social externalism, which are correct on the assumption that content exists. The more immediate and important conclusion is that the expressive theory of communication is mistaken. From the way Burge persists in using the expressivist's proprietary concept of content in theoretical work, I infer that he does not accept this conclusion. The question I would like him to answer is: Why not?

9 Acknowledgments

Many of the present defenses of my prima facie reductio originally had to be concocted in response to Ausonio Marras's criticisms, which he first put to me in a correspondence concerning his review of my 1994 (Marras 1996) and some of which he reiterated in his comments on a draft of this paper. I thank him for his patient endurance. Thanks also go to Steven Davis for his correspondence with me concerning some of the points in section 3. This work was supported by a grant from the Taft Memorial Fund of the University of Cincinnati, which I gratefully acknowledge.

References

Bennett, Jonathan, 1976, *Linguistic Behavior*, Cambridge University Press.

Bezuidenhout, Anne, 1997, "The Communication of *De Re* Thoughts", *Noûs*, 31: 197-225.

Burge, Tyler, 1979, "Individualism and the Mental" in Peter A. French, Theodore E. Uehling, Jr., and Howard K. Wettstein (eds.) *Midwest Studies in Philosophy*, Vol. 4, *Studies in Metaphysics*. University of Minnesota Press. Pp. 73-121.

Burge, Tyler, 1986a, "Individualism in Psychology", *Philosophical Review* 95: 3-45.

Burge, Tyler, 1986b, "Intellectual Norms and the Foundations of Mind", *Journal of Philosophy* 83: 697-720.

Burge, Tyler, 1992a, "Philosophy of Language and Mind: 1950-1990", *Philosophical Review* 101: 1-51.

Burge, Tyler, 1992b, Review of Paul Grice, *Studies in the Way of Words*, *Philosophical Review* 101: 619-621.

Burge, Tyler, 1993, "Content Preservation", *Philosophical Review* 102: 457-488.

Davidson, Donald, 1990, "The Structure and Content of Truth", *The Journal of Philosophy* 87: 279-328.

Davis, Steven, 1997, "Social Externalism and the *Elm/Beech* Thought Experiment", in Paul Weingartner, Gerhard Schurz and Georg Dorn (eds.), *The Role of Pragmatics in Contemporary Philosophy: Papers of the 20th International Wittgenstein Symposium*, Vol. 1 (Kirchberg am Wechsel, Austria, 1997), pp. 199-203.

Gauker, Christopher, 1987, "Language as Tool," *The American Philosophical Quarterly* 24: 47-58.

Gauker, Christopher, 1991, "Mental Content and the Division of Epistemic Labor," *Australasian Journal of Philosophy* 6: 302-318.

Gauker, Christopher, 1994, *Thinking Out Loud: An Essay on the Relation between Thought and Language*, Princeton University Press.

Gauker, Christopher, 1997, "Domain of Discourse", *Mind* 106: 1-32

Gauker, Christopher, 1998, "What is a Context of Utterance?", *Philosophical Studies* 91: 149-172.

Grice, Paul, 1968, "Utterer's Meaning, Sentence-meaning and Word-meaning", *Foundations of Language* 4: 225-242. Reprinted in Grice 1989.

Grice, Paul, 1989, *Studies in the Way of Words*, Harvard University Press.

Lewis, David, 1975, "Language and Languages", in Keith Gunderson (ed.), *Language, Mind and Knowledge*, University of Minnesota Press. Pp. 3-35.

Marras, Ausonio, 1996, Review of *Thinking Out Loud: An Essay on the Relation between Thought and Language*, *Philosophical Quarterly* 46: 422-426.

Schiffer, Stephen, 1972, *Meaning*, Oxford University Press.

Sellars, Wilfrid, 1963, "Empiricism and the Philosophy of Mind", in his *Science, Perception and Reality*, Humanities Press. (Originally published 1956.)

2

Terms and Content*

Tobies Grimaltós

1 Introduction

In 'The Meaning of "Meaning"'[1], Hilary Putnam defended that the natural environment contributes to the meaning of natural kind terms. Meanings are not in the head; intension does not determine extension[2]. In 'Individualism and the Mental' and 'Other Bodies'[3], Tyler Burge claimed that the social environment contributes also to the meaning of many terms, as well as to the content of thoughts through the meaning of terms that take part in them. Different natural or social environments can produce different meanings in two homophonic terms and by means

* Research for this paper has been funded by the Spanish Government's DGICYT as part of the projects PB93-0683 and PB93-1049-C03-02. My thanks to this institution for its generous help and encouragement. Thanks are also due to Josep Corbí, Christopher Hookway, Carlos Moya and Dora Sánchez for their valuable comments on previous versions of the paper. A version of this paper was read at the VIII Seminario de Filosofía y Ciencia Cognitiva, University of Granada, May 1996, I am grateful for the comments and suggestions received from the attendants.

[1] "The Meaning of 'Meaning'" in K. Gunderson (ed.), *Language, Mind and Knowledge, Minnesota Studies in Philosophy of Science,* University of Minnesota Press, 1975.

[2] In the sense that sameness of intension does not entail sameness of extension.

[3] "Individualism and the Mental" in *Midwest Studies in Philosophy,* Vol. 4, P.A French *et al.* (Eds.), 1979. "Other Bodies" in *Thought and Object. Studies on Intentionality*, A. Woodfield (ed.) Clarendon Press, Oxford, 1982.

of this can produce different thought contents in subjects that are physically identical. It is the real meaning (determined by the environment) of the terms we use in thinking or expressing our thoughts what determines the content of the thought we have. If Oscar and Twin Oscar both believe what they express by "I have developed arthritis in my right thigh", but Oscar inhabits a world in which arthritis can only be developed in the joints (because it means inflammation of the joints), while Twin Oscar inhabits a world in which arthritis also applies to inflammation of thighs, their beliefs have different content. One has a belief about arthritis, the other about *tarthritis* (twin arthritis).

In this paper I would like to question the universal validity of that claim. I assume the externalist claims that meanings are not in the head, extension is not determined by intension, and the environment contributes to the meaning of terms. I also accept that usually the content of our thoughts is partially fixed by the environment through its contribution to the meaning of terms that take part in those thoughts. However, in spite of granting all this, I intend to argue that the meaning of the terms we use in thinking or in expressing a thought does not always determine (not even partially) the content of the thought we have. I think that we can distinguish between a *deferential* and a *referential* use of terms such as common names and adjectives, and that it is only when we use a term in a deferential way that the "real" meaning of the term contributes to the content of our thought. I judge that by means of this distinction we can throw some light on the current debate upon whether externalism is compatible with the direct knowledge of the content of our thoughts. I shall briefly treat this question in the last part of this paper.

My thesis will consist more or less in the claim that it is the speaker's intention that fixes the reference of her terms. Usually, this intention is to defer to the community with respect to the real sense and extension of the terms she uses. But, on some other occasions, her intention to refer to a particular kind of things will be stronger than her deferential intention. In such cases and when the mismatch between speaker's reference and semantic reference is produced, what contributes to the content of the thought is the former and not the latter. The speaker's intention is usually governed by the natural and social environment, but when, for instance, the environment is altered in such a way that it produces the alluded mismatch, it is not always the conventional meaning of the terms which compose the thought that has the last word in order to fix its content. I will also maintain that the inferential origin of a thought fixes its content in spite of the meaning of the terms by means of which the thought is thought or expressed. The premises we use in order to arrive to a conclusion affect in an essential way the content of such a conclusion-thought.

2 Two externalist intuitions

In order to prove that the meaning of the terms we use does not always determine the content of our thoughts and begin to motivate the relevance of distinguishing between deferential and referential uses of terms, I would like to examine a few claims in Paul Boghossian's 'Externalism and Inference'[4], as well as make a rather liberal use of one of the cases he presents. In this paper, Boghossian holds that it is a consequence of externalist accounts that "if there were thoughts whose typical causes continued to be Earthly, in spite of their being tokened on Twin Earth, then those thoughts would retain their Earthly interpretations, even on Twin Earth"[5]. Candidates to be thoughts of this type are, according to him, memories and beliefs about the past based on those memories. Such thoughts "are caused and sustained by *previous* perceptions long gone"[6]. And Boghossian concludes: "In the normal case, they owe little, if anything, to current perceptions and cognitive transactions with one's environment. They would be expected, therefore, to retain their Earthly interpretation when tokened on Twin Earth"[7].

On this basis he explores the case of someone who is suddenly and unwittingly transported to Twin Earth. I shall examine here a variant of his case. Imagine that Peter was so transported to a Twin Earth, where lakes and rivers are full of XYZ, instead of H_2O. Of course, this liquid is superficially identical to water and is called 'water' by Twin Earthians. It is also clear, that Peter has no suspicion about 'water' not being water. After some time, because the typical cause of his thoughts about that liquid is *twater* (twin water) his thoughts would be about twater and not about water. However, imagine that after that time, Peter remembers an experience he had on Earth: he was swimming in a river and the water was chilly. He thinks:

---

[4] In Enrique Villanueva (ed.), *Rationality and Epistemology*, Ridgeview, Atascadero, California, 1992; pp. 11-28. It is true that Boghosian makes these claims in order to articulate a *reductio ad absurdum* against externalism, but I shall take them in a positive sense. This kind of *reductio* is challenged by Tyler Burge's "memory and Self-Knowledge", in P. Ludlow and N. Martin (eds.), *Externalism and Self-Knowledge,* CSLI Publications, Stanford, California, 1998; pp. 351-370. See specially pp. 364 and ff.

[5] *Ibid.* p. 19

[6] *Ibid.*

[7] *Ibid.*

A) "Water was chilly in that river"

According to Boghossian—if we hold externalism—, this thought, since it is a thought about the past based on memories, is about water and not twater. And, maybe because Boghossian thinks it to be a clear consequence, he goes further and claims that—according to externalists intuitions—tokens of 'water' "in sentences expressing memories and beliefs about that [occasion] will refer to [...] water [...]; whereas other tokens of that type, in sentences expressing beliefs about his current environment [...] will refer to [twater][8]."

I agree with Boghossian that thought A) is about water. Peter can be remembering that occasion and having a sort of mental image of the river, the water, etc.; he can be reviving the chilly feeling of the water in contact with his skin. I also agree with him that the token of 'water' refers on such an occasion to water. However, this externalist consequence does not easily harmonise with another externalist intuition upon which Burge bases a lot of his claims about the content of thoughts. This intuition is that we use our terms deferentially to the community we are living in. So, the expression token has to refer to whatever that expression type refers to on Twin Earth. There exists a sense of 'means' in which I am not so sure that the token in question means water instead of twater; on the contrary I am quite convinced that, in such a sense, it means twater and not water. But I also believe that both things are not incompatible.

3   Two uses of terms

Let us think a bit about this. If deference is to outweigh the speaker's intention or the causal origin of the thought, and if 'water' is a natural kind term, which refers rigidly, then the token of 'water' in such an utterance refers to twater and not to water. Since Peter is living on Twin Earth long enough to use his terms deferentially to his new community, his 'water' means (semantically refers to) twater. It has to be so because, as a consequence of his wanting to adjust the use of his terms to its conventional meaning, he is now a twin-English speaker, and in twin-English 'water' means (refers to) 'twater'. I think this is right. The meaning of our terms (if our use is not absolutely deviant) is fixed by the conventions of the community we are part of and by the world (the natu-

---

[8] *Ibid.*, p. 21

ral environment) we live in. As Burge says in 'Belief and Synonymy'[9], "the willingness of the speaker to submit his statement to the arbitration of a dictionary indicates a commitment to having his words taken in their conventional sense, *whatever that sense is*"[10]. So we want to use our terms with its 'semantic reference' or with its 'attributive use' if we can use this later denomination in this way. We want to mean by them whatever they mean. If we believe that we have arthritis in a thigh and we learn that arthritis means inflammation of the joints (and only inflammation of the joints), we shall have to say that we had a false belief. We want to refer to that inflammation of our thigh as arthritis, but we want to mean arthritis by 'arthritis' whatever it is, so if that inflammation is not arthritis, we have to say that our belief is false. The case is not different if we want to refer to the liquid in a particular pool by 'water'; we want, at the same time, to mean water by 'water', whatever water is; and if that liquid is not water, we should have to say that our belief is not true.

So far, so good. However, Boghossian's intuition seems also powerful. Peter is remembering an Earthian river that contains water. So his thought, based on memory, has to be about water. If it was water what that river contained and if he is thinking of that experience, it seems difficult that his thought is about twater. Water is what is in some way causing his present thought through memory. If a fact caused a memory, the memory cannot be of another fact[11].

But we should not be confused. We quoted a Boghossian's sentence which said: "If there were thoughts whose typical causes continued to be Earthly, in spite of their being tokened on Twin Earth, then those thoughts would retain their Earthly interpretations, even on Twin Earth". But, in the same page in Boghossian's paper it is said that the "principles of content fixation [that] underlie the standard Twin Earth cases [...] is this: the contents of thought tokens of a given syntactic type are determined by whatever environmental property is the typical cause of the perceptions that cause and sustain tokens of that type". Well, I have to say that this claim is not valid at the level of individual subjects or, if it

---

[9] *The Journal of Philosophy*, 75, no. 3 (1978); pp. 119-138

[10] *Ibid.*, pp. 130-131. *Cf.* note 12 on p. 131.

[11] This does not mean, *per se*, that in the content of his memory thought could not intervene a concept that does not apply to that particular sample of liquid. For instance, suppose that I once saw a glass full of alcohol, but I thought it was full of water. If, on that occasion, I thought "This glass is full of water", then when I remember that experience, what participate in my thought content are the concept 'water' and not the concept 'alcohol'. So, my thought, although it was caused by alcohol, was *of* alcohol, is—and was—*about* water.

is, this "environmental property" has to be, not a physical property, but a social one: a social convention determining the meaning the term really has. Let me explain this. What I want to say is that what determines the content of a thought is not the *res* of the thought, but what the thought is *about*, and what the thought is about is not the *res* that causes the thought *per se*, but what the speaker intends to talk about. So, this claim cannot be true of individuals, but only of communities (such as Earthians or Twin Earthians, for instance). An example can clarify this. Imagine that someone has been in perceptual contact only with fake gold. Even so, when this person talks about gold, she wants to refer to gold and not to fake gold (if she inhabits a world in which 'gold' means gold). Of course when she says 'My pieces of gold are shiny and yellow' she wants to refer to the pieces of her fake gold, but she wants to refer to them as part of the extension of gold. The fact that she takes as gold the pieces of fake gold does not alter the meaning of 'gold' when she utters it. The immediate reference of her sentence does not constitute a part of the content of her thought, only the social meaning of 'gold' does[12]. It is not fake gold what she wants to talk about when she uses 'gold', but about gold. Her belief *de re* is *of* fake gold, but her belief is *about* gold: she believes of fake gold that it is gold[13]. This person wants to mean gold by 'gold', even if she has not been in causal interaction with any sample of gold. The community conventions are more powerful than her beliefs about the putative elements of the kind. If it really is the "typical cause of the perceptions that cause and sustain tokens of that type", then those tokens have to be tokens of the experts in a community (or something in that way), not tokens of a particular person or other[14].

But Boghossian's case fulfils in my opinion this requisite and it is really about water, and not only of water. As Peter grew up on Earth, has been in contact with water, and has learned to use 'water' in that community, his thought based on memory is very probably about water. It is really water what contributes to the content of his thought token.

What to do then? It seems that in this case there exists a mismatch between what Kripke has called 'semantic reference' and 'speaker's

---

[12] If we counterfactually replace her pieces of fake gold with pieces of real gold, then her belief would be true. So her belief has the same truth conditions whether the pieces immediately referred to be fake gold or real gold.

[13] In the same way, if Oscar says 'My arthritis in the right thigh is disturbing me' when what he has in his right thigh is a contusion, the contusion or 'contusion' does not constitute a part of the content of his thought.

[14] And even this should have to be qualified, taking into account normative elements.

reference'[15]. His general intention is to use his words with its semantic reference, but, on this particular occasion, this general intention does not fit in with his intention to refer to water. He wants to refer to water, but his general intention to use terms with its real meaning fixes that the word he uses to refer to water should mean 'twater'.

What has the primacy? As Donnellan[16] has shown, the fact that we want to use 'champagne', 'glass' and 'man' with their real meaning does not prevent us from referring by 'the man with the glass of champagne' to a man who in fact is holding a glass of water. It is possible to use a definite description to pick out a particular and state something of it independently of whether it fulfils the description or not. I think that, in a similar way, we can refer to water by using a term, which really (semantically) means (or refers to) twater. We have the commitment to use our terms with their real meaning, and we should have to admit that the sentence we used is not true if it has not the meaning we thought it had, but this fact does not preclude that we can state something of a thing by means of terms that, as a matter of fact, do not semantically refer to it. So, we can believe of someone that he is bored by means of the description 'the man with the glass of champagne', whether he is drinking champagne or whether he is drinking water. I think that in a similar vein we can believe that water in that river was chilly whether 'water' means water or whether it means twater. We use 'water' to refer to that water and state something of it. To do that, it does not matter whether 'water' means water or twater.

4 Referential use of terms

I would like now to dedicate, however, some lines to clarify what I understand by 'referential use' of a term and show a difference between Donnellan's 'referential use' and mine. As Donnellan understands the referential use of definite descriptions, it is possible to pick out a particular and state something about it independently of its fulfilling the description. Nevertheless, we have to say that in the case, in which the thing does not fit the description, not only the sentence we use but also the belief we have is (or can be[17]) not completely true. We are, in some way, considering an individual as a member of a class when, as a

---

[15] Saul Kripke, 'Speaker's Reference and Semantic Reference' in *Contemporary Perspectives in the Philosophy of Language*, ed. by Peter A. French, Theodore E. Uchling, Jr. and Howard K. Wettstein, University of Minnesota Press, 1977.

[16] Keith Donnellan, 'Reference and Definite Descriptions', *Philosophical Review*, 75 (1966).

[17] For the rationale of this, *cf.* Donnellan's paper, section IV.

matter of fact, the individual does not pertain to that class. When we say "Her husband is kind to her" referentially, we can pick out a subject and state something true of him, even if he is not the woman's husband; but we are considering him her husband and that is mistaken. According to Donnellan's use, our subject in the case of fake gold is stating something true of the pieces of fake gold. But it seems also true that she believes that it is gold. She believes that the pieces she is talking about are gold and are shiny and yellow: they are shiny and yellow gold. She not only wants to refer to the tokens but also to the kind, she believes that the tokens are part of the kind 'gold'. In such a sense, not only the sentence she uses is not true; the belief she has is not true either. In Peter's case, however, he is not only stating something true of a sample of water, he is talking of that sample of water and wants to mean water by 'water', he is correctly identifying the sample as a member of a kind. In my use of referential use, the speaker not only gets to state something true of something, but to classify it correctly in the class he wants to refer to. The only problem is that the term he uses does not conventionally mean (in the world he is) what he thinks it means. We can say that Donnellan's use of 'referential use' has a remainder of attribution, which is absent in my use. In sum, the case of Peter on Twin Earth is different from the case of fake gold, because the subject in the latter case wants to mean gold by 'gold', even if her thought is of fake gold, while in the present case, the subject not only wants to refer to a sample of water, but to mean water. In the case of gold, the believer thinks of fake gold as gold, in the case of Peter, he thinks of water as water.

So there is a difference with respect to our beliefs when terms intervene in them referentially or when they intervene in a purely deferential way: when we use terms in a deferential way, we have to admit that our belief is not true if the term we used has not the extension we thought it had and that makes untrue the utterance we believed to be true. But when we use it referentially, we have only to accept (if we do have to accept it) that the utterance was false without having to accept at the same time that our belief was false or untrue.

5   Thinking of water by means of 'twater'

Taking into account the qualifications we have introduced so far, I think we can accept Boghossian's claims about the typical causes being responsible for the content of our thoughts, and combine them with the externalist intuition about the deferential use of our terms. Peter's thought based on memory and caused by water on an Earthian river is about water. So he uses 'water' referentially. However, since he is now a

Twin-English speaker, his 'water' means twater. The consequence is that

    a) His thought is about water
    b) He thinks it by means of a term that means twater.

His thought is based on memory; he wants to refer to water and wants to mean water by 'water'. But his commitment to use words with their real meaning makes him use a term that means twater in order to think about water. It is possible to have a belief about water, even if the term by which we formulate it means twater. Peter has a true belief about water, which he expresses (or thinks) by means of an inappropriate sentence. He *believes* truly that *water* was chilly in that river and *believes* untruly that *it is true* that *twater* was chilly in that river.

    Maybe things will appear clearer if we slightly modify the example. Imagine that on Twin Earth the name for XYZ is 'twater'. Peter is transported to Twin Earth and is told that he has been transported there. He realizes that everything on Twin Earth is exactly similar to Earth, except, he thinks, the fact that—and these are his words—"Twin Earthians refer to water by the name 'twater'". In such a situation, Peter comes to remember his experience in the river and the chilly water. He is talking to a Twin Earthian fellow and he sincerely says:

    B) "Twater was chilly in that river"

What is the content of his thought? What are the truth-conditions of the utterance he makes? Again his thought is about water, but he thinks it in terms of 'twater' which means twater. If a difference in truth-conditions entails a difference in propositional content, then i) "Water was chilly in that river" (said on Earth) and ii) "Twater was chilly in that river" (said on Twin Earth) express two different propositions. So, the propositional content of i) and ii) is different. i) Is true if and only if that river contained water (and was chilly), ii) is true if and only if the river contained twater (and was chilly). So, he believes of two different propositions that are true. But since both thoughts are, in the case of Peter, about water, the content of both thoughts has to be the same. He has the same thought in both occasions, but he expresses it differently in each of them, correctly in one case, incorrectly in the other. Only i) picks up the propositional content of his thought. He believes on both occasions that water was chilly on that river but he also believes on Twin Earth that it is true that twater was chilly in that river[18].

Imagine, however, that in such circumstances, Peter says, while he is touching the liquid of a Twin Earthian river:

C) Twater in that river was as chilly as twater in this river

What can we say in this case? I think that the first occurrence of 'twater' refers (in the speaker's intention) to Earthian water, so to water. But it seems that in its second occurrence it refers to twater. Is this true? It is true that in the second occurrence, 'twater' refers to a sample of twater. But it is not so clear that the sample is classified as pertaining to the kind twater; it is not clear then that he is meaning twater by 'twater', as I have contended above. Contrarily, since C) is perfectly equivalent to

C') Twater in that river was as chilly as *it* is in this river,

The kind referred to in the intention of the speaker has to be the same in both cases[19]. Maybe that kind of liquid is water[20] and for this reason his belief is not true.

Suppose that Peter knows that water is H_2O, for him, then, C' is a synonymous[21] of

---

[18] When someone believes that p, she also believes that it is true that p, but when one believes that it is true that p she does not always believes that p. One can believe that q and for this reason and because she believes that the sentence S (which really expresses p) expresses q, can believe that S (which expresses p, has the truth-conditions of p) is true, and so can believe that p is true. But then her belief on p is only a belief on the truth value of a proposition, not a real belief or a belief about the world; it is almost a linguistic belief, the belief that S express something true (the proposition p), which belief is false. See T. Grimaltós and C. Hookway "When Deduction Leads to Belief", *Ratio*, vol. VIII, no. 1 (1995), pp. 24-41 and T. Grimaltós and C. Moya, "Belief, Content and Cause", *European Review of Philosophy. Cognitive Dynamics*, vol. 2 (1997), pp. 159-171 for more details on this.

[19] The 'it' is anaphoric and has to refer to the same kind of thing as 'twater' in the intention of the speaker.

[20] This is, as I understand it, Carlos Moya's position in 'Externalism and Self-knowledge'. According to this position, Peter's belief that water in this river is chilly is not true, since it is not water what the river contains. This is relevant to what Boghossian says about inferences in 'Externalism and Inference'; at least as far as natural kind terms are concerned.

[21] When I say that C' is, for him, a synonymous of C", I mean that, for Peter, C" is an alternative way of expressing the belief expressed by C' or by C.

C") H_2O in that river was as chilly as H_2O in this river.

6 The responsibility of inference for the content of our thoughts

Up to now, I have argued that the content of thoughts in which a natural kind term intervenes is not always fixed by the meaning of that term. I think the case is reproducible in the case of terms whose meaning is conventionally fixed by (only) the social environment. I shall now offer a couple of examples to illustrate this. At the same time I shall try to show that the inferential origin of thoughts contributes to their content. The contents of reasons that serve as premises affect, in an essential way, to the content of the conclusion.

First, I am going to use a variation of an example in Burge's 'Belief and Synonymy'[22]. Imagine that Peter wants to be gone for twelve days. Peter has a good number of true beliefs about what a fortnight is. He believes for instance, that a fortnight is more or less the duration of Spanish Easter holidays, he believes that the seventh consulate of Marius lasted less than a fortnight, that in a month's time there is room for two fortnights and not for three, etc. But, Peter also believes that a fortnight is a period of twelve days. He makes an inference and says that he wants to be gone for a fortnight. Does he really want to be gone for a fortnight? But he believes that he wants to be gone for a fortnight, or that is what it seems. Does not he know what he wants? If he does not want to be gone for a fortnight, but only for twelve days, how is it that he believes that he wants to be gone for a fortnight? Compare this case with the case of John: he has heard that Mary wants to go to Paris for a fortnight. He does not know exactly how much time a fortnight is (he knows only that it is a period of time among ten and fifteen days) but he wants to be in Paris during the time Mary will be there. John really wants to be in Paris for a fortnight (whatever a fortnight is) and he wants to mean a fortnight by 'a fortnight'.

Let us make now a thought experiment in the way of Putnam or Burge. Suppose that there exists a Twin Earth in which 'fortnight' means a period of twelve days instead of a period of two weeks or fourteen days. In such a Twin Earth, Peter, who is a Twin Earthian, believes that

1) The seventh consulate of Marius lasted exactly twelve days

---

[22] *Loc. cit.*

and he infers for this reason (and his certainty that 'fortnight' means a period of twelve days) that

2) The seventh consulate of Marius lasted exactly a fortnight.

His latter belief is not, in a sense, different from the previous one. He could not accept the latter if he believed that the sentence 'the seventh consulate of Marius lasted exactly a fortnight' could express something different (a different fact) from 'The seventh consulate of Marius lasted exactly twelve days', because in believing (imagine that he believes it with certainty) that it lasted twelve days, he is excluding any possibility whatsoever which results incompatible with 'twelve days'. He can only accept, then, 'The seventh consulate of Marius lasted exactly a fortnight' as a synonym of 'The seventh consulate of Marius lasted exactly twelve days'. For Peter 'The seventh consulate of Marius lasted exactly twelve days' is the only correct answer to the question 'How long did the seventh consulate of Marius last?' You can ask him about the circumstances in which he would say that it is true that the seventh consulate of Marius lasted a fortnight. You can ask him whether it is true or false that the seventh consulate of Marius lasted a fortnight if it lasted twelve days, if it lasted nine, if it lasted fourteen, etc. He would only say that it is true if it lasted twelve days. In such a situation, 2) is not, in the case of Peter, a different belief of 1), but a different expression of 1). Of course, Peter usually employs 'fortnight' deferentially; he wants to mean by 'fortnight' whatever it means. But in this case, we have to say that he uses it referentially (although there is no mismatch), he wants to refer to (or mean) a period of twelve days and only to a period of twelve days, and because of the reasons we have offered. 2) Wants only to be an alternative expression of 1) and it is accepted only as far as he believes 1). Peter cannot refuse 1) and accept 2); neither refuse 2) and accept 1), in such a situation. Maybe we can say that 1) and 2) are (in Peter's use) alternative sentences to express one and the same belief content (at least as far as truth conditions are concerned).

Suppose now that Peter, instead of being a Twin Earthian, is an actual Earthian (or a Twin Earthian unwittingly transported to Earth and living here for some time) and that his inference has taken place on Earth[23]. We would have to account for the story in terms similar to this. He believes that

---

[23]For the sake of argument, suppose that the Marius being referred is the same on Earth and Twin Earth; you can imagine that in Twin Earth, people study Earth's ancient history and believe that it is their own history. So when they talk about Marius

1') The seventh consulate of Marius lasted exactly twelve days.

He (falsely) believes that a fortnight is a period of twelve days and for this reason and only this reason he infers and accepts that

2') The seventh consulate of Marius lasted exactly a fortnight.

It seems to be a consequence of Burge's claims that we should have to say that the beliefs Peter would have after the inferences in Twin Earth and Earth have different contents. If one is true, the other is false. 2) and 2') have different truth-conditions and, then, different content. But in what sense his beliefs would have different contents? Can we say that he believes on Twin Earth that the seventh consulate of Marius lasted twelve days, while on Earth he believes that it lasted fourteen days? Clearly not. But if terms have to determine the content of a thought, it has to be by their meaning, not by their own. The beliefs 1) and 2) or 1') and 2') would have to be different, not because in one case it appears 'twelve days' and in the other 'a fortnight', but because in one case he should have to believe that the seventh consulate of Marius lasted twelve days and in the other that it lasted a fortnight (a real fortnight, whatever it is), what is not obviously the case. He would believe in both places that it is true that the seventh consulate of Marius lasted a fortnight. But this only shows that he considers true two different propositions, truly in one case, falsely in the other. He would not have two beliefs with different content, but believe true two different propositions. He would use two different sentences, with different content (different propositions expressed), to express the same belief (the same belief content) and, consequently, with different fortune. Peter has a belief about a particular period of time, and he can think and express it with the correct terms or not. He can incorrectly think about twelve days in terms of a fortnight, but the mere fact that 'fortnight' means fourteen days does not make his belief to be about a period of fourteen days. If the beliefs in the conclusions are for Peter alternative ways of expressing the same belief as in the premises, and if 1) and 1') have the same content, what he believes first orderly when he believes 2) and 2') to be true cannot have different contents, although the propositional content of 2) and 2') is different. When Peter believes that the seventh consulate of Marius lasted twelve days, he is attributing a truth condition to his be-

---

and his seventh consulate they are talking about our Marius, and not about a Twin Marius.

lief: it would be true if the seventh consulate of Marius lasted twelve days, it would be false if it lasted less or more. In believing that it lasted a fortnight, he is using 'fortnight' referentially to mean the same period of time; otherwise, Peter would be irrational. So if he chooses an incorrect sentence to express this belief, this fact does not prove that he has a different belief, but a false higher order belief about the truth-value of a proposition. (This has not to be news to Burge[24]). Again,

     a') His thought is about twelve days
     b') He thinks it in terms of 'fortnight', i.e., by means of a term that means fourteen days.

Not only the causal origin (through the social influence) of a thought has a role in determining its content; its inferential origin has a role too.

    The situation would differ if what happens to Peter in the actual world and in a counterfactual world, where 'fortnight' means twelve days, were one of the two following things:

    a)   Peter, who has not a clear idea of how much time a fortnight is, reads on an encyclopaedia that the seventh consulate of Marius lasted a fortnight. Peter trusts completely encyclopaedias, so he believes it.

    In such a case what Peter would believe on Earth and on Twin Earth, would be in fact different. His beliefs would have different contents, because in such beliefs 'fortnight' would have a purely deferential use.

    b)   Peter believes (on Earth and Twin Earth) that the seventh consulate of Marius lasted a fortnight, because he read it in an encyclopaedia which he completely trusts, and he also believes that a fortnight is a period of twelve days, but he believes this with less confidence than he believes what the encyclopaedia says. In such a case, if he comes to believe that a fortnight is not a period of twelve days, he would reject that the seventh consulate of Marius lasted twelve days as false, but he would not reject that the seventh consulate of Marius lasted a fortnight.

---

[24] *Cf.* 'Belief *de re*', *The Journal of Philosophy*, vol. LXXIV (1977), pp. 338-362; p. 342, note 4.

A last case. In 'Normativism and the Mental: A Problem of Language Individuation', Adèle Mercier explains the semantically change of the word 'bead'[25]. She says: "In the Middle English, the word 'bead' meant prayer (from Old English 'biddan', to pray -cf. the current verb 'to bid'), and praying folk used rosaries to "count their beads". Now, at least one person, but probably many, misunderstood (or only partially understood) what the praying folk where doing (i.e. counting their prayers) and misunderstood (or only partially understood) the priests who explained: "They are counting their beads". What they understood, or if you don't like that way of putting it, what they took the praying folk to be doing, is counting the little doodads on the rosary"[26].

Now suppose that Peter was one of the first persons who first misunderstood (or only partially understood) 'bead' as meaning a little doodad in a rosary or in general as what today 'bead' means. He believed that prayers were counting the little doodads on the rosary. Of course when he first believed that, 'bead' still meant 'prayer', but as Peter used it referentially to refer to the little doodads, his thought was about the doodads and not about the prayers. Imagine that Peter lives time enough to think that thought again when the semantically change has (unknown to him) been produced, when the definition for 'bead' in dictionaries was (as it currently really is) "small pieces of colored glass, wood, plastic, etc, usually round in shape with a hole through the middle"[27]. Would his thought on that occasion have a different content from the thought he had the first time, when 'beads' meant prayers? Of course the sentences he used in one and another occasion have different content, and he believes two different propositions to be true, but I do not think that this fact affects the content of his first order thoughts. He thinks both times that prayers count the doodads on rosaries, but one time he thinks or expresses this thought by means of a term that means prayers and the other with a term that means beads.

7 Some conclusions on belief content and on self-knowledge

To say that two thoughts are different (have different content) because the sentences one uses to express them could have different truth-conditions (can have different propositional content) is as poor and un-explaining as saying that two people (or the same person in different

---

[25] *Philosophical Studies, 72 (1993), 71-88.*

[26] *Ibid.* p. 84.

[27] Collins Cobuild, *English Language Dictionary,* HarperCollins, London, 1978.

times) have the same thought if they believe the same proposition to be true. Imagine that Peter believes that Smith is a lecturer in the Department of Philosophy. As he also believes that Smith is Nancy's husband, he infers that

(a) Nancy's husband is a lecturer in the Department of Philosophy

and believes this proposition to be true. Now, Peter tells John that (a). John has not any other information on the subject. Both, Peter and John, believe (a) to be true. But, do both of them have the same belief? To say that both have the same belief is to offer a poor account of their beliefs' content. If, John comes to believe that Smith is not Nancy's husband, he will not immediately abandon his belief in (a), instead he will conclude that Nancy's husband has to be one of the other lectures in the Department of Philosophy (and if he really does not know anything about who are the members of the Department of Philosophy, he will also conclude that Smith is not a lecturer in that Department). However, if Peter comes to believe that Smith is not Nancy's husband, he will have to abandon his belief in the truth of (a) (he should have to believe that (a) was false or suspend his judgment). (a) represents the content of John's belief in a faithful way. That is not the case for Peter. Peter believes (a) only as an alternative expression of his belief that Smith is a lecturer in the Department of Philosophy[28]. If he comes to believe that Smith is not Nancy's husband, he cannot conclude that it has to be another lecturer in the Department of Philosophy who married Nancy, neither he will conclude that Smith is not a member of the Department of Philosophy). Peter has a complete answer to the question "Who is Nancy's husband?" and this answer excludes any other possible one. (a) contains answers that Peter has excluded and which he cannot rationally accept. Peter is using "Nancy's husband" referentially; (a) has for Peter the same content, as "Smith, who is married with Nancy, is a lecturer in the Department of Philosophy".

---

[28] Or the belief that Smith is Nancy's husband and is lecturer in the Department of Philosophy. That's the reason why he has to abandon his belief in a). Many times when a belief of the form "The F is G" is believed referentially, one does not only believe that an a (picked out by the description, which can fulfill or not) is G, but also that a is F. So, very frequently when one believes "The F is G" referentially, one believes '$Fa \wedge Ga$' and not only 'Ga'. This, of course, does not mean that the proposition one believes to be true (the proposition expressed by the sentence one uses to express her belief) is not always analyzable in Russellian terms. Carlos Moya and I develop this in 'Proper and Improper Beliefs' (manuscript).

In a similar vein, it does not matter what 'fortnight' means, if one believes that it is true that he will be gone for a fortnight because, and only because, he believes that he will be gone for twelve days, then the meaning of 'fortnight' has no role in order to determine the content of his or her belief.

I think that this position can be fairly identified as externalist. It maintains that the meaning of terms is fixed by the contribution of the environment, and it also accepts that environment often contributes to partly fix the content of our thoughts through the meaning of terms which intervene in them. Besides, it accepts that beliefs are to be evaluated by the conventional meaning of the terms and not by the speaker's meaning, except when terms have a referential use[29]. After all, when a subject believes a sentence S to be true, but the content of his thought does not correspond with the proposition expressed by this sentence, the content of his thought is also partly fixed by the environment (although, maybe the environment that contributes is not the present one as in the case of people transported to Twin Earth or to Earth).

If this is so, then it is my opinion that the qualifications made so far facilitate the conciliation between externalism and direct knowledge of our own thoughts, which some philosophers have put in question. Only when terms are used deferentially, the content of our thoughts is determined by the actual meaning of the terms that figure in them. Otherwise, the terms we employ do not determine what our thoughts are about. So, when our terms are used referentially, we can know perfectly well, without carrying out any empirical research, the content of our intentional attitudes. When they are used deferentially, we perfectly know what the contents of our thoughts are, since they are as indeterminate as in the case in which we use a definite description attributively. When we believe that the murderer, whoever he is, is insane, it does not affect the knowledge of the content of our thought the fact that the murderer is John or that it is Paul. In the same way when we use 'fortnight' deferentially it does not affect the knowledge of our thought content that it means fourteen days or twelve days, since we are being deferential about its exact duration. On the other hand, if we use it referentially it does not matter either what its real meaning is, because we are using it to mean a particular period of time and only that period of time. It is like when we use 'the murderer' referentially to talk about John; it does not matter if he really has not killed anyone; we have managed to talk about him even if the sentence we have used is false (or untrue, I am

---

[29] Recall the quotation above from Burge's 'Belief and Synonymy'.

not going to argue about that here). Our thought is about John even if John does not fulfill our description.

3

On Orthodox and Heterodox Externalisms*

JORGE RODRÍGUEZ MARQUEZE

1 Introduction

My goal in this paper is to show, in a rough outline, how McCulloch's externalism, as presented in his book *The Mind and Its World*[1], is exposed or open to a basic, general criticism made by Bilgrami, in his book *Belief and Meaning*[2], against any form or type of what he calls 'orthodox externalism'. First, I will sketch Bilgrami's argument against orthodox externalism. Later, I will briefly present McCulloch's externalist thesis and I will devote the rest of the text to examining whether his position is threatened by Bilgrami's argument.

* Research for this paper has been partly funded by the Spanish Government's DGICYT through project PS-92-DG-0121-206. I appreciate this financial support. Also, I am very grateful to José A. Díez-Calzada for his valuable written comments on a previous draft of this work.

[1] Routledge, 1995. All quotes from McCulloch used in the text are from this book.

[2] Blackwell, 1992. All quotes from Bilgrami present in the text are from this book. I have used the first paperback 1994 edition.

Meaning, Basic Self-Knowledge and Mind: Essays on Tyler Burge.
María J. Frápolli and Esther Romero (eds.).
Copyright © 2003, CSLI Publications.

2 Bilgrami's argument against orthodox externalism

2.1 What does Bilgrami understand by orthodox externalism?

He understands by such any externalism based on or linked to what he calls orthodox theories of reference (p. 32); that is, causal theories of reference or theories that accept the notion of direct reference. In Bilgrami's view, classic formulations of orthodox externalism can be found in "The Meaning of 'Meaning'"[3] (henceforth, '*MM*') by Putnam and in "Naming and Necessity"[4] by Kripke. Bilgrami distinguishes three different orthodox externalisms and directs his attack against all of them. It suffices for us to know that one of these orthodox externalisms is the one he calls 'causal-essentialist', attributed to Putnam and (with variants) also to Kripke.[5] This is of interest to us because, as we shall go on to see, McCulloch's externalism is greatly indebted to the Putnamian theory of content for natural kind-terms (or as McCulloch prefers to call them, 'substance-words'), and can be seen as a version or adaptation of the latter. Therefore, we will do well to take a look at Bilgrami's criticism of Putnam's externalism as a preliminary step to dealing with McCulloch.

2.2 Bilgrami's argument

In a nutshell, Bilgrami's criticism towards orthodox externalism, whether Putnamian or otherwise, can be put thus: It is not possible to reconcile the obvious pre-theoretical supposition that the content of our beliefs and other psychological states is efficacious in the ordinary psychological explanation of the behavior of human beings with the idea that content is what the orthodox externalist theory says it is. If content is as the orthodox externalists understand it to be, then (external) content lacks explanatory efficacy.[6]

---

[3] Putnam, H., in *Mind, Language and Reality: Philosophical Papers*, vol. 2, Cambridge U. P., 1975.

[4] Kripke, S., in D. Davidson and G. Harman (eds.), *Semantics for Natural Language*, Reidel, 1972.

[5] The two other types of orthodox externalism are, according to Bilgrami: 1) what he calls 'causal-informational externalism', attributed mainly to Fodor and supposedly based on the kind of information-based semantics proposed by Dretske and Stampe; and 2) social externalism, whose most influential and interesting proponent—to put it in Bilgrami's own words—is Tyler Burge. It may be useful to mention here that although this paper does not deal directly with Burge's views, most of the issues touched upon could be very naturally reformulated in ways plainly relevant to Burge's position.

[6] Bilgrami, a professed externalist himself, takes pains to distinguish his own externalism (and hence, externalism as such) from orthodox externalism. To keep this paper

According to Bilgrami, the sterility for psychological explanation plaguing orthodox externalist content emerges as the result of studying two types of examples: the so-called Fregean puzzles and the Putnamian, Twin-Earth style thought-experiments—in fact both types of examples are typically used by internalists in their attacks on externalism. In the Fregean examples, this sterility is shown by the fact that wide (orthodox externalist) content is too coarse-grained. In the Twin-Earth cases this sterility is patent from the fact that wide content is too fine-grained. As Bilgrami says:

> [T]he taxonomy [of content] dictated by [orthodox] externalism in the twin-earth example has us attributing two beliefs where [psychological] explanation requires one, whereas [orthodox] externalism in [the Fregean] example dictated that there be one belief where explanation requires two (p. 20).

The argument used by Bilgrami to substantiate his accusation against all types of orthodox externalism can be formulated thus: Orthodox externalists inescapably face or encounter a fatal trilemma when dealing both with the so-called Fregean puzzles regarding content and with cases directly related to Twin-Earth style thought-experiments. The trilemma is the following: 1) Either they must uncharitably attribute implausibly inconsistent or, at best, very bizarre beliefs and other propositional attitudes to subjects of belief; 2) or they must bifurcate content; 3) or, finally, they must admit that subjects lack self-knowledge of their own contents

Let us briefly look at how the trilemma arises for each of the two examples when the starting externalist theory is of the "causal-essentialist" type in Putnam's style.

2.3 The Fregean puzzles

Let us first focus on the Fregean puzzles.[7] Since they are designed to throw light on the analysis of singular terms, we need to modify them appropriately for the purpose of our discussion: the analysis of sub-

---

manageable, I have had to leave the discussion of Bilgrami's heterodox externalism entirely untouched.

[7] When speaking of Fregean puzzles, I naturally refer to the very famous examples examined and introduced by Kripke in "A Puzzle about Belief" (for example, the one whose main characters are Pierre, London and the names 'London' and 'Londres'; and also the one which talks about Paderewski, his name 'Paderewski' and his two facets of pianist and politician), but also to its more basic or less sophisticated versions put forward by Frege himself (among others, his classic example of Venus, the Morning Star and the Evening Star).

stance-words (which as I have already advanced, is the type of term for which McCulloch designs his theory). But of course, the modification is straightforward. Let us take the case of two terms used to refer to the same natural substance: 'water' and 'ice'. Let us also suppose that there is a speaker, Oscar, or a group of English speakers to which Oscar belongs, who although acquainted with water in its normal, liquid state and in its solid state, think that water and ice are different substances (they do not know the chemical constitution of water and ice, and moreover, they have never seen a lump of ice melt nor have they experimented the freezing of a portion of liquid water, etc.) Thus, this community associates the term 'water' only with portions of water in liquid state and associates the term 'ice' with ice without knowing that what its members call 'ice' is water. It seems reasonable to specify the relevant beliefs of Oscar by sentences 1) and 2):

Oscar believes that ice is ice.

Oscar believes that ice is not water.

But if substance-words have the meaning that the standard interpretation of Putnam's theory of meaning (as set out in *MM*) seems to attribute them, then, assuming identity or a close connection between semantic and mental content (that is, assuming what Kripke calls "the principle of disquotation"), it seems that the joint truth of 1) and 2) requires us to accept that Oscar holds a pair of beliefs which are scandalously inconsistent. In fact, according to Putnam's theory (in its standard interpretation), substance-words are rigid designators, which refer directly, and so their contribution to the semantic (truth-conditional) content of the sentences in which they occur is nothing other than their reference. However, this means that any co-referential substance-words are identical in semantic content). And so, in our Fregean case concerning 'water' and 'ice', the semantic content of

3) Ice is Ice.

and
4) Ice is water.

is literally the same, since 'water' and 'ice' are co-referential. Now, given the mentioned principle of disquotation, this entails that the content of the beliefs expressed by the utterances of 3) and 4) is the same.

That is to say, attributing the belief that ice is ice to Oscar and attributing the belief that ice is water to Oscar are attributions of one and the same belief. And similarly, attributing the beliefs that ice is ice and that ice is not water to Oscar is tantamount to attributing to Oscar an absurdly inconsistent pair of beliefs.

This being so, three options arise: 1) either we conclude that Oscar is absurdly irrational in his beliefs and behavior concerning water and ice. 2) Or we conclude that the content specified by Putnam's theory is not the only type of content associated to substance terms but is complemented with another type of content which is much more fine-grained than the former (that is, more sensitive to the different ways of conceiving substances which a subject can have), and so the really efficacious one as regards psychological explanation.[8] 3) Or else we assume that subjects of belief lack self-knowledge about their belief contents.

2.4 Twin-Earth cases

Let us now look at Twin-Earth cases.[9] We suppose that a planet, Twin Earth, coexists with Earth and is similar to Earth in all aspects except for one very specific feature: what is called 'water' on Twin Earth has a chemical composition different from H_2O. It is not H_2O but XYZ. Nevertheless, its superficial or macro-molecular properties are exactly the same as those of H_2O. Also, we imagine an inhabitant of Earth, Susana (let us say), and her twin on Twin Earth, Twin-Susana, who are molecule for molecule identical (and so "internally identical"). Given the theory of meaning and content attributed to Putnam, the beliefs of Susana and Twin-Susana specified in 5) and 6), respectively, are different.

5) Susana believes that water (= H_2O) is good for quenching thirst.

6) Twin-Susana believes that water (=XYZ) is good for quenching thirst.

---

[8] It is to this position that Bilgrami is referring when he talks about the bifurcationist solution to the Puzzle. It is important to notice that Putnam (or the standardly interpreted Putnam that Bilgrami presents) would openly acknowledge the bifuracationist implications of his doctrine on meaning\content. But he would not see them as a drawback or as an embarrassment. Quite to the contrary, he would see them as part of the solution to the problems discussed in the text. Neither Bilgrami nor McCulloch can take this attitude because they both hold the thesis of the unity of content (See, infra, p.).

[9] Just as happens with the Fregean puzzles, this is a very popular case and very widely known since its conception by Putnam in 1975. So I will be extremely brief in its description.

However, from the design of the example, it again seems that these differences in content are absolutely irrelevant in explaining the respective behavior of the two twins concerning H2O and XYZ, given the supposition that both twins are ignorant as to the chemical composition of the substances they call 'water'. For example, they both drink a glass full of a substance they both call 'water' because both are thirsty and both believe that drinking this (respective) substance will quench their thirst. As Bilgrami points out:

Our interest as explainers or rationalizers of their actions is simply not in a chemical fact that neither of them is aware of. As far as the interests of such explainers is concerned, that chemical fact does not have the effect of showing that their respective actions must be differently described. And so it does not have the effect of showing that they must have different water-beliefs and different water-desires. (p. 20).

In its official version, just as it has been arranged, the Twin-Earth example does not directly lend itself to the attribution of inconsistencies, because the beliefs compared in the example involve different subjects and not just a single individual. But a slight variation of the example brings us back to the danger of inconsistency. The variation consists simply in focusing on only one of the two twins, Susana or Twin-Susana. Would we not have to accuse Susana of inconsistency if she uttered (sincerely, etc) 7):

7) Water is not H2O.

even in the case that Susana had no knowledge of chemistry? And equally, would we not have to accuse Twin-Susana of inconsistency if she uttered 8):

8) Water is not XYZ?

Exactly as in the Fregean examples, the orthodox externalist faces the three undesirable alternatives of: 1) assuming the subject of belief to be absurdly irrational, 2) bifurcating content (taking care, this time, that the type of additional content introduced to save the rationality of each of the twins be of a coarser grain than orthodox externalist content), or 3) denying self-knowledge.

3 McCulloch's externalist theory

I will start with three warnings:

First, an important restriction in the scope of the theory should be borne in mind: it is a theory of content intended in principle only for natural kind-terms and concepts or for sentences and thoughts about natural kinds. The second and third warnings merely make clear two basic presuppositions that this theory shares with many others (in particular, with that offered by Bilgrami himself) First, the presupposition that there is an identity between semantic and psychological content. In particular and given the above-mentioned restriction in scope, the presupposition is that the meaning of a substance-word and the concept associated with it are one and the same entity. Second, the presupposition already referred to in a previous note[10] that an adequate theory of content must be one that maintains the unity of content (pp. 190 ff.)—that is, "[the claim] that there is only one notion of content, which is externally determined and which explains actions" (Bilgrami, p. 3)[11].

What is, according to McCulloch, the meaning of a substance-word? That is to say, what is the nature of a concept associated to a substance-word? A concept associated to a substance-word is, in McCulloch's terminology, an in-the-world Wittgensteinian sense. We can understand in-the-world Wittgensteinian senses as the result of interlacing three different notions: The notion of meaning as use, taken from Wittgenstein's *Philosophical Investigations*; Putnam's notion of meaning as "essence revealed or revealable by science"; and the Fregean notion of sense (Sinn), but devoid of its "descriptional" or "definitional" standard interpretation, so discredited since Kripke's and Putnam's objections.

The mixture or fusion of these three notions boils down to this: From Frege's sense, only its feature of being a mode of presenting reference is taken. However, *mode of presentation* is understood in terms of Wittgenstein's notion of meaning as use. We could say that, for McCulloch, the mode of presenting the reference (for a natural kind-term) is through a certain practice grounded on this reference. McCulloch's senses are practices or forms of life or sets of abilities grounded on or associated with references. Or rather, given a term of natural kind N whose reference is substance t, the sense of N is a practice grounded on t.

---

[10] See note 3.

[11] The quote is from Bilgrami, not from McCulloch. But the thesis would be wholeheartedly subscribed by the latter if formulated at this high level of generality. Their differences surface, no doubt, when proceeding to detail their respective views concerning what may count as "external determination" of content.

In turn, the Wittgensteinian notion of practice or form of life or use is complemented with and specified by the application of what McCulloch describes as the Putnamian doctrine that "the understanding tracks real essence" (p 163). That is, for our purposes, with the thesis that the extension or the reference of substance-words is or forms part of their sense (meaning).

To my understanding, and although McCulloch himself offers nothing by way of a quasi-formal representation of his senses/concepts, we can represent them as pairs with the following form:

<Practice grounded on $t-t$, t>

where t is a substance denoted by a substance-word, '−' is the arithmetical sign 'minus' and the expression '$t - t$' should be read as 't minus t'. The reason for 't' appearing three times in the former representation is that the substance t grounding a certain practice is itself a constituent of this practice. Hence, the occurrence of t as the second element of the pair. But, on the other hand, a practice grounded on t is not exhausted by (does not merely comprise) the grounding substance. It is in order to refer to these "residual" features making up the practice grounded on t that I represent the first element of the pair by the expression 'practice grounded on $t - t$' (this expression should be read as "practice grounded on t minus t").

This highly succinct description of McCulloch's doctrine suffices for my purposes of evaluating how it stands up against the type of criticism Bilgrami directs against orthodox externalism.

4 McCulloch's senses faced with Bilgrami's trilema

Very briefly, the result of my evaluation will be the following: Confronted with the Fregean puzzles, McCulloch's senses are unable to overcome the trilemma formulated by Bilgrami. McCulloch's solution to the puzzles presupposes a veiled appeal either to bifurcation of content or to denial of self-knowledge. Independently of this, disregarding the problem posed by the Fregean puzzles, McCulloch's senses are also vulnerable to Bilgrami's trilemma in confrontation with Twin-Earth cases. But now they are vulnerable only on condition that a certain type of interpretation of a variant of these cases is acceptable. If this interpretation is rejected, McCulloch's senses avoid the trilemma. However, this occurs at the cost of having to admit what I think is a rather bizarre or extravagant notion of *substance-word*.

I now move on to a detailed examination of the points under debate:

4.1 McCulloch's senses and the Fregean puzzles

4.1.1 McCulloch's solution

Let us first see how McCulloch applies his notion of in-the-world Witt-gensteinian Sense to face up to the Fregean puzzles. I will simply help myself to a relatively long quote of McCulloch's. His words are, I think, eloquent enough to omit additional comments on my part.

On [my] approach, to say that one associates a certain sense with a substance-word is to say that the word is part of a practice or form of life involving the substance. But even when this is intended, as [in my doctrine], so that forms of life track real essence, it does not follow that forms of life have to be sensitive to *nothing but* real essence. Hence it does not follow that the 'water'-involving practice has to be identified with or include the 'ice'-involving practice, even though they both in fact track the same real essence. And of course, [given an incurious group of people who knew water from the hot plain and later encounter ice on the cold mountain, who had never seen the former freeze or the latter melt, and who supposed that water and ice are as different as Chablis and Cheese], on no sane interpretation of 'ability' do the members of the group [so described] acquire just the one ability in acquiring 'water' and then 'ice'. Down on the plain they are inducted into one practice involving water in liquid form, then later up on the mountain they begin or are inducted into an entirely distinct practice involving water in the solid form. Clearly they could engage in either practice without engaging in the other. Obviously to supplement one by the other is to extend their linguistic repertoire and hence their scope for forming propositional attitudes. On our Wittgensteinian approach, then, their uses of 'water' constitute one exercise of understanding, and their uses of 'ice' constitute another. *In other words, the contents ascribed in [7] They do not realize that ice is water] and [8] They do not realize that ice is ice] are distinct contents, even though they are also wide and track the same real essence.* So there is no reason to suppose that they have the same explanatory powers. (p. 210. Emphasis mine)[12].

4.1.2 Bilgrami's trilemma

Given McCulloch's line of defense, the Bilgramian counterattack strategy is clear and simple. In fact, with the McCullochian senses represented in this way, it is easy to directly accuse McCulloch of incurring in bifurcation. And so of being trapped by the second horn of Bilgrami's trilemma.

---

[12] The sentence enclosed in square brackets is an almost literal quotation from a previous fragment of McCulloch's text (pp. 208–9).

We must realize that McCullochian senses\concepts, the practices grounded on substances and trackers of the real essence of such substances, surreptitiously reproduce the duality of aspects that the Putnamian theory attributes to substances from the point of view of our cognitive access to them. Natural substances can be described attending either to their "superficial" features or to their "intrinsic", "deep" or "underlying" features. Similarly, the concepts we use to think about them seem to be amenable to identical treatment. They also accept two types of characterization, according to what we may call their superficial aspects and their deep aspects. By 'superficial aspects' I mean, for instance, those aspects, which distinguish the practices grounded on liquid water and on frozen water, when it is not known that water is ice. In general, I mean those features of McCullochian concepts, which, in our canonical form of representation, are expressed by the first element of the pair. In turn, by 'deep aspects' I understand those represented by the second element of the pair, in our canonical representation.

Now, in the above quote, it is only the supposition that self-knowledge of our concepts is of their superficial aspects, but not of their "deep" or "underlying" aspects, which allows one to solve the Fregean puzzles. When Oscar, a member of the community imagined by McCulloch, believes that ice is ice but that ice is not water, what happens (if we describe the situation in McCullochian terms) is that Oscar has two different concepts. One with the form <Water-practice grounded on H2O - H2O, H2O>; the other, with the form <Ice-practice grounded on H2O - H2O, H2O>. Moreover, Oscar by having these two different concepts knows they are different. But his knowledge or his grasping of them is, we could say, not complete but partial. It is not sufficiently transparent or detailed to embrace or include the fact that they have a very important aspect in common. Actually, if Oscar had a full knowledge of both aspects of his two concepts of H2O, then he would probably cease, strictly speaking, to possess two different concepts of H2O. They would immediately evolve into partial components of a single, richer and more complex H2O concept, which would include both. The amount of self-knowledge we suppose Oscar to have concerning his two concepts grounded on water is not total but is just the right one to rationally explain Oscar's linguistic and extra-linguistic behavior. If his knowledge were total or complete, then he could recognize both concepts as being of the same substance, and so it would not be reasonable to suppose that Oscar believes that water and ice are different substances. On the other hand, if Oscar were not conscious of the difference between his two concepts, if he did not recognize them as different in the aspect in which they are different (if he were not in a position to recognize that the practices which constitute them are different), neither could we guarantee a rational explanation of Oscar's behavior. If he does not know that his concepts of water and ice are different we do not know how to justify that he believes that ice is ice but not water.

But to speak in these terms of partial self-knowledge is hardly different to talking about self-knowledge restricted to an aspect of the concepts in question. And that, after all, seems to amount to the surreptitious admission of two different aspects or factors in the constitution of content: One responsible for its efficacy in psychological explanation (the factor corresponding to the narrow content of bifurcationists), and another responsible for the externalist character of content (the factor corresponding to the wide content of bifurcationists). Perhaps these do not constitute two different contents in the strictest sense, but the acknowledgment of these two factors and their different role is enough to leave one open to the accusation of bifurcationism.

4.2 McCulloch's senses and Twin Earth

How does McCulloch's conception stand up to the Twin-Earth cases?

4.2.1 McCulloch's solution to the Twin Earth cases

The first point to notice is this: If despite its vulnerability—which I have just tried to show—we go along with McCulloch's strategy to block the Fregean puzzles; i.e., if we ignore the objection I have just made against it, then the replacement of the Putnamian, purely referential meanings\concepts by McCulloch's senses\concepts has the intended effect of sufficiently refining the grain of externalist content so that the trilemma arising from the Fregean puzzles can be deactivated. But such a replacement gains nothing with respect to Twin-Earth cases. Regarding these cases, the solution will have to come from making the grain of orthodox externalist content coarser. And nothing in McCulloch's senses\concepts constitutes an advance in this direction. Their grain is still fine enough to allow the concepts associated with 'water' by Susana and Twin-Susana to be different. And they are different exactly in the same way as or for the same reason that the Putnamian meanings\concepts were different.

For this reason, McCulloch's strategy when facing Twin-Earth cases, unlike the one he adopts for the Fregean puzzles, cannot consist in exploiting any adjustment or correction in grain supposedly provided by his new notion of sense for substance-words. As concerns Twin-Earth cases, McCullochian senses continue being—I repeat—as excessively fine-grained as Putnamian meanings\concepts are.

What is McCulloch's solution for the Twin-Earth cases?

McCulloch's defense against a possible internalist objector (or against an externalist in Bilgrami's sense) consists essentially in accusing his attacker of begging the question against (McCullochian) externalism. As in the case of the Fregean puzzles, I will practically limit myself to quoting those texts of McCulloch's, which I consider relevant:

McCulloch acknowledges (p. 212) that the problem posed by Twin-Earth cases for his in-the-world Wittgensteinian senses is entirely similar to the one it poses for a standard Putnamian externalist: they seem to be too fine-grained to be efficacious for the purposes of psychological explanation:

> The point is that the observable parallels between [Susana and Twin-Susana] are themselves evidence that common explanations should be given, and hence common mental states ascribed. (p. 212).

And a few paragraphs below, to avoid a possible reply by a McCullochian externalist, he reformulates the problem thus:

> The thought now is that [Susana] and [Twin-Susana] have the same causal powers in [the sense in which sameness of causal powers requires only same reaction *given the same context*]. Although (...) their careers are actually different ([Susana] drinks and swims in water, [Twin-Susana] drinks and swims in twin-water), it is also the case that they live in different contexts. But imagine that (say) [Twin-Susana] had been born and raised on Earth (...). Then she would have followed much the same career as [Susana] actually did follow, and as far as her dealings with water (H2O) are concerned, there is no doubt that they could have been exactly the same. But this indicates sameness of causal power after all: just as two metal balls have the same causal powers if and only if they would react the same in the same contexts, so presumably the same goes for agents too. [Susana] and [Twin-Susana], it seems, have the same causal powers as far as psychology is concerned, since they would react the same in the same contexts (...). (pp. 214-15).

Faced with this attack, McCulloch's response consists, as I mentioned above, in accusing his attacker of begging the question:

> This is neat, but it begs the most important question of all. We are willing to allow that two metal balls are mechanically equivalent if they have the same (mechanical) causal powers because we have already accepted that causal powers are all that matters from the point of view of mechanics (...) Mechanical nature is in this sense self-contained with respect to context: the ball can retain its own mechanical nature even though the context is varied (...) In comparing [Susana] and [Twin-Susana] to metal balls in the above way, the [argument against McCulloch senses] clearly begs the question against [them]. To assume that sameness of causal power in the above sense is tantamount to psychological equivalence is just to assume that the mind is self-contained with respect to changes in context such as that between Earth and Twin Earth. But that is precisely

the question at issue. (...) Our in-the-world Wittgensteinianism (...) sees the differences in actions performed between [Susana] and [Twin-Susana] not as inessential reflections of their difference in context, but as part of the stuff of the psychological differences between them. (pp. 215-16).

4.2.2 Bilgrami's trilemma

Whatever our opinion may be about McCulloch's counter-argument against his possible objector; that is, even supposing that he succeeds in his confrontation with the Twin-Earth cases he considers in his text,[13] what I want to underline is that such a defensive strategy is barren when dealing with other Twin-Earth versions. Or more exactly, that the adoption of this strategy paves the way for brandishing Bilgrami's trilemma against McCulloch's senses again. If we accept McCulloch's defense for his senses, we must understand the term 'water' as ambiguous in the Twin-Earth version considered by McCulloch himself; that is, as possessing two different McCullochian senses depending on whether this term is grounded on H2O or on XYZ, depending on whether 'water' is used by earthlings or Twin-earthlings. However, there are versions of the Twin-Earth case, like the one I am about to present, where such a supposition of the ambiguity of the term 'water' confronts us with Bilgrami's trilemma once again. It is of course true that, in these versions, it is not clear that we have to understand 'water' as an ambiguous term. However, the only alternative to this interpretation I can think of, although allowing the trilemma to be avoided, leads to a bizarre notion of substance-word.

Let us consider a Twin-Earth version, which I deem to be harmful for McCulloch. First of all, it is necessary to recognize that in order to construct a Twin-Earth version, which allows us to pose Bilgrami's trilemma it is, no longer possible to use the simple device we exploited to attack Putnamian meanings. It is not enough to imagine that Susana, an Earthling uneducated in chemistry, assents to or utters a sentence like

9) Water is not H2O.

According to the McCullochian analysis of substance-words, it is perfectly possible to suppose that the terms 'water' and 'H2O' have differ-

---

13 In fact, as I see it, McCulloch's strategy is not very convincing because it probably leads to a never-ending cross-fire of accusations and counter-accusations of having appealed to question-begging intuitions. (See Bilgrami, pp. 214 ff., and Larson & Segal, Knowledge of Meaning, MIT Press, 1995, secs. 13.1 and 13.2).

ent meanings for Susana. She would associate different practices grounded on H2O with each of the two terms. The sense of 'water' for Susana could be represented thus: <Aqueous practice grounded on H2O - H2O, H2O>. The sense of 'H2O', perhaps in this way: <"H2O-ous" practice grounded on H2O - H2O, H2O>.

To generate the danger of inconsistency or irrationality for Susana, given McCulloch's notion of content, we need to construct a case, which makes it possible to simultaneously ascribe to a single individual two McCullochian concepts that are entirely similar except for being grounded on different but qualitatively identical substances. Besides, this has to be a case, which makes it possible to suppose that the individual in question associates a single substance-word with both concepts, and of course with both substances.

The problem which arises, however, once a case of this type has been constructed, is that there are at least two possible ways of interpreting it: a) As a case in which the term 'water' is an ambiguous substance-word. b) As a case in which the term 'water' is not a substance-word, correctly speaking, but rather a general term similar to 'jade', 'liquid', etc. Only in the first case is it possible to submit McCulloch's thesis to Bilgrami's attack.

Here is, at last, an attempt to construct an example of the type I have just referred to: Let us imagine a Twin Earth where, together with water, that is, together with H2O, there exists a substance superficially or macro-molecularly identical to H2O but with a different chemical structure, XYZ. Let us further suppose that water (H2O) happens to be distributed throughout the European continent but not (or only scarcely) on the American continent. And inversely, that XYZ is (mainly) located on the American continent but is not found (except, perhaps, very scarcely) in Europe. Let us also imagine Susana, a person born in Dublin before the development of chemistry and so before the discovery that H2O and XYZ are different substances. English-speaking Americans call 'water' that which comes out of the taps of washbasins in their homes and fountains in their cities, etc.; just as their English-speaking counterparts in Europe call 'water' that which comes out of their washbasins and fountains, etc. Europeans in general, although not traveling much and having no (direct) contact with the aqueous substance from America, possess some information about the American continent. They believe that there is also water there and that what the Americans call 'water' is the same substance that abounds in Europe. And the same holds, *mutatis mutandis*, for Americans. But Susana is not a typical European, although perhaps she is a typical Dubliner, and emigrates as a teenager to Boston. Later as an adult, after a long period, she returns to Ireland and from then on alternates stays of quite a considerable length on each of the two sides of the Atlantic. Susana, who learns English in her native country and so associates its term 'water' with the aqueous substance which abounds in Europe, H2O, possesses as a child a McCullochian concept associated with 'water' different from that of any Bostonian. Remember that a McCullochian sense for a substance-word is a practice (or a set of abilities) grounded on the substance referred to by that term and a "tracker" of its "real essence". When Susana learns the meaning of the term 'water', what she learns is a practice resulting from her dealing with H2O, a practice based on H2O and a tracker of H2O. And given the identity between semantic and psychological content assumed by McCulloch, this practice also constitutes the McCullochian concept that Susana associates with the term 'water'.

Upon moving to Boston and after a certain period of time, Susana, who is no longer in contact with H2O but does have contact with XYZ, associates a new practice with her term 'water', that is a practice based on XYZ, not on H2O. Naturally, the new practice is completely identical to the previous one except for the chemical constitution of the substance, which grounds it.

If we accept that Susana's new aqueous practice, grounded on XYZ, is added to but does not wipe out or fuse with her previous one, grounded on H2O, the situation in which Susana finds herself can now be described, in McCullochian terms, as a case in which the term 'water' is ambiguous in Susana's mouth: Susana associates this term with two different McCullochian senses.

Let us now consider Susana's behavior, once she possesses her two different aqueous concepts, in the following context: Susana takes part in a contest which is similar except for period differences, to the current, popular television contests and almost of as poor intellectual demand for the contestant as their present-day counterparts. Among the tests Susana has to be submitted to in order to win a brand new carriage of the latest model with two horse power and life-long coachman service included is the following: She is asked, when faced with a set of containers with samples of diverse substances, to mix together only the contents of those containers having samples of the same substance. That is, it is a question of making a partition of the samples offered into equivalence classes according to the relation "being a sample of the same substance as". The test is considerably facilitated by the fact that the containers have labels with the names of the substances on them and also that the contestant is explicitly warned that their labels are not deceptive, that they correspond to their contents. As the test is so absurdly easy, Susana promptly carries it out and is very careful to mix together the content of all those containers labeled thus: 'Water from Dublin' and thus: 'Water from Boston'. Her mixing behavior is rewarded with the promised carriage, since all those involved in the contest share (although for different reasons) Susana's mistake, but we know that Susana has not fulfilled the requirements to win the prize.

How should we interpret Susana's mixing behavior? Should we judge it simply as erroneous but not irrational or as erroneous and also wildly irrational (=interpretable only as the result of possessing inconsistent beliefs)? The intuitively most obvious way of interpreting Susana's behavior is the former: We simply suppose that Susana does not know that water from Dublin and water from Boston are different substances. She mistakenly believes that both are the same substance. But given McCulloch's position, such an interpretation is forbidden. Or rather, it is forbidden unless one assumes that Susana, although possessing two different concepts associated with water from Dublin and water from Boston, does not know that they are different--that is, unless one assumes that Susana lacks self-knowledge about her own substance-concepts; about the ambiguity which affects her term 'water'. However, if we are willing to accept this diagnosis, we have already conceded too much to the Bilgramian objector—accepting it amounts to surrendering McCulloch's theory to the third horn of Bilgrami's trilemma. If we dismiss this diagnosis, the only justifying route left is that based on bifurcating the notion of content. Hence, the trilemma reappears in full strength.

However, the force of this conclusion, so adverse for McCulloch, weakens (as I have already mentioned) because there seems to be a way of reinterpreting my example which does not allow the trilemma to arise: McCulloch could simply argue that a situation strictly as the one described cannot arise, that it is incoherent. McCulloch could point out that in the case imagined, contrary to what I assumed when I described it, the term 'water' Susana associates with the two substances is not a substance-word, is not a term of natural kind, but a term similar to those such as 'gas', 'liquid' or (perhaps more accurately) similar to 'jade'. A genuine substance-word for water (= H_2O) would have to have as its extension (reference) only portions of H_2O. Such a term is impossible to find in the situation imagined. The important thing here is that the concept that Susana would have associated with her term 'water' would not be a McCullochian concept, would not be of the form:

<Practice grounded on $t - t, t$>,

but perhaps, of the type:

<Practice grounded on (t and t') - (t and t'), t or t'>.

But a term associated with a concept of this type—McCulloch could say—is not a (genuine) substance-word.

Why do I think that McCulloch would respond by denying the condition of "genuine" substance-word to 'water'? Because of the way he deals with a case similar to our example in his discussion and explanation of his Putnamian theory that "understanding tracks real essence" (p. 163). McCulloch, after quoting the following famous text of Putnam's:

I point to a glass of water and say 'this liquid is called water' (...) My 'ostensive definition' of water has the following empirical presupposition: that the body of liquid I am pointing to bears a certain sameness relation (say x *is the same liquid as* y...) to most of the stuff I and other members of my linguistic community have on other occasions called 'water' (...) The key point is that the relation [*same liquid as*] is a *theoretical* relation: whether something is or is not the same liquid as *this* may take an indeterminate amount of scientific investigation to determine. (Putnam, MM, p. 225). After quoting this text, McCulloch comments:

According to Putnam, we understand [substance-words] as having their correct application ultimately determined not by the superficial characteristics which guide our day-to-day judgments, but by a supposed, perhaps unknown, unifying real essence. So if it had turned out that we had been applying 'water' to a mixture of two or more different but superficially indistinguishable chemicals, then we should have said that there is no *one* substance water, just as there is no one mineral jade and no one gas air. Equally, we should have said that our pre-discovery understanding of 'water' was to that extent defective: we thought we meant a single substance by it, but we did not. (p. 163). [14]

It is difficult to resist the temptation of "completing" this passage by adding: "We thought that 'water' was a substance-word but it was not. Our understanding of the term 'water' was to this extent defective".

It is true that this way of blocking my Bilgramian attack amounts to adopting a rather peculiar notion of substance-word. A peculiar notion, because, to put it crudely, it implies that speaker intentions are irrelevant in determining whether a general term belongs to the (lexical) category of substance-word: the essential factor involved is the envi-

---

[14] McCulloch introduces this claim as one held by Putnam. But it is clear that McCulloch himself agrees with it.

ronment surrounding the subject or linguistic community that uses such a term. That is to say, whether the English word 'water' is a substance-word or not depends on whether there is, in the world where 'water' is used, one or several chemically different substances which are qualitatively identical. It depends on whether the earth contains only H2O with its usual macro-molecular properties or whether in addition it contains at least XYZ in amounts similar to those of H2O and in a way that H2O and XYZ are distributed more or less promiscuously throughout the planet. Precisely, the planet I have imagined in order to create difficulties for McCulloch would be one of those planets, with the exception that the distribution of both substances would be hardly promiscuous, if at all. But such a circumstance could be compensated for if it is supposed that the inhabitants of the planet travel frequently and are sufficiently advanced in transport and communications technology; that is, if we assume that there is an easy, relatively frequent and continuous access to different regions of the planet where the twin substances are found. For the same reason, a world extraordinarily poor and scarce in variety of liquids; that is, a world with only one liquid, water, would be a world, it seems, in which the English term 'liquid' would denote a single substance and would qualify as a substance-word. 'Liquid' would be at least co-referential with 'water' and, provided that the community of English speakers met certain conditions not very different from those described by McCulloch himself when presenting the case of the "incurious group of people" who mistakenly believe that (liquid) water and ice are different substances,[15] it seems that 'liquid' would be not merely co-referential but "synonymous" with 'water'.[16] The McCullochian concept associated with both terms would be one and the same. At the other extreme, a world extraordinarily rich in liquids and natural substances of all types (a world that, together with every natural substance S with macro-molecular properties P, included at least one twin substance S' with identical macro-molecular properties P) would be such that no English term spoken there would be a substance-word, at least not before the development of chemistry. Also, worlds like the "Dry

---

[15] Cf. supra, p.

[16] The required difference with respect to McCulloch's case is not important. It merely amounts to this: this time, the incurious group of people would have to believe, not only that liquid water and solid water are different substances, but also that they are both different from gaseous water. In general, the relevant case may be described as one in which the community of speakers believes that samples of substances in different states (solid, liquid, gaseous) are samples of different substances.

Earth" imagined by Paul Boghossian[17] would constitute cases in which the term 'water', although used with the (failed) intention to talk about a substance, would not be a substance word. Now, the problem is not that there is more than one substance to which 'water' applies, but rather that there is not any to which it may apply. No McCullochian concept could be associated with 'water' since there is no substance whose essence is to be tracked, no substance on which a practice could be grounded.

No doubt, this consequence about the behavior of substance-words, given McCulloch's hypothetical response, is considerably bizarre. But I am not sure it can be used to disqualify the latter, because, after all, we do not have a sufficiently clear idea about the conditions of material adequacy that a semantic theory for natural kind-terms should meet.

In summary, there are (at least) two possible ways of interpreting the Twin-Earth version that I have proposed: a) as a case in which the term 'water' is an ambiguous substance-word. b) As a case in which the term 'water' is not a substance-word, correctly speaking, but a general term similar to 'jade', 'liquid', etc. Only in the first case is it possible to submit McCulloch's thesis to Bilgrami's attack against orthodox externalism.

Before finishing this last section, I would like to draw attention to one more point: As I have tried to show above, if we adopt interpretation a) of my version of Twin Earth (if we judge that 'water' is ambiguous in Susana's mouth), then we fall into the third horn of Bilgrami's dilemma: we have to suppose Susana's lack of self-knowledge regarding her two aqueous McCullochian senses\concepts. But notice also—and this is what I would like to emphasize now—that the supposition that Susana lacks self-knowledge with respect to her own concepts of water from Dublin and water from Boston is undesirable for McCulloch, not only because it makes him vulnerable to Bilgrami's objection in his version designed for Twin-Earth cases, but also because it precludes him from adopting his solution for the Fregean puzzles. The strategy McCulloch uses to solve the Fregean puzzles is nothing other than a refined version

---

[17] Boghossian describes Dry Earth thus: "[L]et us imagine a planet just like ours in which although it very much seems to its inhabitants that there is a clear, tasteless and colorless liquid flowing in their rivers and taps and to which they confidently take themselves to be applying the word 'water', these appearances are systematically false and constitute a sort of pervasive collective mirage. In point of actual truth, the lakes, rivers and taps on this particular Twin Earth are all dry" ("What the externalist can know a priori", p. 279. In Wright, Smith and Macdonald (eds.), *Knowing Our Own Minds*, Oxford U.P., 1998. Originally published in *Proceedings of the Aristotelian Society* (97), 1997).

of the strategy followed by Frege himself: it boils down to holding that a subject of belief, *H*, has two "properly distinct"[18] concepts of a different substance. Let us recall, it is because Oscar has two different concepts of the same substance, H2O, associated with 'water' and 'ice' that we can "explain" that Oscar holds, at the same time, the two beliefs specified in 1) and 2):

1) Oscar believes that ice is ice

2) Oscar believes that ice is not water

It suffices to invoke this disparity of concepts to save Oscar's rationality.

But if the fact of having two different concepts were not a sufficient reason to know that one has two different concepts (if we reject the hypothesis of self-knowledge with respect to our ordinary substance-concepts), then to adduce the possession of different concepts of water and ice by Oscar would not suffice, contrary to what McCulloch's strategy supposes, to reconcile Oscar's rationality with the fact that he holds the beliefs specified in 1) and 2). It would still be necessary to ensure or guarantee that Oscar not only has two different concepts, but that he also knows or is aware that they are different.

I would like to conclude by drawing attention to what I think would be a rewarding task for me to tackle now but which will have to remain untouched for the time being. The question is this: Assuming that I have succeeded in showing that McCulloch's conception is vulnerable to Bilgrami's type of objection, we can interpret this result in two ways, depending on whether we take McCulloch's position as a particular version of orthodox externalism or as a variety of externalism different from or not falling under the general heading of Orthodox externalism. In the first case, our contention that McCulloch's thesis is vulnerable to Bilgrami's criticism could be seen as merely further or additional evidence confirming Bilgrami's general critical assessment of orthodox externalism. In the second case, we can take our contention against McCulloch as an indication that Bilgrami's argument may be more powerful than expected, that it is effective against a wider range of externalisms than

---

[18] As I understand McCulloch's theory, if someone initially unaware that ice is water discovered that ice is water, then his two former concepts of ice and water would fuse into one single, richer and more complex concept of water. We could no longer talk of two different concepts but, rather, of two partial aspects of the same concept. Although (as far as I can tell) McCulloch says nothing explicit concerning "concept fusion", I think my suggestion is (plausibly) in accordance with McCulloch's view.

those he describes as being orthodox. If we follow this second line, one question would immediately arise: How relevantly distant, or how foreign from orthodoxy is McCulloch's externalism? This and related questions are interesting because should we find McCulloch's idea to be sufficiently different from orthodox externalism, our contention that the former is open to the same criticism as the latter can be taken as reasonable ground to at least wonder whether Bilgrami's objection is too powerful. Once we have started along this path, it would become necessary, or at least natural, to explore whether Bilgrami's own heterodox externalism is immune to the very criticism he directs against orthodox externalism. A negative result in this matter would obviously discredit Bilgrami's general objection.

4

Arguments for Externalism

STEVEN DAVIS

1 Introduction

On Putnam's account of what he takes to be the traditional theory of meaning (TTM),[1] TTM is committed to two assumptions:

(1) Knowing the meanings of a term is a psychological state of the individual.

(2) The meaning(s) (intension) of a term determines the semantic referent(s) (extension) of the term, if it has one[2] (Putnam: 1975, 218).

Hence, to know the meaning of a term is to be in a psychological state that determines the semantic referent of the term, if it has one. The individual's psychological states are determined by his inner states that do not presuppose anything 'outside' the individual, including both his

---

[1]Putnam mentions Frege and Carnap as the philosophers that he has in mind. Others include Locke within the traditional view that is the target of Putnam's attack. See Donnellan (1993, 155).

[2]An intension of a term is a set of necessary and sufficient conditions for membership in the extension of the term (Putnam: 1975, 222).

Meaning, Basic Self-Knowledge and Mind: Essays on Tyler Burge.
María J. Frápolli and Esther Romero (eds.).
Copyright © 2003, CSLI Publications.

physical and social environments. Consequently, on TTM since these psychological states are the internal states of the individual that has them, the semantic referents of the terms in the individual's idiolect are determined by what is internal to the individual. Let us call this view 'semantic internalism'. Burge describes a similar view about an individual's *de dicto* intentional states, a view that he calls 'individualism'.[3] This view is that the nature of such states, including the conditions for their individuation, is wholly determined by what is internal to the individual. It follows that those individualist accounts of the individuation conditions of *de dicto* intentional states make no reference to anything outside the individual, including his physical and social environment.

Semantic internalism and intentional state individualism[4] have been called into question by a series of arguments that have their origin in Hilary Putnam's famous *water* and *elm/beech* Twin Earth thought experiments.[5] Putnam, himself, applies the arguments to semantic internalism. And Tyler Burge applies modified and extended versions of Putnam's Twin Earth thought experiments to intentional state individualism.[6] It is commonly assumed that although Burge's and Putnam's thought experiments have different conclusions, they are essentially the same arguments. In a recent paper Keith Donnellan calls into question this assumption (Donnellan: 1993).

Donnellan does not consider the full range of Putnam's and Burge's Twin Earth thought experiments, but concentrates his attention on Putnam's *water* thought experiment and Burge's *arthritis* thought experi-

---

[3]Sometimes individualism is characterized as the view that the *de dicto* intentional states of an individual supervene on his internal physical states. This is too narrow a view of individualism, since it leaves outside the range of individualist accounts dualist views about the nature of *de dicto* intentional states, although there is some indication that Descartes, himself, ascribes to some elements of anti-individualism. (See Burge: 1979, 103-104)

[4]There are two important differences between Putnam's and Burge's views that should be mentioned at this point. First, at least in the arguments that Putnam gives against semantic internalism Putnam, himself, is an individualist about *de dicto* psychological states. Second, Putnam is not concerned with questions about individuation; rather his focus is on what determines the semantic referents of the terms in a speaker's idiolect.

[5]Putnam also presents two other thought experiments that turn on aluminum and molybdenum and on gold. Both of these are variants of the *elm/beech* thought experiment (Putnam: 1975, 223-229).

[6]In "Other Bodies" Burge makes use of a version of Putnam's *water* thought experiment and in his earlier "Individualism and the Mental" extends the range of the thought experiment to 'arthritis', 'sofa', 'mortgage', 'brisket', etc. (Burge: 1979 & 1982).

ment. One might think it would be more appropriate to compare Putnam's and Burge's *water* thought experiments, since both turn on a difference across Earth and Twin Earth in natural kinds, or to compare Burge's *arthritis* thought experiment with Putnam's *elm/beech* thought experiment, since they both appeal to different linguistic practices on the two planets. *Donnellan* gives as his reason for concentrating on Burge's *arthritis*, rather than his *water* thought experiment that the latter is merely a variant of the original *arthritis* thought experiment (*Ibid.*, 155). His reason for not comparing Putnam's *elm/beech* with Burge's *arthritis* thought experiment is that the former thought experiment is not really an argument against TTM, since it is compatible with (2) and a modified version of (1).

Let us consider Putnam's *elm/beech* thought experiment. It is supposed to show that it is possible for a speaker, whom I shall call 'Oscar', to have the terms 'elm' and 'beech' in his idiolect, but who is not able to tell an elm from a beech. On Putnam's account of TTM, this amounts to his not knowing the intensions of the terms. Let us imagine that Oscar has a *doppelgänger*, Boscar, on Twin Earth who is "molecule for molecule 'identical' with [him]" (Putnam: 1975, 227). Thus, he too is not able to tell an elm from a beech. The difference between Earth and Twin Earth is that 'elm' and 'beech' are switched in their extensions. Despite not being able to tell an elm from a beech, the terms in Oscar's and Boscar's idiolects have their standard, but different extensions. Yet, according to Putnam, Oscar and Boscar have the same psychological states. Hence, it cannot be Oscar's and Boscar's psychological states that determine the extensions of the terms in their idiolects. Putnam's hypothesis to account for reference determination of the terms in Oscar's and Boscar's idiolects is that there is a division of linguistic labour between Oscar and Boscar, on the one hand, and on the other, the 'experts' in their respective linguistic communities who are knowledgeable about elms and beeches and to whom Oscar and Boscar have a disposition to defer.[7]

The upshot of the thought experiment is that (1) does not apply to Oscar and Boscar. Neither can be said to know the meanings (intensions) of the terms, since they cannot tell an elm from a beech. What about (2)? Do the intensions of the terms determine their extensions? Putnam's *elm/beech* thought experiment, claims Donnellan, leaves open

---

[7]'Experts' occurs in quotations marks to indicate that the persons to whom Oscar and Boscar are disposed to defer need not be experts in the sense that they have scientific knowledge about elms and beeches. It might only be that they are able to recognize an elm or a beech when they see one.

the possibility that it is the 'experts' knowing the intensions of 'elm' and 'beech' that determines the extensions of the terms in *their* idiolects (Donnellan: 1993, 163). In turn, extension determination for the terms in Oscar's and Boscar's idiolects would ride piggyback on the extension determination in the idiolects of the 'experts'. On this view, extension determination for their terms would not be determined by their psychological states, but rather by the psychological states of the 'experts' to whom they are disposed to defer. Consequently, according to Donnellan, Putnam's *elm/beech* thought experiment leaves open the possibility that TTM could give an indirect account of extension determination for some of the terms in the idiolects of speakers like Oscar and Boscar and a direct account for the 'experts' to whom they are disposed to defer. It is, argues Donnellan, Putnam's *water* thought experiment and not his *elm/beech* thought experiment that forces us to give up TTM and to adopt a radical new theory about how the extension of terms is determined. Consequently, Donnellan concentrates his attention on Putnam's *water* thought experiment and compares it to Burge's *arthritis* thought experiment.

Let us return to Donnellan's claim that Putnam's *water* and Burge's *arthritis* thought experiments, despite surface similarities, are in important respects different arguments. According to Donnellan, the difference between them is that they make use of different principles. The principle to which the Putnam thought experiment is supposed to appeal is that for each natural kind term there is a semantic rule that makes indexical reference to paradigms the nature of which determines the extension of the term, natures, which might well not be known to those who know the semantic rule (Donnellan: 1993, 156). Burge's *arthritis* thought experiment, on Donnellan's view, turns on a speaker's incomplete mastery of a notion and on his linguistic community's setting the standards for what constitutes mastery of the term (*Ibid.,* 160). In this paper I shall show that Donnellan is mistaken about Burge's views,[8] and that he is misled about them because he concentrates his attention on his *arthritis*, rather than his *water* Twin Earth thought experiment. Moreover, I shall also show that Donnellan mischaracterizes Putnam's *water* Twin Earth

---

[8]It might seem to be unfair to charge Donnellan with a faulty exegesis of Burge's work. Donnellan, himself, claims that he is not so much concerned with what Burge's views are in detail, but rather with a certain philosophical view that he argues that he has taken from Burge's earlier papers. I think, however, that by not paying more attention to the details of Burge's views Donnellan gives us a mischaracterization of them and misses some of Burge's important insights into the nature of intentional states (Donnellan: 1993, 165, n.5).

thought experiment and his positive views about reference determination.

2 Putnam's *Water* Thought Experiment

Both Putnam's and Burge's thought experiments have negative conclusions and lead to positive suggestions. I shall begin with Putnam's *water* thought experiment and the negative conclusion that he draws from it and then turn to his positive suggestion about how the reference of 'water' is determined. Putnam argues that the aim of the thought experiment is to show that (1) and (2) cannot be conjointly satisfied by any theory. Before turning to Putnam's argument for this conclusion, we must be clear about his account of the nature of the psychological states in (1) to which he claims TTM is committed. There are two features of this account that are important for our purposes. The first is to spell out what knowing the meaning of a term comes to. This can be brought out by considering what it is for Oscar to know the meaning of a term, A, that has associated with it two intensions, I_a and I_b. According to Putnam's account of TTM, Oscar's knowing the meaning of A is his knowing both that I_a is an intension of A and knowing that I_b is an intension of A. The second is a more controversial claim about the nature of the psychological states to which TTM is supposedly committed. According to Putnam, TTM presupposes 'methodological solipsism', namely, that the sorts of psychological states involved in (1) do not "... presuppose the existence of [anything] other than the individual to whom that state is ascribed"[9] (Putnam: 1975, 220). Putnam calls the psychological states to which methodological solipsism commits TTM "...psychological states in the narrow sense," that he contrasts with 'wide psychological states', states like being jealous or envious that presuppose the existence of individuals other than the person who is jealous or envious (*Ibid.*, 220). Thus, Oscar's psychological states involved in knowing the meaning of A are distinct "psychological states *in the narrow sense*"[10] (*Ibid.*, 221). Tyler Burge has shown, I believe, that 'psychological states in the narrow sense' are *de dicto* intentional states and 'psychological states in the wide sense' are *de re* intentional states (Burge: 1982, 107-

---

[9]The way that Putnam puts the point in his famous assumption of methodological solipsism is somewhat different from the way I have put it here. "... No psychological state ... presupposes the existence of any *individual* other that the subject to whom the subject is ascribed" (The italics are not in the original; Putnam: 1975, 220). I have broadened Putnam's point, in keeping with what I take to be his intention, to include not just other individuals, but any other thing. See McDowell (1996, 306).

[10]Italics are in the original.

110). Hence, a necessary condition for a psychological state's being a psychological state in the narrow sense is that a report of it not contain a non-anaphoric use of an indexical. For if it did, it would be a report of a *de re* intentional state, an intentional state that presupposes the existence of something other than the individual.[11]

I would now like to turn to Putnam's *water* thought experiment. Consider again Oscar and a term in his idiolect, A, that we shall take to have two extensions, {A} and {B}. The first step in Putnam's argument is to show that Oscar's psychological states, his knowing the meaning of A, determines the extensions of the term. As we have seen, on Putnam's account of (1)

(3) Oscar knows that I_a is an intension of A.

(4) Oscar knows that I_b is an intension of A.

From (3) and (4) the truth of (5) and (6) follows.

(5) I_a is an intension of A.

(6) I_b is an intension of A.

Consequently, given (2), (5) determines that A has as one of its extensions {A} and (6) determines that A has as one of its extensions {B}. Thus, Oscar's knowing the meaning of A determines the intensions and extensions of the term (*Ibid.*, 221).

Let us imagine that besides Oscar we have Ruth and suppose that Oscar and Ruth have A in their idiolects, but each understands the term differently; they use it in different idiosyncratic ways.

(7) Oscar understands I_a to be the intension of A.

(8) Ruth understands I_b to be the intension of A.

It is obvious that (7) and (8) are distinct psychological states. In turn (7) and (8) determine that the extensions of A in Oscar's and Ruth's idiolects are different. In Oscar's idiolect the extension of A is {A} and in Ruth's idiolect it is {B}. For their terms to have different extensions the

---

[11]This will become important when we turn to a discussion of Donnellan's account of Putnam's thought experiment. See Burge's account of *de re* attitudes (Burge: 1977, 339-347 and 1982, n. 1, 118-119).

psychological states that constitute their knowing the meaning of the term must be different. What is impossible on TTM, Putnam claims, is (a) that Oscar and Ruth know the meaning of *A,* (b) that in their idiolects the term has distinct extensions and (c) that Oscar and Ruth are in the same psychological states (Putnam: 1975, 222). The purpose of Putnam's *water* Twin Earth argument is to show, contrary to TTM, that it is possible that (a), (b), and (c) can be true together.

Putnam asks us to imagine a possible world in which there are two planets, Earth and Twin Earth, between which there has been no physical contact.[12] Twin Earth is type identical to Earth, except that on Earth there is water and on Twin Earth there is another substance that has the same perceptual properties as water's, that flows in rivers and streams and that is used in the same ways as water is used on Earth. The difference between water and the substance on Twin Earth is that the substance on Twin Earth has a different chemical composition from water's that Putnam abbreviates as *XYZ*. Since *XYZ* is not H_2O, the substance on Twin Earth is not water. Let us take this to be the first premise of Putnam's argument.

> I There is a possible world in which there are two planets, Earth and Twin Earth, that are type identical, except that where Earth has water, Twin Earth has *XYZ*.[13]

Let us consider Oscar, a typical speaker of English, and his type identical[14] counterpart on Twin Earth, Boscar, who are, according to Putnam, "...exact duplicates in appearance, feelings, thoughts, interior monologues, etc.," including having 'water' in their idiolects (Putnam: 1975, 225). Yet, given the description of the thought experiment, Oscar's and Boscar's uses of the term have different extensions. When Os-

---

[12]Twin Earth thought experiments have also been presented as involving two possible worlds, rather than a possible world with two planets. See Burge, (1979, 77-79). In places Putnam also appeals to two possible worlds, rather than a possible world with two planets (Putnam: 1975, 233). But for Putnam there does not seem to be any important difference between the two sorts of arguments.

[13]There are various problems that arise for this thought experiment because, for example, there are different isotopes of water that are not H_2O, and water and *XYZ* is the main constituents of humans on respectively, Earth and Twin Earth. The same thought experiment could be run using another substance, say gold or aluminum, but since it is Putnam's original example that other authors have taken up, I shall stick with water.

[14]Oscar and Boscar are supposed to be molecule for molecule type identical, but see the previous footnote.

car says, "Water is good to drink," the extension of 'water' is water, but when Boscar uses the same sentence, his tokening of 'water' has as its extension *XYZ*. The difference in extension of 'water' in their idiolects follows from I, since there is no *XYZ* on Earth, and no water on Twin Earth. This gives us the second premise in Putnam's thought experiment.

II In Oscar's idiolect 'water' has water as its extension; in Boscar's idiolect 'water' has *XYZ* as its extension.

Since Oscar and Boscar are type identical in their psychological states, they are type identical in their narrow and not their wide psychological states, that is, in their *de dicto*, but not their *de re* intentional states. Obviously, they are not type identical in their *de re* intentional states, since such states presuppose the existence of something other than the person to whom the state is attributed and thus, cannot be narrow psychological states. Moreover, *de re* intentional attitudes are held of or about something and are individuated by virtue of what they are of or about. Hence, Oscar's and Boscar's *de re* attitudes expressed with 'water' are not type identical, since Oscar's 'water' *de re* intentional states are about water, while Boscar's are about *XYZ*. Thus, the condition on their being type identical with respect to their psychological states applies, if at all,[15] only to their narrow (*de dicto*) psychological states. This gives us the third premise of Putnam's argument.

III Oscar and Boscar are type identical in their narrow (*de dicto*) psychological states.

Both Oscar and Boscar know how to use 'water', abilities that on TTM are exhausted by their narrow psychological states.[16] Hence from III it follows that

IV (a) Oscar and Boscar are type identical in their narrow (*de dicto*) psychological states that constitute their knowing the meaning of 'water'.

---

[15]Burge argues that Oscar and Boscar are *not* type identical with respect to their *de dicto* psychological states (Burge: 1982, 99-100)

[16]It could be argued that 'water' in Oscar's and Boscar's idiolects is not the same term type, since in Oscar's and Boscar's uses of 'water' tokens of it have different extensions. To avoid this problem we can take term identity to be phonetic rather than semantic.

That is to say,

> IV (b) Oscar's knowing the meaning of 'water' is type identical
> to Boscar's knowing the meaning of 'water'.

IV (a) and (b) follow from III, since on Putnam's interpretation of
TTM knowing the meaning of a term is a narrow psychological state.

Since on TTM a speaker's knowing the meaning of a term is his
knowing of some particular intension that it is the intension of the term,
it follows that

> V (a) Oscar knows that W_a is the intension of 'water'.
> V (b) Boscar knows that W_b is the intension of 'water'.

Hence, from IV (b) and V (a) and (b) we have

> VI Oscar's knowing that W_a is the intension of 'water' is type
> identical to Boscar's knowing that W_b is the intension of 'wa-
> ter'.

It follows from VI that

> VII W_a and W_b, the intension of 'water' in Oscar's and Boscar's
> idiolects, are identical.

However, from VII and (2) it follows that

> VIII In Oscar's and Boscar's idiolects 'water' has the same ex-
> tension.[17]

Obviously, II and VIII are contradictories. Given the description of the
thought experiment, II is true. Hence, it must be VIII that is false. Since
VIII follows from IV (a) (that is, (1)) and (2), it follows that at least one
of these must be abandoned.

There is nothing in the Putnam's description of his thought experiment that presupposes or provides a positive suggestion about how the
extensions of terms like 'water' are to be determined. There is, however,
a feature that Putnam includes in the thought experiment that although
it does not play a role in the argument above, it does exclude one way

---

[17] VIII really follows from VII alone, since (2) merely tells us what intensions are.

in which the extension of 'water' could be determined. Putnam asks us to imagine that the time of the thought experiment is in 1750, when no one on Earth or on Twin Earth knew anything about the chemical composition respectively, of water or of *XYZ*. Hence, there were no experts on Earth about water and Twin Earth about *XYZ*. Consequently, there was no one to whom Oscar or Boscar could defer about their uses of 'water' or about water or *XYZ*. Hence, social practices involving deference and experts play no role in Putnam's description of his *water* thought experiment and thus, in reaching the conclusion that he draws from it. One way of interpreting the thought experiment, then, is to view it as showing that there are cases of the reference determination of natural kind terms that do not involve the division of linguistic labour.[18]

3   Putnam's Positive Suggestions and Indexicality

I would now like to consider Putnam's positive suggestions for replacing (1) and (2). Rather than hold onto either, Putnam abandons both and opts for a theory to account for semantic competence and reference determination that is radically different from TTM.[19] His theory appeals to social practices and indexicality (Putnam: 1975, 245). As we have seen, it is the indexical aspect of reference determination and semantic competence that Donnellan thinks is fundamental to Putnam's theory and it is to this I would now like to turn my attention. Putnam's theory, unlike TTM, is not a unified theory of semantic competence and reference determination across individuals. Consider again 'elm' and two English speakers, Oscar, an 'expert', and Ruth, a non-expert, about elms. Putnam's theory gives a different account both for what it is for Oscar and for Ruth to be semantically competent in their use of 'elm' and for how the semantic referent of 'elm' is determined in their idiolects. No such difference arises for those terms for which there is no distinction between 'experts' and non-experts, for example, for 'water' in Putnam's *water* thought experiment. As we have seen, in the thought experiment Putnam asks us to suppose that we are in 1750, when no one on Earth or on Twin Earth knew anything about the chemical composition, respec-

---

[18]It seems that Donnellan is interpreting Putnam's *water* thought experiment in this way (Donnellan: 162-165).

[19]In summarizing his views at the end of the "Meaning of 'Meaning'" Putnam claims that he abandons (1), but keeps (2) (Putnam: 1975, 270). The (2) that he claims that he keeps, "Meaning determines extension" is not the same as the (2) that figures in his presentation of TTM, "Meaning (in the sense of 'intension') determines extension" (*Ibid.*, 219). The 'meaning' of his summary remarks is not to be understood as 'intension'.

tively, of water or of *XYZ*. Hence, on Earth and Twin Earth there would be no experts about either. Consequently, a uniform account across individuals can be given for the 'water' semantic competence of English speakers on Earth and of *English speakers on Twin Earth and also for what determines the referent of 'water' in their idiolects. But as we shall see, it does not follow from this that a unified account must be given for semantic competence and for reference determination. It still leaves open the possibility that what accounts for their 'water' semantic competence might not play a role in accounting for the semantic referent of 'water' in their idiolects.

Let us return then to indexicality and the role that it plays in Putnam's theory.[20] One way in which indexicality enters into our linguistic practices with natural kind terms, Putnam claims, is in what he calls 'meaning explanations' (Putnam: 1975, 230). According to Putnam, there are two ways in which a meaning explanation can be given for a natural kind term: A speaker can explain the meaning of a natural kind term by giving an ostensive definition or by giving a description of the normal or stereotypical members of the kind. It is not clear that in a descriptive meaning explanation indexicality plays a role. For this reason I shall exclude it from the discussion. In giving an ostensive definition of 'water' Oscar could explain the meaning of 'water' by pointing to some water, say in a river or lake, and saying, "This is water." The purpose, says Putnam, "...is simply a way of pointing out a standard..." (*Ibid.*, 232). The standard is the liquid to which the speaker's use of 'this' refers (*Ibid.*, 230). For something to be water it must be the same liquid as the liquid picked out by the ostension. In a ostensive meaning explanation the standard does not play an explicit role in what is uttered, since no standard is mentioned in what the speaker says. Putnam claims that in

---

[20]Putnam claims that 'water' is an indexical (Putnam: 1975, 234). As Burge has shown, natural kind terms, like 'water', are not indexicals, since the semantic referent of 'water', unlike 'he', 'I' and 'this', remains constant across utterance contexts (Burge: 1982, 104-107). This does not rule out, however, indexicals from playing a role in the linguistic practices involving natural kind terms (Donnellan: 1993, 157). Consider for example my naming my dog "Fido" by a naming giving ceremony in which I point to my dog and say, "I'll call that 'Fido'." The name giving contains the use of an indexical and fixes the referent of 'Fido' in my idiolect. In my subsequent uses of the name the semantic referent of 'Fido' is determined by there being a causal/historical connection with my name giving ceremony and hence, with the use of an indexical. Hence, even though 'Fido' is not an indexical in my idiolect, indexicality plays a role in determining the semantic referent of my uses of the name. Burge recognizes this point. (1982, 105-106)

the ostensive definition "... the force of [Oscar's] explanation is that..." (*Ibid.*, 231).

(9) (For every world W) (For every x in W) (x is water if and only if x bears the same$_L$ to the entity referred to as 'this' *in the actual world W_l*).[21]

Putnam suggests that the way in which (9) enters into Oscar's ostensive definition is that in saying, "This is water," he intends (9) (*Ibid.*, 213). The paradigmatic instances are picked out by being the semantic referent of 'this' on the occasion in which Oscar gives his ostensive meaning explanation.

There are two problems with (9) as an account of how indexicality is connected to natural kind terms. First, it does not mention 'water' and hence, it is not clear in what sense it is a meaning explanation for 'water'. Second, there is nothing in it that would distinguish the use of 'water' on Earth from its use on Twin Earth, since in the *water* thought experiment both Earth and Twin Earth are imagined to be in the same possible world. Hence, 'in the actual world W_l' does not distinguish between Earth and Twin Earth, since both are in the same world. Consequently, contrary to what Putnam claims, if on his account of ostensive meaning explanations, Oscar were to give an ostensive meaning explanation for 'water' on Earth and Boscar for 'water' on Twin Earth, there would be nothing to differentiate their meaning explanations. Let me suggest (10), which is similar to proposals of Putnam and Donnellan, as a first approximation to a way out of these problems.[22]

---

[21]The italics are in the original. Here Putnam switches from talk about Twin Earths to talk about possible worlds.

[22]This is not exactly what either Putnam or Donnellan proposes. One of Putnam's proposals is "'Water' is the stuff that bears a certain similarity relation to the water around here" (Putnam: 1975, 234). This is incoherent with 'water' in quotation marks. If the quotation marks are removed we no longer have a rule for 'water'. In addition it will not do to have 'water' used, as it is in its second occurrence, rather than mentioned. For what the rule is supposed to provide is an account of how the semantic referent of 'water' is determined. There cannot then be a part of the rule in which 'water' is used to refer to water, since that is what the rule is supposed to explain. If we drop the second occurrence of 'water', a problem arises with 'around here'. As Burge points out, it would give us XYZ in the extension of our 'water'. Imagine that Oscar is transported to Twin Earth with something like the Putnam rule. 'Around here' then would change its extension to what is around Oscar on Twin Earth, namely XYZ (Burge: 1982, 102-103).

Donnellan's version of the rule does not fare any better. It comes in two forms:

(10) 'Water' refers to the liquid, and any liquid similar to it, in our lakes and rivers.[23]

We can suppose that Putnam's claim is that anyone who gives an ostensive meaning explanation for 'water' intends (10) or something similar to it.[24] There is a minor problem with (10). It is not in the form of a rule, but closely related to (10) is the rule,

(10a) Apply 'water' to the liquid, and any liquid similar to it, in our lakes and rivers.

In what follows I shall talk about (10a), rather than (10), although (10) is closer to Putnam's and Donnellan's proposals. This still leaves open the question about how (10), and similar rules, are to be understood in Putnam's theory.

Let us look more closely at (10a) and suppose that in accordance with Putnam's description of his *water* thought experiment that we are in 1750 prior to the time that anyone knew what the nature of water was. There are two ways in which the (10a) could play a role in Putnam's theories of semantic competence and reference determination. First, it can be regarded as a rule that is known by every Earth English speaker and Twin Earth *English speaker who has 'water' in his idiolect, includ-

---

(a) 'Water' is whatever has the underlying nature of the stuff in *our* lakes and oceans (Donnellan: 1993, 158).

(b) Water is the stuff which has the important underlying physical characteristics of the stuff we (or I) have been used to calling 'water' (*Ibid.*, 170 n.16).

(a) makes no sense with 'water' in quotation marks and without the quotation marks, (a) is not about 'water'. (b) does not fare much better. It does not give us a semantic rule for 'water'. Moreover, it seems on the face of it to be false. Suppose that the stuff I have been calling 'water' is not water, but something that looks like water. I am mistaken about what I took to be water. It cannot be the case, as (b) would have it, that if I am mistaken about what I am calling 'water', my calling something 'water' makes it and anything that shares its 'important underlying characteristics' water. There is more to say about Putnam's and Donnellan's versions of (10), but since my main concern is not with getting (10) right, I shall not pursue this matter further.

[23]The definite description, 'the liquid in our lakes and rivers', is used indexically; it can change its semantic value from one context of utterance to another.

[24]I say something similar, since it is not necessary that every speaker of English who gives an explanation of the meaning for 'water' intends (10) with 'our lakes and rivers'. We can imagine that there could be variants from speaker to speaker that would contain other indexicals or definite descriptions.

ing those who give meaning explanations. Their knowing the rule constitutes what it is for them to have 'water' in their idiolects, their 'water'
semantic competence, and what they know, the rule, determines the
extension of their term. Hence, this way of construing (10a) gives an
account of semantic competence and reference determination similar to
TTM, since in both, a speaker's psychological state determines the semantic referent of 'water' in his idiolect. Although this way of understanding the role (10a) plays in reference determination and semantic
competence is similar to TTM, there is an important difference. Contrary to TTM, there is no appeal to an intension, a set of necessary and
sufficient conditions for water, that speakers who have 'water' in their
idiolects know and which determines the extension of the term. Rather,
the function of the definite description used indexically is to pick out
paradigmatic instances of the kind, the properties of which determine
the extension of the term, properties that need not be known to the
speaker or to anyone in his linguistic community who has the term in his
idiolect (*Ibid.*, 245). Second, (10a) can be taken to play a role in determining semantic reference, but not to be a rule that plays a role in semantic competence. This could arise if English or *English speakers in
1750 were unacquainted with water or with *XYZ*. If this seems implausible for 'water' and water or *XYZ*, the thought experiment could be run
with some other natural kind term, for example, 'magnesium'. Despite
this, (10a), or something akin to it, could still figure in the determination of the semantic referent of 'water' in the idiolects of English or
*English speakers by playing a role either implicitly or explicitly in fix-
ing the referent[25] of 'water'.[26] This would also require that English
speakers are related in the appropriate way with the initial baptizing of
water with 'water' and *English speakers of *XYZ* with 'water'. Since
their being so related is not a psychological state, it would follow that in

---

[25]This does not mean that in the act that introduces the term and fixes its referent
the person who introduced the term, the initial baptizer, actually utters (10a), or anything like it, but only that something like (10a) figures in the intention that the baptizer has when the name is introduced. In addition terms can be introduced into a
language in a variety of ways, for example, by an explicit act in which something like
(10a) is used to introduce the term or by a term being applied to something without its
being introduced with anything like (10a) being uttered. Some nicknames are introduced into a language in this way.

There is an obvious difficulty with this as a necessary account of reference fixing.
There are cases in which a baptizer need not introduce a term by using an indexical,
but can introduce it using a definite description attributively in a sentence that does
not contain any indexicals. See Kripke (1980, 53-164) for the distinction between reference determination and reference fixing.

[26]This assumes that the baptizer is not part of the linguistic community in 1750.

the second scenario, unlike the first, their psychological states do not determine the semantic referent of 'water' in their idiolects.[27] In the second way in which (10a) could play a role in Putnam's theories of semantic competence and reference determination, then, for the non-baptizers who have 'water' in their idiolects neither their 'water' semantic competence, nor what determines the semantic referent for the term in their idiolects consists in their knowing (10a). There are a variety of theories that have been proposed to account for their semantic competence, but for our purposes what is important is that it does not consist in their knowing (10a). We have then two ways in which rules like (10a) involving terms for which there are no experts might play a role in Putnam's theories of semantic competence and reference determination.

4 Donnellan's Interpretation of Putnam's Thought Experiment

I would now like turn to Donnellan's interpretation of Putnam's thought experiment and his views about how (10a) is to be incorporated into Putnam's theories of reference determination and semantic competence. Donnellan thinks that there is a direct connection between (10a) and Putnam's thought experiment. As we shall see, he thinks that a necessary part of the thought experiment is that (10a) determines the semantic referent of 'water' in the idiolects of Oscar and Boscar. Donnellan claims that Putnam's *water* thought experiment give us "...a new way of thinking about how a term [like 'water'] might determine its extension" (Donnellan: 1993, 157). We can take Donnellan's proposal to be that something like the rule in (10a) plays a role in determining the extension of 'water'. Moreover, argues Donnellan, the rule is "in us" in the sense that the rules of grammar, on a Chomskyian view of linguistic competence, are in us (Chomsky: 1965, 3-15). That is to say, a speaker who has 'water' in his idiolect has tacit knowledge of (10a). On this view, the semantic rule for 'water' is in our heads and thus, what is in our heads determines the extension of the term. It does this because of the indexical element in the rule having as its referent paradigms of water or of *XYZ*, the underlying nature of which determines the extension of the term (*Ibid.,* 158). On Earth anything that has the same under-

---

[27]This is not to suggest that psychological states would play no role, since the links in the causal/historical chain might well pass through speakers' intentions. The point is that on the causal/historical account a speaker's psychological states are not sufficient for reference determination.

lying structure as water, anything that is H_2O, is in the extension of 'water;' on Twin Earth anything that is *XYZ* is in the extension of 'water'.

We cannot take Donnellan to be making a general point about how for every speaker the extension of any natural kind term in his idiolect is determined. Putnam's *elm/beech* thought experiment shows that there are terms in speakers' idiolects the extension of which cannot be determined by their having tacit knowledge of rules like (10a).[28] The most conservative interpretation of Donnellan's proposal is to take it to be about Oscar in Putnam's *water* thought experiment, and any speaker similarly situated. That is to say, it applies to speakers, like Oscar, with respect to terms in their idiolects about which there are no experts in their linguistic communities to whom they defer about the use of the terms or about their extensions, if the terms have extensions. That Donnellan's proposal applies at least to Oscar and similar speakers can be seen from how he interprets the role that indexicality plays in the thought experiment. Donnellan argues that (10a), in particular the indexical element in it, "...becomes important..., when we want to generate the Twin Earth examples," since it is, he claims, a necessary condition for the Twin Earth thought experiments (Donnellan: 1993, 159). "It is in the service of Twin Earth examples that indexicals *must* enter in"[29] (*Ibid.*). The reason he gives for why indexicality must enter into (10a) is that "...we want the semantical rule for 'water' on Twin Earth to be indistinguishable, except for the context in which it is applied, from the semantical rule on Earth" (*Ibid.*). And his reason for this is that it is a requirement of Putnam's Twin Earth thought experiment that Oscar and Boscar have type identical psychological states (*Ibid.*). Earth and Twin Earth are supposed to be type identical, except where Earth has water, Twin Earth has *XYZ*. The type identity of the two planets, argues Putnam, brings in its wake the type identity of Oscar and Boscar, including the type identity of their psychological states. What enables the rule to be the 'same', according to Donnellan, is that (10a) specifies the paradigms indexically. Consequently, (10a) specifies different paradigms for an English speaker and for a Twin Earth *English speaker for whom (10a) plays a role in the reference determination of 'water' in their idiolects, but yet Oscar's and Boscar's semantic rule for 'water', Donnellan claims, is the same.

Donnellan draws on Kaplan's distinction between character and content to provide the conceptual framework for his proposal that the semantic rule for 'water' is the same for Oscar and Boscar, but that the

---

[28]Donnellan seems to recognize this (Donnellan: 1993, n. 22, 170).

[29]Italics in the original.

rule determines different paradigms (Kaplan, 1989, 500-507). It is the character expressed by (10a), which Donnellan identifies with the semantical rule, that is the same in Oscar's and Boscar's idiolects (*Ibid.*). Since if Oscar and Boscar were to use, 'This is water', the indexical would have different referents on Earth and Twin Earth. Hence, the content of the rule would be different and with this difference in content there would be a difference in paradigms for the two idiolects.

5 Problems with Donellan's Interpretation of Putnam's Thought Experiment

There are three problems with Donnellan's claim about the role that (10a) is supposed to play in Putnam's Twin Earth *water* thought experiment. First, Putnam's requirement that the psychological states of Oscar and Boscar be type identical is a requirement that their narrow psychological states be identical. As I have pointed out above, Burge has shown that the only plausible interpretation of this requirement is that the psychological states in question are *de dicto* psychological states. On Putnam's own account of the distinction between wide and narrow psychological states, psychological states, like *x's being jealous of y*, are not psychological states in the narrow sense, but in the wide sense and as such, are not the sorts of states, according to Putnam, to which TTM appeals in (1) (Putnam: 1975, 220). Mapping narrow psychological states onto the distinction between *de dicto* and *de re* psychological states, such states are *de re* psychological states. Hence, on Putnam's view about TTM, (1) does not appeal to *de re* psychological states. Consequently, Putnam's *water* thought experiment is designed to show that Oscar and Boscar can be in the same *de dicto* psychological states, but yet 'water' in their idiolects can have different extensions. What *de re* psychological states that Oscar and Boscar have is irrelevant to the thought experiment. Since (10a) contains an indexical, someone's believing what it expresses would have a *de re*, rather than a *de dicto* belief. Consequently, contrary to Donnellan, sameness of (10a) is irrelevant for Putnam's thought experiment.

The second problem for Donnellan's claim about the relevance of (10a) for Putnam's *water* thought experiment is that Donnellan's way of incorporating it into the thought experiment does not give the right result. Putnam takes as a requirement of the thought experiment that Oscar and Boscar are type identical and thus, that they have the same psychological states. Donnellan claims that for this requirement to be met Oscar and Boscar must have the same semantic rule for 'water', namely, (10a) as the semantic rule for the term. But this is not sufficient for the requirement of the thought experiment that Oscar and Boscar be type identical in their psychological states. A necessary condition for sameness of psychological state is sameness of content. Let us assume that Donnellan is correct in suggesting that since in Oscar's and Boscar's idiolects the character of (10a) is the same, their semantic rule for 'water' can be taken to be the same. But sameness of character does not guarantee sameness of psychological state. What is required is sameness of content. However, what Oscar believes in believing what is expressed by (10a) is not the same as what Boscar believes in believing what is expressed by (10a). The reason for this is that in their idiolects the indexical in the rule has different referents.[30] Hence, Oscar's psychological state, his believing what is expressed by (10a) is not type identical to Boscar's psychological state, his believing what is expressed by (10a). Consequently, if as Donnellan contends, (10a) were to play the sort of role he ascribes to it in Putnam's *water* thought experiment, Oscar's and Boscar's psychological states would not be type identical. Hence, the thought experiment would not meet the requirement of type identity that Putnam lays down for it.

The third problem for Donnellan's account of Putnam's *water* thought experiment is that contrary to what he claims, (10a) does not play a necessary role in it. What differentiates Putnam's *water* thought experiment from his *elm/beech* thought experiment is that in the latter, but not the former there are experts in the speaker's current linguistic community to whom he has a disposition to defer.[31] By hypothesis there are no experts about water or *XYZ*, or the use of 'water' in Oscar's or Boscar's speech communities. That is to say, in the two communities everyone knows as much as anyone else about water or *XYZ* and about the use of 'water' and everyone has the same recognitional abilities concerning the two substances. Yet in Oscar's idiolect 'water' has as its semantic referent water and in Boscar's idiolect *XYZ*. Donnellan claims that the only way that this could be the case is for Oscar and Boscar to have (10a) as the semantic rule for 'water' in their idiolects. But this is not required for the consequences that Putnam wishes to draw from the thought experiment. It is not part of the thought experiment that Oscar and Boscar have whatever abilities and capacities are necessary so that 'the liquid in our lakes and rivers' has the relevant semantic referent.

---

[30]Take, 'I am tired'. If Oscar and Boscar were to believe what is expressed by this sentence, there would be sameness of character, but not sameness of content. Hence, they would not be in type identical belief states.

[31]The disposition need not be a disposition to defer to anyone in particular, but it could be a disposition to defer to whomever is an expert, if there are any (Davis, 17).

Let us suppose that they and everyone else in their linguistic communities lacked the appropriate abilities and capacities, by, for example, being unacquainted with water.[32] It would follow that in Oscar's and Boscar's idiolects the description in (10a) would not have water and *XYZ*, respectively, as its semantic referents.[33] Hence, their supposed tacit knowledge of (10a) would not be able to provide different paradigms for the term in their idiolects. Thus, it would not determine the extension of 'water' in the two idiolects. But this does not rule out that in the thought experiment in the two idiolects 'water' has different semantic referents. All that would be required is to suppose that there are causal/historical connections between their dispositions to use the term and reference fixing events that fix the semantic referent of 'water' on Earth as water and on Twin Earth as *XYZ*. If this were the case, in Oscar's and Boscar's idiolect the semantic referent of 'water' would be determined appropriately without either having anything in their heads resembling (10a) that determined the referents of the term in their idiolects.[34] This does not rule out the possibility that something like (10a) plays a role in fixing the referent of 'water' and thus, plays an indirect role in determining the semantic referent of 'water' in Oscar's

---

[32]See my remark about 'magnesium' and magnesium above.

[33]Care must be taken here not to confuse the deictic and anaphoric uses of 'the liquid in our lakes and rivers'. Suppose that Ruth in Oscar's linguistic community is able to recognize water in normal circumstances, when she sees it. She tells Oscar that water is the liquid in our lakes and rivers. Oscar then uses 'the liquid in our lakes and rivers', intending to refer to the stuff to which Ruth referred. The description used anaphorically would then have water as its semantic referent. But this sort of case is ruled out by Putnam's description of the thought experiment, since no appeal is to be made to experts. That is to say, everyone in Oscar's and Boscar's linguistic communities is supposed to be on an equal footing with respect to their knowledge about the relevant liquids on Earth and Twin Earth.

[34]It might be thought that this objection can be turned aside by placing as a condition on Putnam's *water* thought experiment that the division of linguistic labour plays no role in reference determination, a condition that is not equivalent to the stricture that there are no experts that play such a role. The causal/historical story provides an account of reference determination that meets the latter condition, since there is no sense in which the baptizer need be an expert, but the causal/historical account does not meet the former condition, since what would determine the referent of 'water' in Oscar's and Boscar's idiolects would involve a division of linguistic labour. There are two problems with forestalling the criticism in this way. First, it is not part of Putnam's description of his *water* thought experiment. Second, and more importantly, it would mean that Donnellan would have to show that 'water' was not introduced by an initial baptizer other than Oscar and Boscar, or if it were, that the reference fixing and its connection with Oscar's and Boscar's 'water' plays no role in determining the referent of the term in their idiolects.

and Boscar's idiolects. Consequently, Putnam's *water* thought experiment leaves open the way in which the semantic referent of 'water' is determined in their idiolects. The conclusion that we have reached is that Donnellan has incorrectly characterized Putnam's *water* thought experiment in claiming that it is a necessary part of it that the semantic referents of 'water' in the idiolects of Oscar and Boscar are determined by their having in their heads a rule like (10a).

Perhaps, we can interpret Donnellan's proposal to be more modest. We could take his claim not to be about Putnam's *water* Twin Earth thought experiment, but to be about a subclass of natural kind terms and natural kinds about which there are no experts. Let us call the class of natural kind terms and natural kinds about which there are no experts, the 'Donnellan class'. Terms in the class are ordinary non-technical natural kind terms that speakers have in their idiolects, but have not, themselves, introduced into the language. Whether a given term belongs to the Donnellan class can change over time. There might be no experts about a natural kind term or the corresponding kind at one time, but at a later time there might develop a distinction between what experts and non-experts supposedly know about the use of the term and the corresponding kind. An example of such a term is 'water'. In 1750 there was no distinction between experts and non-experts about water or the use of 'water'. We can take Donnellan's proposal to be that the semantic referent of 'water' is determined by the underlying nature of paradigms of water, about which no one, including those who have the term in their idiolects, had any knowledge. The paradigms could be picked out in two ways: either indexically in the way in which instances of water are determined for English speakers by (10a) or non-indexically by "... a purely descriptive description denoting the paradigms" (Donnellan: 1993, 159). In either cases speakers who have the term in their idiolects would have tacit knowledge of a rule that specified paradigms of the kind either indexically or descriptively and their tacit knowledge of the rule would constitute their 'water' semantic competence. The revolutionary idea, according to Donnellan, is the way in which paradigms determine the extension of a term. "...The important feature of the rule will be that the extension of the term is determined by the underlying nature of some set of paradigms and the paradigms are fixed by the rule itself" (*Ibid.*, 157). (10a), then, is an instance of what Donnellan regards to be "...a new kind of semantic rule for a term utterly different from the classical model..." (Donnellan: 1993, 162).

The question is whether Donnellan's proposal about there being a new kind of semantic rule is an accurate account of what determines the semantic referent for the Donnellan class of natural kind terms. I think that it does not. Consider the natural kind term 'gold', a time before anyone knew what the underlying nature of gold was and Oscar who has 'gold' in his idiolect and who has acquired it in the same way that a normal speaker of English acquires the term. Oscar is able to use the term appropriately in a variety of situations. Hence, there is good reason for taking gold to be the semantic referent of 'gold' in Oscar's idiolect. Let us suppose that Oscar has various items that are made of gold, his wedding band, a gold coin, a gold locket, etc., that he is able to identify as being made of gold. But none of these is picked out as paradigms by his 'rule' for 'gold'. Rather, he mistakenly believes that his King's crown is made of gold. We can imagine that the original crown that had been made of gold was replaced by a crown that looked the same, but was made of some base metal. Since the crown is the most important thing supposedly made of gold in the kingdom, it is this that is picked out as the paradigm by Oscar's 'rule' for 'gold'.[35]

(11) 'Gold' refers to the metal, and any metal similar to it, in our King's crown.

Obviously, (11) does not yield gold as the semantic referent of 'gold' in Oscar's idiolect. Hence, it gives the wrong result, since by hypothesis the semantic referent of 'gold' in his idiolect is gold. The problem is that Oscar is mistaken about the King's crown being made of gold, and hence, is mistaken about (11), a mistake that he can come to recognize, the recognition of which would lead him to change his view about 'gold' being true of the King's Crown and thus about (11). As Putnam puts the point, (11) is a *defeasible* condition on reference determination (Putnam: 1975, 225).

Putnam suggests that in such a situation "...one of a series of ... 'fallback' conditions becomes activated" (*Ibid.*). One might suppose that there is something else that Oscar could identify as being made of gold and thus, could serve as a paradigm that would determine the semantic referent of 'gold'. Oscar could have, perhaps, tacit knowledge of something like,

(12) 'Gold' refers to the metal, and any metal similar to it, in my wedding band.

---

[35]I assume that Oscar is not using 'gold' idiosyncratically. He intends to use it in the way that others use it in his linguistic community.

(12), and similar rules, however, do not help with the determination of the semantic referent of 'gold' in Oscar's idiolect, when it is (11) to which he appeals before he discovers that he is mistaken about the King's crown. This can be seen by considering an ostensive meaning explanation for 'gold'. Ruth asks Oscar what 'gold' means. He points to the King's crown and says,

(13) This is gold.

In so saying he intends (11) that is supposed to determine the semantic referent of his use of 'gold' in (13). But if it does, it gives the wrong semantic referent; the King's crown is not made of gold. (12) does not play any role here, since it is (11) that Oscar intends in saying (13).

If this is not convincing, suppose that all of Oscar's gold objects have been replaced with fakes. Hence, any rule, similar to (11) or (12), which on Donnellan's proposal Oscar knows tacitly and determines the semantic referent of 'gold' in his idiolect, would not give gold as the semantic referent of 'gold'. What then determines the semantic referent of 'gold' in (13) and gives the correct result that what Oscar says in uttering (13) is false? What we can fall back on is some version of the Kripke causal/historical chain between Oscar's disposition to use 'gold' and the referent fixing ceremony in which 'gold' was introduced into English. Consequently, Donnellan has given us no reason to suppose that in standard circumstances for ordinary speakers, even when there are no experts, what determines in their idiolects and in their use of sentences like (13) the semantic referent of 'gold', or of any other natural kind term, must be a new kind of semantic rule that is "...utterly different from the classical model..."[36] (Donnellan: 1993, 162).

6   Burge's Thought Experiments

I would now like to turn to Burge's *water* and *arthritis* Twin Earth thought experiments. They are standardly treated as being very different sorts of arguments that have the same negative conclusion, but lead to different positive suggestions. The negative conclusion that Burge draws

---

[36]This is not to suggest that my argument against Donnellan shows that there cannot be speakers, circumstances and natural kind terms for which a plausible account of reference determination for the terms would involve a Donnellan rule. But I do not think that Donnellan has given us any reason to think that the semantic referents of natural kind terms in the idiolects of ordinary speakers in standard situations is determined by a Donnellan rule in the way that Donnellan suggests.

from his *water* thought experiment and the positive suggestion that he makes about the nature of *de dicto* intentional states parallel Putnam's conclusions and suggestions about semantic knowledge and reference determination. The negative conclusion is that an individual's intentional states, Oscar's, say, are not individuated by his inner states, that is, by his dispositions, his internal physical states, the stimuli impinging on his sensory organs, his local functional states, etc., all non-intentionally described. The positive suggestion is that some of Oscar's intentional states are individuated by his physical environment. Let us call this sort of externalism 'kind externalism'. In an earlier paper, "Individualism and the Mental," Burge presents another version of the Twin Earth thought experiment that also has negative and positive results, but that appeals to a wider range of terms, for example, 'arthritis', 'sofa', 'brisket', and 'mortgage' (Burge: 1979). The negative result is the same as for kind externalism; Oscar's inner states, non-intentionally described, do not individuate his intentional states. The positive proposal is that some of his intentional states are fixed by his social environment, that is, by how the terms are used by his linguistic community. Let us call this variety of externalism, 'social externalism'.

In both kind and social externalism it is something that it is external to an individual that individuates his intentional states. In the former it is his physical environment that does the trick; in the latter his social environment. Burge's two kinds of thought experiments can be seen, then, to lend support to different sorts of externalism, the *water* thought experiment to kind externalism and the *arthritis* thought experiment to social externalism. So it might seem. As we shall see, in Burge's *water* Twin-Earth thought experiment an individual's social environment also plays a role in individuating his *water* intentional states. Thus, both thought experiments can be viewed as arguments for social externalism.[37] I shall argue that Donnellan has mischaracterized Burge's *water* thought experiment. I shall begin by laying out Burge's *water* thought experiment and show how in some respects it is similar to and different from Putnam's *water* thought experiment.

The first steps in Burge's *water* thought experiment are similar to Putnam's. Burge asks us to imagine a possible world in which there are

---

[37]Burge presents four different thought experiments. The two already mentioned and two others in Burge: 1986a and 1986b. In the arguments in Burge, 1979, 1982 and 1986b, but not in 1986a, a feature of an individual's social environment plays a role in the individuation of his *de dicto* intentional states. In 1986b, however, "Even where social practices are deeply involved in individuating mental states, they are often not the final arbiter" (Burge: 1986b, 706).

two planets, Earth and Twin Earth the physical environments of which look very much the same, but differ in that where Earth has water Twin Earth has *XYZ*. In addition there are two people, on Earth, Oscar, and on Twin Earth, Boscar, who are physical twins of one another, hence, who are type identical in their internal states, stimuli impinging on their sensory organs and dispositions to behavior, all described non-intentionally. Moreover, both Oscar and Boscar have 'water' in their idiolects, but in Oscar's idiolect 'water' has water as its semantic referent and in Boscar's idiolect, *XYZ*. As Burge points out, Boscar's 'water' cannot be translated into our 'water'. To avoid confusion Burge suggests that we coin a new term, 'twater', for translating Boscar's 'water' into' English (Burge: 1982, 100).

It is in the second step of his thought experiment, a step that will become important in what follows, that Burge parts company with Putnam. Putnam asks us to imagine that we are in 1750 before anyone knew about the underlying physical structure of water or about *XYZ*. Hence, in Putnam's thought experiment neither on Earth nor on Twin Earth are there experts about the use of 'water' or about water or *XYZ*. Burge's thought experiment does not follow Putnam on this point. On Earth and Twin Earth there are experts in the two scientific communities who know, respectively, that the molecular structure of water and of twater. Moreover, Burge has it that this knowledge has spread beyond the two scientific communities into the corresponding non-scientific communities, but it does not extend to all the members of the linguistic communities, in particular to Oscar and Boscar who are ignorant of the structure of, respectively, water and twater (*Ibid.*, 100-101).

Burge also parts company with Putnam in the conclusion that he draws from the thought experiment. It is part of Putnam's description of his thought experiment that Oscar and Boscar are type identical in their narrow psychological states, that is, in their *de dicto* intentional states. Burge argues that Oscar and Boscar do not have the same *de dicto* intentional states. Let us suppose that both Oscar and Boscar utter in the course of an ordinary conversation,

(14) I believe that water is good to drink.

In so uttering (14) Oscar expresses the belief that water is good to drink. Boscar can express no such belief, since there is no water on Twin Earth. Hence, neither Boscar nor anyone else in his linguistic community has had contact with water.[38] The belief Boscar expresses is that twater is good to drink. Since 'water' and 'twater' are not true of the same things and hence not translations of one another, the content of the beliefs that Oscar and Boscar express in uttering (14) are not the same. The point can be generalized: Any beliefs that Oscar and Boscar would express using the same sentence in which 'water' occurs are not the same. Hence, the difference in Oscar's and Boscar's intentional states cannot rest on their internal physical properties, stimulations of their sensory organs and their disposition to behavior, all non-intentionally described, since for Oscar and Boscar they are type identical. The question is, then, what individuates the beliefs that Oscar and Boscar express in uttering (14). Before considering this question, I wish to consider Donnellan's characterization of Burge's thought experiments.

7 Donnellan's Interpretation of Burge's Thought Experiments

As we have seen, Donnellan concentrates his attention on Burge's thought experiments in "Individualism and the Mental," and in particular on his *arthritis* thought experiment. His reason for doing so is that he regards Burge's *water* and other thought experiments in later papers to be variants of the *arthritis* thought experiment (Donnellan: 1993, 155). In important respects Burge's *arthritis* and *water* thought experiments are different. The *arthritis* thought experiment, unlike the *water* thought experiment, does not follow Putnam and consider a possible world in which there are two planets, Earth and Twin Earth and two type identical persons on the different planets. Rather, in the *arthritis* thought experiment we are asked to consider one person, Oscar, across the actual world and a possible world. This difference, however, has no bearing on Donnellan's interpretation of Burge and Putnam or on the conclusions that Burge draws about the individuation of intentional states.[39]

The first step of the *arthritis* thought experiment has it that Oscar is able to use 'arthritis' in various contexts so that we are warranted in ascribing to him a variety of beliefs in which the belief ascriptions have 'arthritis' in the content clause. For example, Oscar believes that having cancer is worse than having arthritis, that taking aspirins helps reduce

---

[38] I shall also suppose that no one on Twin Earth has a theory about water. Having a theory about something does not require that one be causally connected with that thing, or that anyone with whom one is associated has such a connection.

[39] The *arthritis*, but not the *water* thought experiment can be used to show that token identity and supervenience theories of brain states and mental states are mistaken (Burge: 1979, 111).

arthritic pain, that his uncle has arthritis, etc. However, Oscar also believes that he has arthritis in the thigh, a belief that he is ready to give
up, when he goes to see his doctor who tells him that arthritis is a disease of the joints (Burge: 1979, 77).

In the second step of the *arthritis* thought experiment we are asked
to consider a counterfactual situation in which there is no change in
Oscar's history, inner physical states, stimulation patterns of his sensory
organs, dispositions to behavior, all non-intentionally described. Moreover, he is able to use 'arthritis' in a variety of contexts, the same contexts, non-intentionally described, that he uses the term in the actual
situation. Hence, both in the actual and counterfactual situations Oscar
utters such sentences as, 'Cancer is worse than arthritis', 'Taking aspirins helps reduce arthritis pain', etc. There are two differences, however,
between the actual and the counterfactual situations. One difference is
that in the counterfactual situation 'arthritis' is used by the experts in
the community in the way that Oscar mistakenly uses it, before he sees
his doctor. That is to say, it is applied to arthritis and other ailments that
can occur in the thighs. Another difference is that in the counterfactual
situation arthritis has not been picked out as a separate disease, or if it
has, another term other than 'arthritis', not widely used and unknown to
Oscar, is applied to it (78).

The final step in the argument is to consider what beliefs Oscar has
in the actual and the counterfactual situations.[40] As we have seen, in
the actual situation, despite Oscar's mistaken belief about arthritis, he
has a range of beliefs that we are warranted in ascribing to him, the ascriptions of which contain 'arthritis' in the content clauses. He has,
claims Burge, none of these beliefs in the counterfactual situation.[41]

---

[40]I talk here of 'an argument'. But the thought experiment is not a deductive argument that has premises and a conclusion that follows from them. Rather, in the first
two steps of the thought experiment two situations are described, an actual and a counterfactual situation. In the final step of the thought experiment we are asked to consider how we would describe further features of the counterfactual situation, in this
case Oscar's beliefs about the ailment that is called 'arthritis', given the characterizations of the actual and counterfactual situations in the first two steps of the thought
experiment (Burge: 1979, 78).

[41]Donnellan mischaracterizes Burge's argument at this point. He claims that
...counterfactually, we can imagine the same person (or his counterpart) having the
same history and (in an important sense) psychological states—up to the point of talking to the doctor—in a community where the word 'arthritis' is given a wider use, a
use that allows that arthritis can occur in soft tissue (Donnellan: 1993, 160).
But it would seem that here Donnellan is attributing the same belief to Oscar and
Boscar, namely, that arthritis can occur in soft tissue. The whole point of Burge's

The reason that he does not have any of these beliefs is that he does not have the concept of *arthritis*. 'Arthritis' in his idiolect does not translate as his term 'arthritis' in the actual situation. In fact the two terms are not co-extensive and hence, cannot express the same concept. There is no difference between the actual and counterfactual situations in Oscar's history, internal physical states, stimulation patterns, dispositions to behavior, etc., non-intentionally described, but yet his intentional states differ. In the actual situation Oscar believes, for example, that cancer is worse than arthritis, but he does not have this belief in the counterfactual situation. What individuates Oscar's beliefs is the difference in the ways that 'arthritis' is used in his linguistic communities in the actual and the counterfactual situations, and his having the disposition to be deferential to these uses.

8 Problems with Donellan's Interpretation of Burge's Thought Experiments

Let us look more closely at the thought experiment. What makes it possible, claims Burge, is that Oscar has an incomplete mastery of the concept of *arthritis,* since he believes that arthritis is a disease that could occur in the thigh (Burge: 1979, 83). It is this, incomplete mastery of a concept, that Donnellan takes to be central to Burge's thought experiments[42], including his *water* thought experiment. As we have seen, he regards Burge's *water* thought experiment to be merely an elaboration of the *arthritis* thought experiment and argues that it appeals to the same principles as the *arthritis* thought experiment. There are two ways in which incomplete mastery arises in Burge's thought experiments in "Individualism and the Mental." First, it can arise because of a subject's having a misconception of a concept, the sort of misconception

---

argument is that they do not have the same intentional states that are attributed using 'arthritis' in the content clauses of *de dicto* intentional state attributions.

[42]Donnellan is mistaken in his construal of how incomplete mastery works in Burge's *arthritis* thought experiment. Donnellan thinks that incomplete mastery of a concept applies to Oscar in both the actual and counterfactual situation. "In the Burge examples, the speech community changes in the counterfactual situation and the subject, unchanged, is credited with an incomplete mastery of the different concept designated by the same word in the new speech community" (Donnellan: 1993, 161). But this is not part of Burge's thought experiment. Let us translate 'arthritis' as used in the counterfactual situation with 'tharthritis'. Thus, in the counterfactual situation what Oscar believes is that tharthritis is a disease of the joints and the thigh. In having this belief he does not differ from others in his concept of *tharthritis*, including the experts, who have 'arthritis' in their idiolects. Hence, he does not have an incomplete mastery of the concept that he would express using 'arthritis'.

that Oscar has in believing that arthritis can occur in the thigh. Second, it can also arise because of a subject's having a partial understanding of a concept. Imagine the *arthritis* thought experiment as before, except that Oscar does not believe that arthritis can occur in the thighs. Rather, he is unsure whether arthritis occurs only in the joints, or whether it can also occur in the thighs. The thought experiment would go through equally well on this assumption (Burge: 1979, 82).

There is very little sense, however, to the idea that in Burge's *water* thought experiment Oscar and Boscar have incomplete mastery of the concepts of *water* and of *twater* in either way in which incomplete mastery can arise. What they lack is scientific knowledge about the molecular structure of, respectively, water and *XYZ*, knowledge that is possessed by the 'experts' of their respective linguistic communities (Burge: 1986b, 708). But this difference between the two communities does not play the same role in the *water* thought experiments that Oscar's lack of mastery of the concept of *arthritis* plays in the *arthritis* and similar thought experiments. In the *arthritis* thought experiment Oscar has the mistaken belief that 'arthritis' applies to a disease that occurs in the joints and to a painful condition in the thighs. Hence, we can say that the speaker referent of 'arthritis' for Oscar is different from the semantic referent of the term in his idiolect. His speaker referent is given in the following:

(15) 'Arthritis' applies to arthritis and to a painful condition in the thighs.

It is (15) taken over into the counterfactual situation that gives the way that 'arthritis' is used by Oscar and others in his speech community. That is to say, in the counterfactual situation (15) gives the semantic referent of 'arthritis' in the idiolects of Oscar and other members of his speech community. Similarly with incomplete understanding. Oscar is unsure whether arthritis occurs just in the joints or whether it can occur as well in the thighs. This gives rise to Oscar's being unsure about whether (15) is the correct way to apply 'arthritis'. As before, (15) is carried over into the counterfactual situation as specifying how 'arthritis' is used, its semantic referent, in the idiolects of Oscar and other members of his linguistic community. In the *water* thought experiment neither Oscar nor Boscar have an intentional state that indicates a misconception or a partial understanding of the concepts of either *water* or *twater* that gives rise to something like (15) that is then carried over to describe on the other planet what determines how 'water' is used in that planet. Hence, nothing like incomplete mastery of a concept plays a role in generating the *water* thought experiment.

9 Conclusion

As we have seen, Donnellan mischaracterizes Putnam's and Burge's *water* thought experiments. A new kind of semantic rule is not an essential part of Putnam's thought experiment and Burge's *water* thought experiment does not turn on an incomplete or mistaken understanding of a concept. There is an important difference between the thought experiments that Donnellan does not discuss. In Putnam's thought experiment neither Oscar nor Boscar, nor anyone else in their communities, knows, respectively, the nature of water or of *XYZ*. In Burge's thought experiment Oscar and Boscar are unaware of the natures of the two natural kinds, but there are experts in their respective communities that know their natures. We can take it that in Putnam's thought experiment the division of linguistic labour does not play a role in determining the semantic referents of 'water' in the idiolects of Oscar and Boscar. In Burge's thought experiment the difference in the *de dicto* intentional states of Oscar and Boscar is

> ...a product primarily of differences in their physical environments, meditated by differences in their social environments—in the mental states of their fellows and conventional meanings of words they and their fellows employ (Burge: 1982, 102).

It appears then that in Burge's thought experiment the individuation of Oscar's and Boscar's intentional states depend upon there being experts and a division of linguistic labor in their social environments. The question I would like to close with is what are the conditions under which the social environment places a necessary role in the individuation of intentional states? In the Putnam's thought experiment, a division of linguistic labor does not play a role. Is his thought experiment deficient in not containing experts and the division of linguistic labor? These are questions that I cannot take up here, but hope to consider at another time. These questions are important, since if it turns out that they have positive answers, it would deepen our understanding of the role that social features play in reference determination and in the individuation of *de dicto* intentional states.

References

Burge, Tyler, 1977, 'Belief *de re*'. *the Journal of Philosophy*. 64: 338-363.

Burge, Tyler, 1979, 'Individualism and the mental'. *Midwest Studies in Philosophy* IV: 73-121.

Burge, Tyler, 1982, 'Other bodies'. In A. Woodfield (ed.) *Thought and Object.* New York: Oxford University Press, 97-120.

Burge, Tyler (1986a). 'Individualism and psychology'. *The Philosophical Review.* 45: 3 - 45.

Burge, Tyler, 1986b, 'Intellectual norms and foundations of mind'. *The Journal of Philosophy* 83, No. 12: 697-720.

Burge, Tyler, 1993a 'Concepts, definitions and meaning'. *Metaphilosophy* 24: 309-325.

Chomsky, Noam, 1965, *Aspects of a theory of syntax.* Cambridge, Mass.: M.I.T. Press.

Davis, Steven (2000). 'social externalism and deference'. In D. Sperber (ed.) *Metarepresentation.* Vancouver Studies in Cognitive Science. Vol. 10. New York: Oxford University Press, 1-30.

Donnellan, Keith, 1993, 'There is a word for that kind of thing: an investigation of two thought experiments'. *Philosophical Perspectives, Language and Logic* 7: 155-171.

Kaplan, David, 1989, 'Demonstratives'. In J. Almog, J. Perry and H. Wettstein (eds.) *Themes from Kaplan.* New York: Oxford University Press.

Kripke, S., 1980, *Naming and necessity.* Cambridge, MA: Harvard University Press.

McDowell, John, 1994, *Mind and world.* Cambridge, MA: Harvard University Press.

Putnam, Hilary, 1975, 'The meaning of 'meaning''. *Meaning, mind and reality.* Volume 2. New York: Cambridge University Press.

5

Externalism, Self-Knowledge and Transmission of Warrant

MARTIN DAVIES

1 Introduction

> The conditions for thinking a certain thought must be presupposed in the thinking. [1]

Externalism about some mental property, M, is the thesis that whether a person (or other physical being) has M depends, not only on conditions inside the person's skin, but also on the person's environment and the way that the person is embedded in that environment. The dependence here is supposed to be conceptual rather than causal; it is the kind of dependence that can be revealed by philosophical theorising. This is an armchair methodology; so, if philosophical theorising yields knowledge, then it is a kind of *armchair knowledge*. Its status as knowledge does not depend on our conducting any detailed empirical investigation of the world around us. The puzzle for discussion in this paper arises when the possibility of armchair knowledge of an *externalist dependence thesis*

---

[1] Burge, 1988, p. 653.

Meaning, Basic Self-Knowledge and Mind: Essays on Tyler Burge.
María J. Frápolli and Esther Romero (eds.).
Copyright © 2003, CSLI Publications.

about mental property M is put together with a thesis of first-person authority for that same mental property.

For the purposes of generating our puzzle, we do not need to be concerned about a precise formulation of the notion of first-person authority. All that we need to suppose is that we each have a distinctively first-personal way of knowing that we ourselves have property M, when we do have it, without needing to conduct any detailed empirical investigation of the environment and our relation to it. This distinctively first-personal knowledge, self-knowledge, is another kind of armchair knowledge.

The puzzle that arises from combining externalism and self-knowledge is clearly visible when we consider the epistemic status of the premises and conclusion of arguments of the following form (Ext):

Ext(1)   I am thinking that p.
Ext(2)   If I am thinking that p then E(me).
Therefore:
Ext(3)   E(me).

('E(x)' is some statement about x's environmental embedding.) The occurrence of the particular mental verb 'think' in Ext(1) is not vital; we could just as well have 'I believe that p'. All that is vital is that the mental property of thinking or believing that p should meet two conditions. First, it should be a property that is subject to first-person authority. Second, it should be a property for which an externalist dependence thesis holds. Philosophical theorising should underwrite the truth of Ext(2), and we can assume that a philosophical theory will underwrite this particular claim by supporting a modal generalisation:

Necessarily($\forall$x)(If x is thinking that p then E(x))

By our assumptions about first-person authority and about philosophical theorising, I can have armchair knowledge of the premises Ext(1) and Ext(2). In neither case does my knowledge depend for its status as knowledge on an empirical investigation of my environment. Given armchair knowledge of those two premises, it is trivially easy to perform the *modus ponens* inference and so, it seems, to arrive at armchair knowledge of the conclusion Ext(3). But this creates a puzzle since Ext(3) is a statement about my environment and my way of being embedded in it, and we normally expect knowledge about such matters to depend on empirical investigation.

2 Transmission of Warrant and the Problem of Armchair Knowledge

In my view, the puzzle that arises from the combination of externalism and self-knowledge is not an isolated phenomenon. Rather, it is one of a number of puzzles that involve arguments of the more general form (MC):

(1) I have mental property M.
(2) If I have mental property M then I meet condition C.
Therefore:
(3) I meet condition C.

Puzzles that are similar to the one under discussion here arise from philosophical theorising about the relationship between descriptions of ourselves as conscious, thinking, language-using persons and descriptions of human animals as information-processing systems (Davies, 2000). For example, there are philosophical theories according to which the cognitive architectural requirements for thought and concept deployment include the truth of the language of thought hypothesis (Davies, 1991a, 1992a). Other philosophical theories have the consequence that the objectivity of linguistic meaning requires the presence of tacit knowledge of a compositional semantic theory (Schiffer, 1993; Davies, 2000). I know from the armchair that I think many things and deploy many concepts, and I know from the armchair what many hitherto unconsidered sentences of my own language mean. But I do not have armchair knowledge about my own cognitive architecture. I cannot know from the armchair that the language of thought hypothesis is true of me; nor that my language processing system embodies tacit knowledge of a compositional semantic theory. These are matters for empirical investigation.

The general form of what I call 'the problem of armchair knowledge' is this. Armchair philosophical theorising supports an inference from A to B. A can be known from the armchair; B cannot be known without detailed empirical investigation of the world. So a thinker can know that A without detailed empirical investigation of the world, and can likewise know that if A then B. But it is obvious that B follows; no empirical investigation is needed to see that. So the thinker's knowledge that A and knowledge that if A then B, and the thinker's ability knowledgeably to draw the obvious inference, seem together to provide a route to knowledge that B—and still without any need to rise from the armchair. Yet B was supposed to be something that could only be known by way of detailed empirical investigation of the world. Knowledge that B was supposed to require an investigative, rather than an armchair, methodology.

If we are to provide a general solution to the problem of armchair knowledge, then we have to accept that, sometimes, knowing that A and knowing that if A then B, and then knowledgeably drawing the conclusion that B, does not constitute a route to knowledge that B. Sometimes, that is to say, the epistemic warrant or justification that we have for the premises of an argument is not transmitted to the conclusion, even though it is obvious that the premises entail the conclusion. The idea of a restriction on transmission of epistemic warrant may seem counter-intuitive at first. But in fact it is quite plausible that something like this is already needed for an adequate account of putative anti-sceptical arguments like G.E. Moore's (1959; see below, section 4). In the remainder of this introductory section, I shall make four general comments by way of clarifying both the problem of armchair knowledge and the form of its proposed solution.

1. The first comment is simply that the issue is not one about validity of arguments. Arguments that seem to give rise to the problem of armchair knowledge, such as arguments of the (Ext) form, are palpably valid instances of *modus ponens*. Our problem is not logical but epistemological.

2. The second general comment is that the issue is not exactly one about closure of knowledge under known entailment. It is true that, if knowledge is not closed under known entailment, then transmission of epistemic warrant must be limited in some way. But the converse is not true in general. In a case where warrant cannot be transmitted from the premises of a valid argument to its conclusion, it might still be that anyone who knows the premises also knows, or can come to know, the conclusion. It might be, for example, that anyone who knows the premises inevitably has an independent warrant for the conclusion. Or it might be that knowledge of the conclusion does not require a warrant.

Since there can be a failure of transmission without a failure of closure, our key question is not whether someone who knows that A and knows that if A then B also knows that B. Rather, the question is whether someone who knows that A and knows that if A then B *thereby* knows that B – whether, that is, drawing the obvious inference is a way of *achieving* knowledge of the conclusion.

3. The third general comment is that the issue is not one about confidence or subjective probability. To propose a restriction on transmission of epistemic warrant is not to suggest that rational subjects who

attach a high degree of confidence to the proposition that A and the proposition that if A then B, should attach a substantially lower degree of confidence to the proposition that B.

There are, of course, cases in which it is rational to be much less confident about the conclusion of a *modus ponens* inference than about either of its premises. The conclusion of a valid argument is no less probable than the conjunction of its premises; but the probability of the conjunction of the premises may be substantially less than the probability of each of the premises taken individually. In the case of *modus ponens* arguments, this can happen if the probability of the conditional premise (if A then B) is high while the conditional probability of B given A is low. In such a case, the conditional is said to be not robust with respect to its antecedent (Jackson, 1987). But the *modus ponens* argument of the (Ext) form is not like this, and we can suppose that if the premises deserve a high degree of confidence individually then they also deserve a high degree of confidence together.

If a thinker is confident that A and confident that if A then B and also confident of their conjunction then she should be no less confident that B. In this sense, believing the premises (together) gives the thinker a reason to believe the conclusion. A thinker who believes that B under these circumstances is not subject to any criticism for doing so; she is not being doxastically reckless or irresponsible. But someone who proposes a restriction on transmission of epistemic warrant says that, even so, epistemically adequate warrants for believing the premises may not themselves add up to an epistemically adequate warrant for believing the conclusion.

4. The fourth general comment is that, in offering putative cases where warrant is not transmitted from premises to conclusion, we must take care to avoid equivocation on key notions that occur in the proposition that A, as between the first premise and the conditional premise. Thus, for example, in the case of (Ext), we must take care to avoid equivocation on the phrase 'believe that *p*' as between Ext(1) and Ext(2). Otherwise we invite a very natural response to the puzzle. Someone may say that it is only in a thin sense of the phrase that I have armchair knowledge that I believe that *p*, while it is only in a thick sense of the phrase that philosophical theory can support an externalist dependence thesis (Raffman, 1998).

3 Externalism about Content

I said at the outset that externalism is a thesis about dependence: whether a person has mental property M depends, at least in part, on the person's environment and the way that the person is embedded in that environment. It is useful to clarify the relationship between externalist dependence theses such as:

Necessarily($\forall$x) (If x is thinking that p then E(x))

and what I have elsewhere called constitutive and modal externalist theses (Davies, 1991b, 1992b, 1993, 1996, 1998).

Constitutive externalism (as it concerns mental property M) says that the fundamental philosophical account of what it is for an individual to have M needs to advert to the individual's physical or social environment. *Modal externalism* says that there are Twin Earth examples for M. That is, according to modal externalism, there are two possible situations w_1 and w_2, differing in environmental conditions, such that an individual, a, has M in w_1 but a duplicate individual, b, lacks M in w_2. According to modal externalism, having M is not a locally supervenient matter. That is, it does not depend only on what is going on inside the individual's skin.

Suppose that an externalist dependence thesis holds for mental property M:

Necessarily($\forall$x) (If M(x) then E(x)).

Then we expect to be able to generate a Twin Earth example for M. To do so, we consider an individual, a, who has M in w_1 and therefore meets condition E in w_1 and a duplicate individual, b, who fails to meet E in w_2 and therefore lacks M in w_2. Thus, unless it is somehow impossible to have a duplicate of a in an environment that fails to meet E, modal externalism goes along with the truth of an externalist dependence thesis. Furthermore, if an externalist dependence thesis for M is supported by philosophical theorising then it seems to be virtually guaranteed that constitutive externalism will also hold for M. So if an externalist dependence thesis holds for mental property M then it is plausible that both constitutive and modal externalism also hold for M.

If M is a constitutively, but not modally, externalist mental property, then we should not expect philosophical theorising to support an externalist dependence thesis about M. But suppose that M is modally externalist. Then it may be tempting to think that it will be a very short step from a Twin Earth example for M to a dependence thesis about M. In a Twin Earth example, a has M in w_1 and b lacks M in w_2 in virtue of a specific difference in environmental conditions between w_1 and w_2.

So, it may be said, whether any individual has M depends on environmental conditions being specifically as they are in w_1 rather than as they are in w_2. But, in fact, it can be quite difficult to derive a specific dependence thesis from a Twin Earth example. To see this, we only have to consider the basic shape of Twin Earth examples that are used to support social externalism (Burge, 1979).

Alf is thinking that arthritis is painful, while TwinAlf is not. Alf has the concept of arthritis, though his understanding of it is incomplete; TwinAlf does not have the concept of arthritis at all. The crucial difference between Alf's social environment and TwinAlf's relates to the linguistic practices of other people. Alf is surrounded by people who use the word 'arthritis' in such-and-such a way while TwinAlf is not. A convincing Twin Earth example of this kind would establish that having the concept of arthritis or thinking that arthritis is painful is not a locally supervenient matter. It would do so by highlighting the difference between meeting and not meeting a social environmental condition. But a Twin Earth example would not motivate the social externalist dependence thesis:

Necessarily($\forall$x) (If x is thinking that arthritis is painful then x is surrounded by people who use the word 'arthritis' in such-and-such a way).

For all that the Twin Earth example shows, it may be that particular features of Alf's internal makeup, or particular features of Alf's non-social environment, make Alf peculiarly dependent on the standard-setting role of the linguistic community around him. If his internal constitution and his non-social environment were the same, but the surrounding community did not play that standard-setting role, then he would not count as having the concept of arthritis. In the example, TwinAlf, who shares both internal constitution and non-social environment with Alf, does indeed lack that concept. But it hardly follows that someone internally unlike Alf, or someone in a different non-social environment from Alf's, would inevitably be without the concept of arthritis unless he enjoyed the support of a standard-setting linguistic community. Nor does it follow from the Twin Earth example that I am dependent on my linguistic community for the concept of arthritis in the way that Alf is.

Let us now consider the basic shape of Twin Earth examples that are used to support externalism about thoughts involving natural kind concepts (Putnam, 1975). Oscar is thinking that water is wet, while

TwinOscar is not. Oscar has the concept of water; TwinOscar lacks that concept. The crucial difference between Oscar's situation and TwinOscar's is that the stuff in Oscar's environment (water aka H_2O) is different from the stuff in TwinOscar's environment (twater aka XYZ). A convincing Twin Earth example of this kind would establish that having the concept of water or thinking that water is wet is not a locally supervenient matter. It would do so by highlighting the difference between meeting and not meeting a physical environmental condition, namely, being surrounded by samples of water. But it would be wrong to think that a Twin Earth example would work by motivating a specific dependence thesis such as:

Necessarily($\forall$x) (If x is thinking that water is wet then x is surrounded by samples of water).

For all that the example of the Oscar/TwinOscar duplicate pair shows, there could be someone else, also in TwinOscar's waterless environment but not a duplicate of Oscar, who did have the concept of water. Perhaps there is something about the way that Oscar is internally that makes his having the concept of water peculiarly dependent on his environmental relations. All the more so, there could be someone in an environment quite different from Oscar's or TwinOscar's but still with twater and no water, who had the concept of water. There could be, for all that the Twin Earth example shows.

The point of these last few paragraphs has been that it is not generally possible to read off an externalist dependence thesis from the difference between worlds w_1 and w_2 in a Twin Earth example. A Twin Earth thought experiment provides a counterexample to a claim of local supervenience and so licenses an existentially quantified statement about worlds and individuals. But an externalist dependence claim involves universal quantification over individuals and universal quantification over worlds. So it is unsurprising that there should be a gap between Twin Earth examples and externalist dependence claims.

4   Externalism and Self-Knowledge

We have seen that it is far from straightforward to motivate a specific externalist dependence thesis even when modal externalism is true. So consider a philosopher who holds that modal externalism is true for the mental properties of thinking thought contents that involve natural kind concepts. This externalist philosopher may still deny that externalist dependence theses about natural kind thoughts lead to the problem of armchair knowledge. Indeed, even a philosopher who accepts both modal and constitutive externalism for a wide range of mental properties could maintain that there are no true externalist dependence theses at all that give rise to the problem of armchair knowledge. I cannot show that such a position is incorrect. But my own view is that problematic externalist dependence theses cannot be avoided and that, in any case, the problem of armchair knowledge arises in many other areas of philosophical theorising. So, in the remainder of this paper, I shall pursue the question of how we might respond to the problem of armchair knowledge as it arises in the case of externalism and self-knowledge.

Let us suppose that it is possible to motivate some such dependence thesis as:

WaterDep   Necessarily($\forall$x) (If x is thinking that water is wet then x is (or has been) embedded in such-and-such ways in an environment that contains samples of water).

Given that assumption, we can consider the following argument, (WaterExt), in which the conditional premise follows from WaterDep:

Water(1)   I am thinking that water is wet.
Water(2)   If I am thinking that water is wet then I am (or have been) embedded in an environment that contains samples of water.

Therefore:

Water(3)   I am (or have been) embedded in an environment that contains samples of water.

It is worth noting two points about this example.

First, the conditional premise, Water(2), and the conclusion, Water(3), speak of an environment that contains samples of water rather than of an environment that contains samples of H_2O. The difference does not matter for the truth of the conditional premise; but it is important for the premise's epistemic status. It would be implausible that armchair philosophical theorising could deliver knowledge of a conditional premise that mentioned water in the antecedent and H_2O in the consequent, without drawing on empirical investigations to support the identity claim that water is H_2O. Speaking of samples of water rather than samples of H_2O protects the status of the conditional premise as a piece of armchair knowledge. But this does not make the conclusion something that is knowable from the armchair. I can and do know that my environment contains samples of water; but that knowledge is achieved by empirical investigation.

The second point to note is that thinking that water is wet is not to be equated with thinking something along the lines of: 'the chemical kind that exists in my actual environment and which falls from clouds, flows in rivers, is drinkable, colourless, odourless etc. is wet'. This is important if we are to avoid a charge of equivocation. (Recall the fourth general comment in section 1 above.)

It is plausible that if I were thinking a thought with the content 'the chemical kind that exists in my actual environment and which ... etc.' then I could know in the special first-personal way that I was doing so. So the first premise, so interpreted, would be a piece of armchair knowledge. But, on this interpretation, the conditional premise is not something knowable from the philosopher's armchair; indeed, it need not even be true. Thinking a thought with that content does not require the thinker to be in an environment that contains samples of water. For a thinker can deploy in thought the description 'the chemical kind that exists in my actual environment and which ... etc.' even though no chemical kind fits that description.

We could patch the conditional premise to make it plausibly true and knowable by way of philosophical theorising if we added a conjunct to the antecedent of the conditional and had it say:

If I am thinking that the chemical kind that exists in my actual environment and which ... etc. is wet *and some chemical kind fits the description that I deploy in thought* then I am embedded in such-and-such ways in an environment that contains samples of water.

But then, to preserve the validity of the argument, we would need to patch the first premise as well and have it say:

I am thinking that the chemical kind that exists in my actual environment and which ... etc. is wet *and some chemical kind fits the description that I deploy in thought.*

Of course, with the second conjunct added, this is no longer something that can be known in the special first-personal way.

In short, if thinking that water is wet were conceived as deploying a definite description in thought, then we would be open to a charge of equivocation between the first premise and the antecedent of the conditional premise. Without the equivocation, it would not be plausible that both premises could be known from the armchair. So (WaterExt) would fail as an example of the problem of armchair knowledge. If we are to use (WaterExt) as an example then we must not regard the thought that water is wet as involving a definite description ('the chemical kind . . . etc.'). It is far from obvious what is the right way to conceive of thoughts about natural kinds, but provisionally we can suppose that the thought that water is wet is about water in somewhat the same way that so-called recognition-based thoughts are about their objects (Evans, 1982; Brown, 1998). Against this presumed background, we can summarise our epistemological commentary on (WaterExt) as follows.

I can know the contents of my own thoughts in the special first-personal way; so I can have armchair knowledge of the first premise, Water(1). Also, we are supposing, externalist philosophical theorising yields armchair knowledge of the conditional premise, Water(2). But, while the conclusion, Water(3), is something that might well be known without any great difficulty, it seems to fall outside the scope of arm-chair knowledge; some empirical investigation is required.

The idea that there is some tension between externalism about content and first-person authority has been developed in more than one way. The problem posed by arguments like (WaterExt) might be called the *consequence problem* for first-person authority given externalism. It should be distinguished from a different problem, which we can call the *achievement problem* for first-person authority given externalism. How can I achieve an especially authoritative kind of knowledge about my own mental states, given that my being in those mental states depends on my environmental relational properties? For I am not, in general, especially authoritative about such properties.

Approaches to the achievement problem typically make some use of the fact that the content of my second-order thought that I am think-ing that water is wet, for example, embeds the content of my first-order thought that water is wet. So the content of the second-order thought is dependent on the environment in just the same way as the content of the first-order thought (Burge, 1988; Heil, 1988; Peacocke, 1999). This does not yet explain how it is that my second-order judgement amounts to knowledge. We still need a general account of how authoritative self-knowledge is possible (Burge, 1996, 1998; Peacocke, 1996, 1998, 1999). But, according to these approaches to the achievement problem, the fact about embedding can be used to show that no special problem for the achievement of self-knowledge flows from the fact that the con-tent of a first-order thought is, in part, externalistically determined.

An account of how self-knowledge is possible has to show how a second-order judgement that I am thinking that water is wet, made on the basis of my (first-order) thinking that water is wet, can be knowledge. According to externalism, quite independently of the epistemic status of the second-order judgement, I can make that judgement only if I have certain environmental relational properties. So, at the very starting point for an enquiry into the epistemic status of the second-order judgement, it is already guaranteed that I meet the externalist conditions for having the first-order thought. Thus, externalism poses no special problem for the achievement of self-knowledge.

In his seminal contribution to this topic, Tyler Burge says (1988, pp. 653–4):

> Among the conditions that determine the contents of first-order empirical thoughts are some that can be known only by empirical means. To think of something as water, for example, one must be in some causal relation to water—or at least in some causal relation to other particular substances that enable one to theorize accurately about water. . . . To know that such conditions obtain, one must rely on empirical methods. To know that water exists, or that what one is touching is water, one cannot circumvent empirical procedures. But to *think* that water is a liquid, one need not *know* the complex conditions that must obtain if one is to think that thought.

Let us agree with this. In order to know that I am thinking that water is a liquid, I do not need to know anything of externalist philosophical theory, and I do not need to know that the conditions required by that theory actually obtain. But to the extent that the truth of externalist dependence theses is no bar to the achievement of self-knowledge, the consequence problem for first-person authority given externalism becomes pressing. Without empirical investigation, I know that I am thinking that water is a liquid. If I learn something about externalist philosophical theory then I can also know that if I am thinking that water is a liquid then certain conditions must obtain. I can draw the obvious consequence that those conditions do indeed obtain. Yet, as Burge says: 'To know that such conditions obtain, one must rely on empirical methods'. This is the consequence problem.

Paul Boghossian presents this problem as a *reductio ad absurdum* of the combination of externalism about mental content and privileged self-knowledge. Externalism is here 'the view that what concepts our thoughts involve may depend not only on facts that are internal to us, but on facts about our environment' (1997, p. 161). The claim about self-knowledge is 'that we are able to know, without the benefit of empirical investigation, what our thoughts are in our own case' (ibid.). The conclusion for *reductio* is that, if both these claims were true, then 'we would be in a position to know certain facts about the world a priori, facts that no one can reasonably believe are knowable a priori' (ibid.). According to Boghossian, one or the other claim has to be rejected. My aim is to show how both claims can be maintained.

In an earlier and influential paper, Michael McKinsey presented a somewhat similar *reductio* (1981, p. 16):

> [I]f you could know a priori that you are in a given mental state, and your being in that mental state conceptually or logically implies the existence of external objects, then you could know a priori that the external world exists. Since you obviously *can't* know a priori that the external world exists, you also can't know a priori that you are in the mental state in question.

But McKinsey's presentation has a number of distinctive features of which one is particularly important for our purposes.

McKinsey says that a priori knowledge is 'knowledge obtained independently of empirical investigation' (1981, p. 9). This sounds just like Boghossian, for whom the notion of a priori knowledge in play is simply that of knowledge that is available 'without the benefit of empirical investigation'. But, in fact, McKinsey makes a significant addition when he talks about the character of self-knowledge (ibid; emphasis added):

> [W]e can in principle find out about these states in ourselves 'just by thinking', without launching an empirical investigation *or making any assumptions about the external physical world*.

The lesson that McKinsey draws from his *reductio* is that we do not have this special kind of knowledge of our own mental states in cases where the truth of an ascription of the mental state depends on the existence of objects external to the subject of the ascription. If the lesson is unpacked in line with McKinsey's characterisation of self-knowledge then it becomes this: We cannot know about our own externalist mental states without launching an empirical investigation or at least making some assumptions about the external physical world.

It is not obvious that this is something with which Burge would disagree. In a sentence just before the passage that I quoted a few paragraphs back, he says (1988, p. 653): 'It is uncontroversial that the conditions for thinking a certain thought must be presupposed in the thinking.' And at the end of that quoted passage, when he says, 'But to *think* that water is a liquid, one need not *know* the complex conditions that must obtain if one is to think that thought', he immediately adds: 'such conditions need only be presupposed.' Perhaps there is a distinction to be drawn here between assumptions and presuppositions. But, on the face of it, Burge is allowing that in thinking that water is wet, or in thinking that I am thinking that water is wet, I presuppose or assume that the conditions necessary for me to think that thought do obtain. In that case, my knowledge that I am thinking that water is wet is not knowledge that I can have 'without making any assumptions about the external physical world'.

McKinsey uses a notion of a priori knowledge that is very strict. Suppose that, in that very strict sense, I could know a priori that I am thinking that water is wet, and could know a priori that if I am thinking that water is wet then environmental condition E holds. Then, according to McKinsey, that strict a priori warrant could be transmitted to the proposition that condition E holds. But, as McKinsey points out and as we must surely agree, it is absurd to suppose that E could be known a priori. So it cannot be that I can both know what I am thinking and know the truth of an exterrnalist dependence thesis a priori, in that strict sense.

An externalist who also accepts a thesis of first-person authority may respond to McKinsey's *reductio* argument by conceding one point but insisting on another. First, an externalist who accepts a thesis of first-person authority may concede that self-knowledge is not a priori in the strict sense. This is what the quotation from Burge (1988) suggests and in any case, quite apart from externalism, it is plausible that self-knowledge is not a priori in the strict sense; there seem to be empirical assumptions or presuppositions in the background (Peacocke, 1999, p. 244–5). But, unless background assumptions always stand in need of justification, this concession is consistent with the idea that self-knowledge is a priori in the weaker sense of not being justificatorily based on empirical investigation (McLaughlin, 2000; see also Field, 1996). So, second, an externalist who accepts a thesis of first-person authority may insist that both self-knowledge and knowledge of externalist dependence theses are a priori in that weaker sense.

Part of the importance of McKinsey's *reductio* argument is that, although McKinsey himself focuses on a priori knowledge in the strict sense, the pattern of the argument can be repeated for the weaker notion of a priori knowledge (Boghossian, 1997; see also Brown, 1995). Suppose that we take a priori knowledge to be knowledge that does not rest on empirical investigation but may still depend on empirical background assumptions (such as the assumption that 'the conditions for thinking a certain thought' are met). This makes it much more plausible that externalist dependence theses can be known a priori and much more likely that first-person authority involves a priori self-knowledge. But it still seems absurd that I could know a priori that I am (or have been) embedded in an environment that contains samples of water.

It does not matter, of course, whether we use the term 'a priori knowledge' at all. Whatever label we use for knowledge that is not justificatorily based on empirical investigation, externalism and self-knowledge together give rise to a problem, an instance of the problem of armchair knowledge. The proposal of this paper is that a solution to the problem involves restrictions or limitations on the transmission of epistemic warrant.

5 Transmission of Warrant and Anti-Sceptical Arguments

Earlier (in section 1), I acknowledged that the idea of limitations on the transmission of epistemic warrant might seem counter-intuitive at first. But I suggested that some restriction is already needed for an adequate account of putative anti-sceptical arguments like Moore's:

> Moore(1)   Here is one hand and here is another.
> Moore(2)   If here is one hand and here is another then an external world exists.
> Therefore:
> Moore(3)   An external world exists.

Of this purported anti-sceptical argument, Barry Stroud says (1984, p. 86):

> Once we are familiar with the philosophical problem of our knowledge of the external world, I think we immediately feel that Moore's proof is inadequate.

The sense that what Moore offered is inadequate as an anti-sceptical argument does, indeed, seem to be compelling. We want to allow, with Moore, that the conditional premise can be known by a very elementary piece of philosophical theorising (or conceptual analysis); and we want to allow that the first premise can be known just by looking at one hand and then the other. The argument is palpably valid; but it seems wrong to suppose that our knowledge of the premises could provide us with a route to knowledge of the conclusion, or that the conclusion has epistemic warrant transmitted to it from the premises.

When I say that epistemic warrant is not transmitted from the premises to the conclusion of Moore's argument, I am not suggesting that someone who confidently believes Moore(1) and Moore(2) would be wrong to believe Moore(3). I am not even suggesting that the belief in

Moore(3) is epistemologically out of order. The proposal is, rather, that the epistemically adequate warrants for believing the premises may not themselves add up to an epistemically adequate warrant for believing the conclusion.

We observed (the second general point in section 1) that it is possible to deny transmission of warrant without denying closure of knowledge under known entailment. Even if warrant is not transmitted from the premises to the conclusion of a particular valid argument, it might be that anyone who knows the premises also knows the conclusion because it is possible to have knowledge of the conclusion without any warrant at all.

Alternatively, it might be that anyone who has a warrant for the premises inevitably has some other, prior and independent, warrant for the conclusion. In principle, it seems that there are two significantly different ways in which this could happen. In one kind of case, anyone who has a warrant for the premises inevitably already has a warrant for the conclusion, and this warrant for the conclusion does not contribute to the warrant for the premises. This pattern of warrants would be consistent with having closure of knowledge without transmission of warrant. But the pattern does not actually guarantee non-transmission, for it might be that the warrant is transmitted from premises to conclusion, but that the warrant for the conclusion is not needed.

In fact, it might be suggested that this is the situation with Moore's argument. On this view, anyone who looks at one hand and then the other and thereby achieves a perceptual warrant for Moore(1) already has a more than adequate warrant for Moore(3) provided by perception of countless other objects. So (continuing with the suggestion), the warrant for Moore(1), provided by perception of two hands, is indeed transmitted to Moore(3). But it is not needed, as the conclusion Moore(3) is already as warranted as can be. According to this suggestion, an illusion of non-transmission is created by a kind of epistemic 'ceiling effect'. It is not easy definitively to rebut this suggestion. But anyone who is convinced, with Stroud, that Moore's premise, 'Here is a hand and here is another', does not warrant the anti-sceptical conclusion is likely to retain their conviction if we add to the premise 'and another and another . . .'. What seems implausible is not just that one little piece of perceptual evidence could defeat the sceptic, but rather that any amount of perceptual evidence could perform that epistemic service.

There is a second kind of case in which anyone who has a warrant for the premises of an argument inevitably has some prior warrant for the conclusion. In this kind of case, the prior warrant for the conclusion figures as a component in the warrant for the premises. This pattern of warrants involves a kind of epistemic circularity, but it is not obvious that it constitutes non-transmission of warrant. Consider, for example, a very simple case of this kind. The premises of the argument are A and B, and the argument proceeds through the conjunction A&B to the first conjunct A. Clearly, anyone who has a warrant for the premises already has a warrant for the conclusion. But it is far from clear that the warrant for the premises is not transmitted to the conclusion. In fact, the most natural account of this case would be that the warrants for the two premises A and B add up to a warrant for the conjunction A&B and that this amounts to a warrant for the conclusion A. But the transmitted warrant for the conclusion A is no more epistemically adequate than the warrant for A&B and this, in turn, is no more epistemically adequate than the warrant for B. So the pointlessly indirect inferential route to the conclusion A results in transmission of the warrant for the premise A; but the transmitted warrant is liable to be contaminated and weakened along the way.

We began from the idea that non-transmission of epistemic warrant is consistent, in principle, with closure of knowledge under known entailment. It might be that knowledge of the conclusion does not require a warrant; or it might be that knowledge of the conclusion is provided by a prior warrant. We have considered two kinds of case in which there is a prior warrant for the conclusion. The first kind of case was consistent with, but did not guarantee, non-transmission; the second kind of case seemed to amount to pointlessly circular transmission of warrant. So, although it remains plausible that Moore's argument is a case of non-transmission of warrant, we do not yet have any account of how this non-transmission arises.

Let us turn to the possibility that knowledge of the conclusion of Moore's argument, Moore(3), does not require a justification or warrant. In our discussion of the priority of self-knowledge (in the previous section), we saw that there seem to be empirical background assumptions for self-knowledge. But, provided that background assumptions do not always stand in need of justification, this is consistent with the claim that self-knowledge is a priori in the sense of not being justificatorily based on empirical investigation. Now I want to focus on the role of Moore(3) as a background assumption for ordinary perceptual knowledge.

Perceptual knowledge does seem to depend on the assumption that an external world exists. Thus, for example, Crispin Wright says (1985, p. 437):

> Once the hypothesis is seriously entertained that it is as likely as not, for all I know, that there is no material world as ordinarily conceived, my experience will lose all tendency to corroborate the particular propositions about the material world which I normally take to be certain.

But we need to be explicit about the relationship between knowledge and justification or warrant. On one conception of this relationship, any proposition that figures as a background assumption in a project of warranting must itself be warranted, or at least be susceptible of being warranted. According to this first conception, unless the conclusion of Moore's argument can somehow be warranted, what we ordinarily take for perceptual knowledge lacks a proper warrant. But there is an alternative conception of the relationship between knowledge and warrant. According to this second conception, the fact that an unwarranted proposition is a background assumption in a warranting project does not always reflect negatively on the epistemic status of propositions that are warranted by the project. There are assumptions that we make without warrant or justification, but not without entitlement or right. It is a substantive task for epistemology to provide an account of the nature of this entitlement. But for present purposes I shall, without giving such an account, simply proceed on the basis of this second conception of the relationship between knowledge and warrant. Some background assumptions are epistemically in good order; and if they are epistemically in good order then we can regard them as cases of knowledge without warrant.

If this conception is correct, then we can offer Moore's argument as a case of non-transmission of epistemic warrant without being committed to saying that it is a counterexample to the closure of knowledge under known entailment. Non-transmission arises because the conclusion of the argument plays a crucial role as a background assumption in the project of warranting the premises. It is only against the background of the assumption of Moore(3) that the perceptual warrant for Moore(1) counts as a warrant.

In an earlier paper (1998), I suggested a limitation on transmission of epistemic warrant along the following lines:

First Limitation Principle (first version):

> Epistemic warrant cannot be transmitted from the premises of a valid argument to its conclusion if, for one of the premises, the truth of the conclusion is a precondition of our warrant for that premise counting as a warrant.

This principle appears to have the desired consequence that epistemic warrant cannot be transmitted from the premises to the conclusion of Moore's argument. But, in this initial formulation, the principle is problematic in a number of respects. It makes use of the unexplained notion of a precondition; and if this is interpreted simply as a necessary condition then the First Limitation Principle is certainly open to counterexamples.

In order to improve the formulation of the principle and to provide it with some clearer motivation, we need to make use of the idea that failure of transmission of epistemic warrant is the analogue, within the thought of a single subject, of the dialectical phenomenon of begging the question (McLaughlin, 2000; Wright, 2000). It is often said that Moore's argument begs the question against the sceptic, but what we need is an explicit account of what makes an argument question-begging.

Here I shall make use of Frank Jackson's account according to which an argument can be said to beg the question when 'anyone – or anyone sane – who doubted the conclusion would have background beliefs relative to which the evidence for the premises would be no evidence' (1987, p. 111). When a speaker advances an argument for a conclusion, he implicitly offers evidence or other considerations in support of the premises. These considerations support the premises against the background of particular assumptions. But the speaker's background assumptions might not be shared by the hearer to whom the argument is directed. In particular, it may be that the background assumptions relative to which the offered considerations support the premises cannot be rationally combined with doubt about the conclusion. In that case, the argument, with its premises supported by those implicitly offered considerations, 'could be of no use in convincing doubters' (ibid., p. 112).

Jackson's account of begging the question, together with the parallel between this and non-transmission of epistemic warrant, suggests a better formulation of the limitation principle.

First Limitation Principle (revised version):

> Epistemic warrant cannot be transmitted from the premises of a valid argument to its conclusion if, for one of the premises, the warrant for that premise counts as a warrant only against the background of certain assumptions and acceptance of those assumptions cannot be rationally combined with doubt about the truth of the conclusion.

In fact, we can slightly generalise Jackson's account of begging the question. An argument will be useless for convincing those who doubt the truth of the conclusion if, for one of the premises, that doubt cannot be rationally combined with acceptance of the background assumptions that are crucial if the implicitly offered considerations are to support that premise. But there are weaker conditions under which an argument will be equally useless for convincing doubters. The person advancing an argument implicitly offers considerations in support of each of the premises. For each premise, there may be crucial background assumptions. If doubt about the truth of the conclusion rationally undermines acceptance of background assumptions in such a way that not all the premises remain supported, then that is enough to render the argument useless. This could happen because doubt about the truth of the conclusion, when combined with acceptance of the considerations offered in support of all but one of the premises, rationally undermines acceptance of the background assumptions that are crucial for support of the remaining premise. This complex relationship of rational influence between doubt about the truth of the conclusion and acceptance of background assumptions may be quite difficult to discern. But it seems appropriate to extend the notion of begging the question to include cases with this more complex and less obvious structure.

Pursuing the parallel with non-transmission of epistemic warrant, we can now propose:

First Limitation Principle (generalised version):

> Epistemic warrant cannot be transmitted from the premises of a valid argument to its conclusion if, for one of the premises, the warrant for that premise counts as a warrant only against the background of certain assumptions and acceptance (i) of those assumptions and (ii) of the warrants for the other premises cannot be rationally combined with doubt about the truth of the conclusion.

No doubt this principle will still face counterexamples. Certainly it could be further improved. But it combines two virtues: it is reasonably clearly motivated and it underwrites the non-transmission of epistemic warrant in Moore's argument.

I hope that this section has made the idea of limitations on the transmission of epistemic warrant less counter-intuitive. But we are still some way from a solution to the instance of the problem of armchair knowledge that arises from externalism and self-knowledge. After all, Moore's argument is not of the (Ext) form or the more general (MC) form; nor is our knowledge of the first premise of Moore's argument armchair knowledge. Furthermore, Moore's argument is a very plausible example of begging the question, but the argument (WaterExt):

Water(1)   I am thinking that water is wet.

Water(2)   If I am thinking that water is wet then I am (or have been) embedded in an environment that contains samples of water.

Therefore:

Water(3)   I am (or have been) embedded in an environment that contains samples of water.

is not intuitively or obviously question-begging (Warfield, 1998). So it is not clear how anything like the First Limitation Principle, which was motivated by the idea of a parallel between begging the question and non-transmission of warrant, could be used to solve the problem that arises from externalism and self-knowledge.

6   Transmission of Warrant and Externalist Arguments

In the earlier paper (1998) that I have already mentioned, I proposed a principle that was intended to apply to arguments of the (Ext) form such as (WaterExt).

> Second Limitation Principle (first version):
>
> Epistemic warrant cannot be transmitted from the premises of a valid argument to its conclusion if, for one of the premises, the truth of the conclusion is a precondition of the knower even being able to believe that premise.

This principle certainly has the desired result. According to externalist philosophical theorising, my being embedded in an environment that contains water is a necessary condition for my believing or even thinking that water is wet. It is also a necessary condition for my thinking any other thought in which the concept of water is deployed; in particular, for my thinking that I am thinking that water is wet. The very same philosophical theory that gives rise to the problem by supporting the externalist dependence thesis:

> Necessarily(If I am thinking that water is wet then I am (or have been) embedded in such-and-such ways in an environment that contains samples of water)

also supports the thesis:

> Necessarily(If I am thinking *that I am thinking that water is wet* then I am (or have been) embedded in such-and-such ways in an environment that contains samples of water).

This thesis triggers the Second Limitation Principle and if the principle is correct then the problem is solved.

However, given just this early version of the Second Limitation Principle, the situation is far from satisfactory. The worry is not, primarily, that the principle is open to counterexamples, but rather that no independent motivation for the principle has been provided. In short, the Second Limitation Principle appears to be completely *ad hoc*.

We need to connect the Second Limitation Principle with the notion of a background assumption so that we can draw on some of the same ideas that were used to motivate the revised and generalised versions of the First Limitation Principle. In particular, as a first step, we need to make it plausible that something like the assumption that I am able to believe that I am thinking that water is wet is a background assumption for my first-personal knowledge that I am thinking that water is wet.

But surely this is plausible. For any proposition (or thought content) A, if there were no such proposition as A then nothing could amount to a justification for believing A. If there were no such thing to think as A, no such thing to believe or doubt, no such thing to confirm or disconfirm, then there could be no prospect of anything counting as an epistemically adequate warrant for A. So, the assumption that there is such a proposition for me to think as *that I am thinking that water is wet* is a background assumption for my first-personal knowledge (and, indeed, for any kind of knowledge) that I am thinking that water is wet.

We are now in a position to generate revised and generalised versions of the Second Limitation Principle. We simply adapt the revised and generalised versions of the First Limitation Principle by focusing on a particular assumption against the background of which a warrant for a premise counts as a warrant; namely, the assumption that there is such a proposition (there is such a thing to think) as that premise. The results are as follows.

Second Limitation Principle (revised version):

> Epistemic warrant cannot be transmitted from the premises of a valid argument to its conclusion if, for one of the premises, acceptance of the assumption that there is such a proposition for the knower to think as that premise cannot be rationally combined with doubt about the truth of the conclusion.

Second Limitation Principle (generalised version):

> Epistemic warrant cannot be transmitted from the premises of a valid argument to its conclusion if, for one of the premises, acceptance (i) of the assumption that there is such a proposition for the knower to think as that premise and (ii) of the warrants for the other premises cannot be rationally combined with doubt about the truth of the conclusion.

It remains to confirm that one or the other of these principles blocks the transmission of epistemic warrant from the premises to the conclusion of the argument (WaterExt) and so provides a solution to the instance of the problem of armchair knowledge that arises from externalism and self-knowledge.

The revised version of the principle is not adequate to this task. There is no immediately obvious incompatibility between, on the one hand, acceptance of the assumption that there is such a thing for me to think as that I am thinking that water is wet and, on the other hand, doubt as to whether I am (or have been) embedded in an environment that contains samples of water. It is only in the context of a philosophical theory of externalism that there is a tension between this acceptance and this doubt.

But the generalised version of the principle does have the consequence that epistemic warrant is not transmitted from the premises of WaterDep to the conclusion. The warrant for the conditional premise, Water(2), is a piece of philosophical theory that supports both the externalist dependence thesis:

> Necessarily(If I am thinking *that water is wet* then I am (or have been) embedded in such-and-such ways in an environment that contains samples of water).

and the thesis:

> Necessarily(If I am thinking *that I am thinking that water is wet* then I am (or have been) embedded in such-and-such ways in an environment that contains samples of water).

The theory supports the externalist dependence thesis because it supports the claim:

> Necessarily(If there is such a thing for me to think as *that water is wet* then I am (or have been) embedded in such-and-such ways in an environment that contains samples of water).

Equally, it supports the claim:

> Necessarily(If there is such a thing for me to think as *that I am thinking that water is wet* then I am (or have been) embedded in such-and-such ways in an environment that contains samples of water).

So acceptance (i) of the assumption that there is such a thing for me to think as Water(1) and (ii) of the warrant for Water(2) cannot be rationally combined with doubt about the truth of Water(3). According to the generalised version of the Second Limitation Principle, then, epistemic warrant cannot be transmitted from the premises Water(1) and Water(2) to the conclusion Water(3).

The combination of externalism and self-knowledge has the consequence that I can know both the premises of the argument from the armchair. This is problematic, because it is implausible that I can know the conclusion from the armchair. The Second Limitation Principle, in its generalised version, provides a solution to this instance of the problem of armchair knowledge.

Earlier, I distinguished between the achievement problem and the consequence problem for first-person authority given externalism. The key idea in dealing with the achievement problem is that the content of my second-order thought that I am thinking that water is wet embeds the content of my first-order thought that water is wet. So the content of the second-order thought is dependent on the environment in just the same way as the content of the first-order thought. This has the result, we noted, that at the very starting point for an enquiry into the epistemic status of the second-order judgement, it is already guaranteed that I meet the externalist conditions for having the first-order thought; so externalism poses no special problem for the achievement of self-knowledge. This same idea, that the conditions for thinking the first-order thought are included amongst the conditions for thinking the second-order thought, also plays a vital role in triggering the application of the Second Limitation Principle and solving the consequence problem.

This is not yet to say that all the resources that we need to solve the consequence problem are present in Burge's (1988) solution to the achievement problem. But Burge also says (1988, p. 653): 'It is uncontroversial that the conditions for thinking a certain thought must be presupposed in the thinking.' If this is right then the conditions for thinking the second-order thought, and so also the conditions for thinking the first-order thought, are presupposed in the thinking of the second-order thought. The truth of the conclusion, Water(3), is presupposed in the thinking of the premise, Water(1). I have been developing the idea that this is why epistemic warrant cannot be transmitted from Water(1) to Water(3) via the externalist dependence thesis, Water(2).[2]

References

Boghossian, P.A. 1997. What the externalist can know a priori. *Proceedings of the Aristotelian Society*, 97, pp. 161–75.

Brown, J. 1995. The incompatibility of anti-individualism and privileged access. *Analysis*, 55, pp. 149–56.

---

[2] Versions of this material were presented at a conference on externalism and self-knowledge held at the University of Bristol in February 1999 and in a symposium at the Pacific Division meeting of the American Philosophical Association held in Berkeley in April 1999. I am grateful to Antonia Barke, Helen Beebee, Paul Boghossian, Bill Brewer, Jessica Brown, Mark Greenberg, Frank Jackson, Brian Loar, Kirk Ludwig, Michael McKinsey, Brian McLaughlin, Michael Martin, Christopher Peacocke, Paul Pietroski, Sarah Sawyer, Stephen Schiffer, Ernest Sosa, Tom Stoneham and Crispin Wright for comments and conversations.

Brown, J. 1998. Natural kind terms and recognitional capacities. *Mind*, 107, pp. 275–303.

Burge, T. 1979. Individualism and the mental. In P.A. French, T.E. Uehling and H.K. Wettstein (eds), *Midwest Studies in Philosophy, Volume 4: Studies in Metaphysics*. Minneapolis: University of Minnesota Press, pp. 73–121.

Burge, T. 1988. Individualism and self-knowledge. *Journal of Philosophy*, 85, pp. 649–63.

Burge, T. 1996. Our entitlement to self-knowledge. *Proceedings of the Aristotelian Society*, 96, pp. 91–116.

Burge, T. 1998. Reason and the first person. In C. Wright, B.C. Smith and C. Macdonald (eds), *Knowing Our Own Minds*. Oxford: Oxford University Press, pp. 243–70.

Davies, M. 1991a. Concepts, connectionism, and the language of thought. In W. Ramsey, S. Stich and D. Rumelhart (eds), *Philosophy and Connectionist Theory*. Hillsdale, NJ: Lawrence Erlbaum Associates, pp. 229–57.

Davies, M. 1991b. Individualism and perceptual content. *Mind*, 100, pp. 461–84.

Davies, M. 1992a. Aunty's own argument for the language of thought. In J. Ezquerro and J.M. Larrazabal (eds), *Cognition, Semantics and Philosophy: Proceedings of the First International Colloquium on Cognitive Science*. Dordrecht: Kluwer Academic Publishers, pp. 235–71.

Davies, M. 1992b. Perceptual content and local supervenience'. *Proceedings of the Aristotelian Society,* 92, pp. 21–45.

Davies, M. 1993. Aims and claims of externalist arguments. In E. Villanueva (ed.) *Philosophical Issues Volume 4: Naturalism and Normativity*. Atascadero, CA: Ridgeview Publishing Company, pp. 227–49.

Davies, M. 1996. Externalism and experience. In A. Clark, J. Ezquerro and J.M. Larrazabal (eds.), *Philosophy and Cognitive Science: Categories, Consciousness and Reasoning*. Dordrecht: Kluwer Academic Publishers, pp. 1–33. Reprinted in N. Block, O. Flanagan and G. Güzeldere (eds.), *The Nature of Consciousness: Philosophical Debates*. Cambridge, MA: MIT Press, 1997, pp. 309–28.

Davies, M. 1998. Externalism, architecturalism, and epistemic warrant. In C. Wright, B.C. Smith and C. Macdonald (eds), *Knowing Our Own Minds*. Oxford: Oxford University Press, pp. 321–61.

Davies, M. 2000. Conscious thinking persons and their information-processing underpinnings. *Philosophical Explorations*, 3, pp. 43–62.

Evans, G. 1998. *The Varieties of Reference*. Oxford: Oxford University Press.

Field, H. 1996. The apriority of logic. *Proceedings of the Aristotelian Society*, 96, pp. 359–79.

Heil, J. 1988. Privileged access. *Mind*, 97, pp. 238–51.

Jackson, F.C. 1987. *Conditionals*. Oxford: Blackwell Publishers.

McKinsey, M. 1991. Anti-Individualism and privileged access. *Analysis*, 51, pp. 9–16.

McLaughlin, B.P. 2000. Self-knowledge, externalism and skepticism. *Proceedings of the Aristotelian Society Supplementary Volume* 74, pp. 93–117.

Moore, G.E. 1959. Proof of an external world. In *Philosophical Papers*. London: Allen and Unwin, pp. 127–50.

Peacocke, C. 1996. Entitlement, self-knowledge and conceptual redeployment. *Proceedings of the Aristotelian Society*, 96, pp. 117–58.

Peacocke, C. 1998. Conscious attitudes, attention, and self-knowledge. In C. Wright, B.C. Smith and C. Macdonald (eds), *Knowing Our Own Minds*. Oxford: Oxford University Press, pp. 63–98.

Peacocke, C. 1999. *Being Known*. Oxford: Oxford University Press.

Putnam, H. 1975. The meaning of 'meaning'. In *Mind, Language and Reality*. Cambridge: Cambridge University Press, pp. 215–71.

Raffman, D. 1998. First-person authority and the internal reality of beliefs. In C. Wright, B.C. Smith and C. Macdonald (eds), *Knowing Our Own Minds*. Oxford: Oxford University Press, pp. 363–9.

Schiffer, S. 1993. Actual-language relations. In J.E. Tomberlin (ed.), *Philosophical Perspectives, 7: Language and Logic*. Atascadero, CA: Ridgeview Publishing Company, pp. 231–58.

Stroud, B. 1984. *The Significance of Philosophical Scepticism*. Oxford: Oxford University Press.

Warfield, T.A. 1998, A priori knowledge of the world: Knowing the world by knowing our minds. *Philosophical Studies*, 92, pp. 127–47.

Wright, C. 1985, Facts and certainty. *Proceedings of the British Academy*, 71, pp. 429–72.

Wright, C. 2000, Cogency and question-begging: Some reflections on McKinsey's paradox and Putnam's proof. *Philosophical Issues*, 10 (published as a supplement to Noûs), pp. 140–63.

6

Anti-Individualism and Basic Self-Knowledge[1]

MARÍA J. FRÁPOLLI AND ESTHER ROMERO

1 Externalism and Anti-Individualism

For the sake of perspicuity, we will take the two dichotomies *internalism* and *externalism*, on one hand, and *individualism* and *anti-*

[1] This paper has been written after a Seminar on some aspect of Tyler Burge's philosophy in which the members of the Area de Lógica y Filosofía de la Ciencia of the University of Granada have been engaged for several months. We are very grateful to our colleagues for making our progressive understanding of Burge's anti-individualism easier. We are especially grateful to Juan J. Acero for encouraging us to write this paper.

Professor Burge hear this paper during the VIII Seminario Interuniversitario de Filosofía y Ciencia Cognitiva (Granada, 23-25 May 1996). He had the kindness and generosity of commenting the paper and explaining his present views. We want to express here our deep gratitude to Professor Burge. Nevertheless, all this help does not preclude the existence of some misunderstandings, of which only our stubbornness is responsible.

individualism, on the other, as non interchangeable.[2] In what follows, internalism and externalism will be categories in philosophy of language: they will represent two different proposals about the status of the elements out of which meanings are made. In internalism, as we use the term, the meanings of words are ideas in the speaker's mind; in (our use of) externalism the meanings will not be subjective. Meanings can be non-subjective in different ways. They might be identical to extensions, they might have extensions as a component, or they might be social. Then, we will distinguish two kinds of externalism: *physical externalism* and *social externalism*. The former would approach meanings using extensions in at least the following sense: that if two words or word-forms do not apply to the same things, their meanings will not coincide. The latter would characterize meanings using the social environment, although it might accept extensions as one of the elements that determine meanings. So, we might distinguish a pure version of physical and social externalisms and also a mixed version: a proposal would be *mixed externalist* if, being externalist, it allowed some room for both physical and social factors. Simplifying somewhat, we would characterize Kripke as a physical externalist because of his extensional theory of meaning, Wittgenstein II would be a social externalist, and Tyler Burge would be a mixed externalist who accepts that meanings are established by the speaker's community and its physical surroundings. Pure externalisms and internalism coincide in that both identify meaning with elements of a single extralinguistic kind, in one case it will be an object or a set of objects, in another case it might be a social practice, and in still another it might be a mental entity. Mixed externalists, on the contrary, allow more than one aspect to determine meaning. In this sense, mixed externalism is a complex theory of meaning.

---

[2] We are aware that this is not the way in which Professor Burge seems to use them. In (1979:73), he says: "But both Cartesian and behaviorist viewpoints tend to feature the individual subject. On the other hand, there is the Hegelian preoccupation with the role of social institutions in shaping the individual and the content of his thought. This tradition has dominated the continent since Hegel. But it has found echoes in English-speaking philosophy during this century in the form of a concentration on language. Much philosophical work on language and mind has been in the interests of Cartesian or behaviorist viewpoints that I shall term "individualistic"." And in (1993a:318): "Modern anti-individualism has its roots in the theory of reference". Nevertheless, there are reasons for making a distinction here. Theories of meaning and theories of mind are usually deeply related, but their relationships depend on the various ways in which meanings and mental contents are connected and these ways are not always straightforward.

It is also possible to account for meanings with a two-factors theory in which meanings have both internal and external aspects; we will baptize such a theory as *semantic dualism*.

The terms "individualism" and "anti-individualism", on the other hand, will classify theories of mind. Individualism, as we use the expression, amounts to saying that all that is relevant for the individuation of the content of mental states belongs to the individual's mind. Anti-individualism, in our sense, defends that some mental states are individuated by reference to entities or events that are external to the individual. The expression "external to the individual" admits of different interpretations: it might refer to the individual's physical surroundings, her socio-linguistic community, and probably others. Thus, Descartes would be an individualist[3] and Burge anti-individualist.

Let's now characterize a mental content as the mental ingredient of thinking that can be expressed by a sentence and by the that-clause after a verb of propositional attitude, among other expressions. Of course, this characterization does not intend to be a definition, but only a minimal approach, as ontologically neutral as possible. Let's say that what we believe in, or what we doubt, judge, wonder, etc. are *thoughts* or, alternatively, that thoughts are the contents of our mental acts of believing, doubting, judging, wondering, etc. Again, we do not need any particular account of thoughts; we just need to take into account that mental contents are articulated in a way that in some sense mirrors the *logical structure* of the sentences or that-clauses used to express them. These logical structures which are the contents of our mental acts have parts that correspond to names, parts that correspond to first-order predicates, parts that correspond to quantifiers, and logical connectives, etc. The structure of thoughts should depend, in a relevant manner, on the linguistic job played by the terms used to express them. We will say that sentences and that-clauses express thoughts, which are the contents of our mental states, and this is the way in which theories of meaning and theories of mind are related.

Unless one maintains that meanings and mental contents are completely independent of each other (which is not Burge's case[4]), the pos-

---

[3] Burge characterizes Descartes sometimes as an individualist, as in, for instance, (1986a:119), and as (almost) an anti-individualist in (1988b:67, n.4) and in (1992:49, n.67).

[4] In (1993a:311), we read: "(4) Concepts are commonly expressed in language. They constitute meanings of the speaker's words." And a bit further, he says: "When we say 'That's a chair', we express a thought that that's a chair; we express the concept chair with the word 'chair'. The concept is not to be distinguished from the meaning of the word 'chair'." (1993a:312). Following modern theories of linguistic meaning, Burge

sibilities of combination of theories of meaning and theories of mind mentioned above are the following: (any kind of) externalism, as a theory of meaning, is only compatible with some kind of anti-individualism, as a position in theory of mind. Internalism, on the other hand, seems to be only compatible with individualism. Semantic dualism, in turn, is compatible both with individualism and with anti-individualism. In one case, one would say that only the internal part of meaning is relevant for the individuation of mental states, and in the other, that the external part has also to be taken into account. But, in any case, an externalist as Professor Burge, who accepts that meanings and concepts are strongly connected[5], has no other alternative but being anti-individualist.

Burge's anti-individualism depends on his assumption of modern theories of reference, as defended by Donnellan, Kripke and Putnam, although he rejects the widespread view that makes of the new conception a refutation of the traditional view of the relations between concepts and meanings.[6] Burge's theory of meaning is many-sided. He admits two kinds of meaning, connected to two kinds of concepts, which he baptizes respectively as "translational meaning" and "lexical meaning". The latter is the aspect of meaning given in definitions, it reflects the speaker's (or the community's) beliefs and her epistemic access to the defined concept. It might change over time depending on the development of knowledge. Translational meaning, on the other hand, is a more deeply-rooted kind of meaning that accounts for the connection between the various definitions a term might go through over time and that explains our ability to use a concept (and a term) without being able to completely characterize what the term is all about. Furthermore, he sometimes speaks of a sort of "meaning" that would correspond to the traditional notions of denotation, extension, reference and the like, although he modifies the traditional (Fregean) interpretation of the relationships between connotation and denotation, or sense and reference,

---

somehow qualifies the severity of these statements and affirms: "Interpreted in the light of our assumptions about meaning, this principle [(4) above] maintains that the content of a concept—and hence the meaning of a term—is codified in ideal lexical entries that capture the cognitive condition under which the speaker would apply the term." (1993a:315).

[5] See footnote 5 above and, in general, Burge (1993a).

[6] Putnam, for example, thinks that meanings are not in the head and that what is in the head has nothing to do with meanings, so Putnam would be externalist and individualist. See, for instance, Putnam (1970) and (1973). Other interesting framework which allows for both externalism and individualism is the proposal put forward by Recanati (1993).

etc. in the light of modern extensional theories. Nevertheless, it is clear that, strictly speaking, extensions are included neither in meanings nor in concepts. Thus, Burgean externalism is different from the version of externalism developed by Kripke or Putnam. What justifies the characterization of Burge's theory of meaning as externalist is the social nature of translational and lexical meanings. This is Burge's originality. Some of his claims offer no doubt. Let's consider some of them. He says:

The work on reference bears on the meaning of terms and on the identity of concepts. For the meaning of a wide range of non-indexical terms and the nature of a wide range of concepts are dependent on the referent or range of application in the sense that if the referent were different, the meaning of the term, and the associated concept, would be different. [...] For example, different meanings or concepts would be expressed by the word-forms "chair" and "arthritis" if the word-forms did not apply exactly to chairs and to instances of arthritis. (1993a:318)

A similar view appeared in (1979). His externalism is also patent in his arguments for anti-individualism. After the explanation of his famous "arthritis" thought experiment, he says: "The word "arthritis" in the counterfactual community does not mean *arthritis*". (1979:79) And then: "The upshot of these reflections is that the patient's mental contents differ while his entire physical and non-intentional mental histories, considered in isolation from their social context, remain the same". (*loc. cit.*)

That is, although what two speakers, *a* and *b*, in two communities, C and D, have in their heads might be the same, this does not entail that the word-form "arthritis" means the same in C and D. It would not mean the same if, for instance, the use of the terms in the two communities has as a consequence that the word-form does not apply to the same type of cases. Let community C make a standard use of "arthritis" and community D a non-standard use so that it would be correct to apply the term to some rheumatoid diseases in the joints and in other parts of the body. In this situation, we should conclude that the word-form "arthritis" has different meanings (and so expresses different concepts) in communities C and D, regardless of what speakers in these communities might have in their minds. Let's also assume that community D does not have an alternative term that plays the job of "arthritis" in community C. Then we should also conclude that community D does not possess the concept *arthritis*, although it has the word-form "arthritis". If this is so, *a* might have thoughts in which the concept *arthritis* were involved, although this possibility would not be open to *b*. The reason is that no one can have arthritis-thoughts unless her community possesses this concept, or unless she has been somehow exposed to arthritis, or ...

Let's insist on the last point still a bit. Adapting an example due to Putnam, one might say that Toscar, Oscar's counterpart in Twin Earth, cannot have water-thoughts. All his thoughts—we assume that he has never been on Earth—will be twater-thoughts because the liquid he calls "water" is XYZ and not H_2O. Toscar would say things like: "I wouldn't swim in this water", "Water is the best thing you can drink", or "Flamingos live in shallow waters". But, in spite of all appearances, none of Toscar's thoughts involves the concept *water*. The reason is that, because there is no water in Toscar's surroundings, Toscar's community has not developed the concept *water*. These two examples show the relationships between the meanings of the word-forms "arthritis" and "water" and the concepts in the minds of the speakers, and so these examples illuminate the way in which externalism and anti-individualism are connected in Burge's view.

Burge's anti-individualism rests on the claim that we think using the concepts of the linguistic community we belong to, these concepts are the ingredients of our thoughts and we use them and not others because these are the concepts we are in contact with and because the concepts available in our community are causally connected to our thoughts. Turning back to our examples, anti-individualism implies that *a* and *b* have different mental contents and are in different mental states because the meanings that their communities relate to the word-form "arthritis" are different. And Oscar and Toscar are in different mental states because their physical surroundings differ. Physical histories might be identical (non-intentionally described) and mental states and contents might still be different.

Anti-individualism and externalism, as defended by Professor Burge, are of a social kind: they stress the role of the believer's linguistic community. His examples do not only involve the sort of terms that other externalists use ("water", "elm", etc.), but rather terms like "arthritis" or "sofa" which do not express any natural kind. The physical environment affects the social environment and both physical and social environments determine mental contents.

The view on concepts maintained by Professor Burge resembles the traditional view (Aristotle, Kant, Leibniz or Frege) in many respects, although it had to be modified by his support, on the one hand, of holism about confirmation, which makes him reject some old claims about the relationships between definitions and meaning, and on the other, by his support to the modern extensional theories of reference, which forces him towards a non-standard interpretation of the traditional relationships between intensions and extensions, in the sense that the external (physical or social) world is projected in our mental states and determines mental contents, and mental states and contents, in turn, determine extensions.[7]

Although Burge tries to stay as close to the traditional view of concepts as possible, his externalism exacts a price: our understanding of the terms we use and the concepts we think with might be—and most of the times is—far from exhaustive[8]. Concepts are the meanings of our words and to use correctly the words and possess these concepts do not mean that we are in the position of characterizing them completely. He says

> [A]n individual can think of a range of entities via such terms and concepts even though the thinker s knowledge of the entities is not complete enough to pick out that range of entities except through the employment of those terms and concepts. What the individual knows about the range of entities [...] need not provide a definition that distinguishes them from all other (possible) meanings or concepts. So the meanings of many terms are what they are even though what the individual knows about the meaning or concept may be insufficient to determine it uniquely. Their identities are fixed by environmental factors that are not entirely captured in the explicatory or even discriminatory abilities of the individual, unless those discriminatory abilities include application of the concept itself. (1993a:318)

That is to say, an individual might think using a concept, expressed in her community by a term, without completely knowing the features that in her community define the concept (or term) or without completely knowing the *essential properties* of the "entities" it is about. In Burge's

---

[7] His support to modern theories of meaning seems to have as a consequence a reinterpretation of the tradition in this point. Burge suggests, as we have seen in n. 2 above, that Descartes is not such an individualist as we are used to think of him. Also in (1993a:310) he introduces as one of the axioms that defines the traditional conception of concepts, the following: "(2a) Concepts' identities are inseparable from their specific intentional properties or functions." And a bit further, he comments on this principle as follows: "Unlike sounds in speech or signs in writing, or paintings, or stone carvings, concepts were not seen as entities whose identities are independent of their intentional functions, independent of the sorts of things they represent. So questions about how they relate to their intentional properties did not arise. The identity of sign and meaning was not a hypothesis of the traditional view because concepts were not construed as signs.[...] There is no reason for the Traditional view to deny that the mind makes use of signs or mental representations in Putnam sense. But concepts are not to be identified with such signs." (1993a:321).

[8] And even in the case that our knowledge is complete we cannot know that it is; we presume that it is because we only doubt when we have strong reasons. This is compatible with the spirit of the Acceptance Principle, Vid. (1993b:469, n.10).

view we do not need to master a concept to be able to employ it in thinking. Nevertheless, our mental contents, and the mental states we are in, are defined, identified, or individuated by the concepts as they stand in the community we belong to (including extension)[9] and not just by those aspects of concepts and meanings that the speaker is aware of. This follows from Burge's anti-individualism.[10] In this sense, Burge's theory distinguishes between concepts and meanings, which have to be anti-individualistically individuated, and our conceptions of them, an epistemological approach to our thought and language.

Physical externalism, as defended by Putnam and Kripke among others, compelled us to carefully distinguish between epistemological and metaphysical perspectives in theories of meaning and mind. Some necessities are no longer a priori. Social externalism and anti-individualism offer no reason for bridging this gap between how things are and how and what we think they are. Anti-individualism implies that we use concepts that we do not master, and so it threatens the old individualistic way (from inside to outside) of getting at truths. Nevertheless, Burge's position is that anti-individualism is compatible with basic self-knowledge. Let's see how this compatibility is possible.

2   Self-knowledge and Mental Content

The map of the subdivisions of knowledge in Burge's view is roughly as follows: We have an indirect and discursive knowledge of the world, including of (some) mental states (my own and other minds') as parts of the world. Besides, we can also have a non-discursive contact with *some* of our mental contents, although we do not have direct access to most of our mental states. Not all knowledge we have about our own minds is immediate, and this feature might be taken as the essential difference between individualism and anti-individualism. Since the development of externalism and its application to the mind, it has been almost a commonplace to defend that externalism and anti-individualism supply language and knowledge with objectivity at the price of abolishing first person's eminent position. Nevertheless, Burge rejects this last thesis affirming that, relative to some of our mental states and contents, anti-individualism is consistent with the authority of the first person. His position is that the authority of the first person does not provide a sufficient

---

[9] In (1993a:310), he says: "(2a) Concepts' identities are inseparable from their specific intentional properties or functions." He attributes this principle to the traditional view of concepts, and he maintains it.

[10] Vid. for instance, (1986b:713).

condition for individualism.[11] Indeed Cartesian epistemic intuitions are compatible with both Cartesian individualism and Burge's anti-individualism.

We will now focus on this kind of authoritative self-knowledge, which is direct, non-discursive, and which is not precluded by anti-individualism. We are not interested in every kind of self-knowledge. One can have indirect self-knowledge, *via* the knowledge of external world and other people. The kind of knowledge relevant for the question we are dealing with is what Professor Burge has called "basic self-knowledge", a kind of self-knowledge characterized as being direct, authoritative, non merely empirical, and self-verifying[12]. An example of basic self-knowledge is my knowing that I am now thinking. Basic self-knowledge is *direct* because it is not inferential (I do not know that I am now thinking as the conclusion of any kind of argument or by interpreting any kind of individual's behaviour); is *authoritative* because my epistemic position about it is different of the position that anybody else can have about my mental contents (I know that I am now thinking in a sense in which you cannot know it—although Burgean basic self-knowledge is fallible); it is *not merely empirical* because it does not completely depend on the information provided by the external senses and it is *self-verifying* because thinking that I am now thinking makes it true (and in this sense they are infallible[13]).

---

[11] Vid. Burge (1986a).

[12] There is another kind of self-knowledge that can also be direct and authoritative. An example of this new kind is "I'm in pain". We have not considered this kind here because it does not seem to possess peculiar features, non-reducible to the kind considered. In (1979:74), Burge says: "Our ordinary mentalistic discourse divides broadly into two sorts of idiom. One typically makes reference to mental states or events in terms of sentential expressions. The other does not. A clear case of the first kind of idiom is 'Alfred thinks that his friends' sofa is ugly' A clear case of the second sort is 'Alfred is in pain'. Thoughts, beliefs, intentions, and so forth are typically specified in terms of subordinate sentential clauses, that-clauses, which may be judged as true or false. Pains, feels, tickles, and so forth have no special semantical relation to sentences or to truth or falsity. There are intentional idioms that fall in the second category on this characterization, but that share important semantical features with expressions in the first -idioms like 'Al worships Buicks'. But I shall not sort these out here. I shall discuss only the former kind of mentalistic idiom. The extension of the discussion to other intentional idioms will not be difficult."

[13] In (1988a: 87-88), he says: "we have a special, strong, intuitively direct, authoritative (though I think not infallible) knowledge of certain of our present mental events." But Vid. (1988b:74, n.8) where he says: "Mistakes about the res in de re judgements are not counterexamples to the claim that basic cogito-like judgements are self-verifying (hence infallible)." Nevertheless, in spite of all appearances, these two claims are not contradictory in Burge's theory. Fallibility in basic self-knowledge has

Burge's characterization of basic self-knowledge is modelled on the Cartesian *cogito* and his examples also follow the Cartesian style:

(a) I am now thinking
(b) I think (with this very thought) that writing requires concentration
(c) I hereby judge that water is a liquid.

Burge (1988b:65) considers examples (b) and (c) as "fuller versions" of the *cogito* paradigm, and they revealed his position about self-knowledge. Example (a) illuminates the most common Cartesian position and is obviously self-verifying. The other two are, nonetheless, much richer. Let's first focus on (b). This example accepts, among others, the following reading[14]:

(d) I think *this* ⭢
         [Writing requires concentration][15]

The important thing here is to realize that if (d) has to be a case of Burgean basic self-knowledge, it has to mean just that *this* (that 'writing requires concentration') is one of *my* thoughts. According to Burge, I have basic self-knowledge because what I am certain about is not the whole content of the referred thought (the content of the first-order thought that writing requires concentration). What I am certain about is that I know that I'm thinking this referred content (and probably that I would express it by the sentence "writing requires concentration", a

---

to do with the contents of first-order thoughts. Infallibility, on the other hand, is something that belongs to some kind of second-order thought.

14 We do not maintain that this is the only acceptable reading, but we think that this reading is compatible and does not force in an unfair way Burge's position. In (1979:88), he says: "The third step, for example, certainly does not depend on a view that contents are merely sentences the subject is disposed to utter, interpreted as his community interprets them. It is compatible to more abstract entities such as Fregean thoughts or Russellian propositions, and those that seek to deny that content-clauses indicate any thing that might be called a content."

15 In this example, and also in the following pages, we will be talking about the "referred" thought, "referring" mental acts, acts of pointing to one of our thoughts, etc. Nevertheless, this should be taken just as a way of speaking. We do not think that, in fact, we point to thoughts in the sense in which we point to external things. We maintain, nonetheless, that there are different ways in which a thought can be individuated. Basic self-knowledge is individuated immediately and non-discursively, without individuation procedures or tests. In this sense we use the analogy with direct reference to external things.

sentence that I understand). So, I know that I am now thinking that writing requires concentration. And I am certain about this second-order thought because I undoubtedly know that I think of *this very thought* (which I directly apprehend) *self-ascriptively* (as one of *my* thoughts). I do not need to individuate it (anti-individualistically or in any other way); it is already individuated by being the thought I'm thinking now[16]. *If* I am thinking *this thought*, I cannot miss the target of my mental "referring" act (I know immediately and non-discursively that I am thinking that writing requires concentration) nor can I fail in attributing it to myself (I know that writing requires concentration is a thought of mine). In this sense, our position relative to some of our thoughts is peculiar, I cannot point to my counterpart's thoughts in this way. That much is clear.

But if some of my mental states are individuated non-individualistically, what is so individuated cannot be what I am immediately certain about (or at least I cannot be certain about its boundaries and the features that make it different from other similar contents). What is individuated non individualistically is the content of a first-order thought (that writing requires concentration, that water is wet, etc.). A thought individuating conditions are the conditions that make this thought possible, what makes it a thought about writing or about water. What partly determines the contents of my mental states are my physical and social surroundings, as they provide the conditions of my having these very thoughts (with these very contents) and not others. And yet I do not need to know that these conditions are fulfilled in order to be certain about my believing these thoughts. The enabling conditions of my having these thoughts are presupposed in my knowing that I am thinking these thoughts. But knowing the enabling conditions is not necessary in order to know that I think what I am thinking. The situation is more or less the following: I cannot have arthritis thoughts if my community does not possess the concept *arthritis*. I cannot have water thoughts if there is no water in my community's surroundings. But once this is granted (my community having the concept of arthritis, or the existence of water in its surroundings), I can know without empirical research that I think that water is wet or that I suffer from arthritis.

---

[16] The causal antecedent of self-knowledge, that is, the thought I'm thinking, is not contingently related to my thinking this thought: we cannot imagine that the mental objects of our self-knowledge are different, although we can imagine that the causal antecedent of some of our thoughts were different and so that our first-order thoughts might be different.

So long we agree with Professor Burge. In an externalism, such as the one maintained by Burge, terms like "water", "sofa", "arthritis" and many others do not mean ideas directly accessible by the subject. Their meanings are the concepts accepted in (or available in) the linguistic community. All these terms incorporate an "external" component (their intensional properties). To explain Professor Burge's position, let's use an analogy from our practice of referring to external objects. Let's imagine that I say, pointing to a human figure running away,

(f) this person is the murderer.

Let's suppose that the referent of my referring act is my friend Jones, although I do not know it. Thus, (f) may have two different interpretations

(g) this person (whoever he or she may be) is the murderer

or

(h) Jones is the murderer.

The Burgian interpretation of (d) is modelled on (g) (I think *this* 'writing requires concentration'). But this is only a metaphor, and metaphors have parts that illuminate the analogy and also unused aspects. Nevertheless, we think that this metaphor, with all its shortcomings, may help to understand Burge's view. We know that we think *this* thought. To know it, we do not need to know the conditions of its individuation, which usually have to do with our physical or social environment. For the same reason, we do not need to know (h) in order to know (g). The same happens with (d): I directly know that I think that writing requires concentration, but to completely know the *content* of my first-order belief, to know all the features of the content in such-and-such circumstances, I would need to know what is the concept (and meaning) that my linguistic community relates to "writing", etc. And the same happens with (c). Of course, I know that I think that water is wet because I know without any doubt that *this* is what I think, namely, that water is wet. And I know it in a direct, non discursive way, and I understand it. But to completely know that the content of my belief is that H_2O is wet (that is, that mine is a water thought) or, alternatively, that XYZ is wet (that is, that mine is a twater thought), I will need an empirical investigation.

Burge's argument for the compatibility of anti-individualism and the authority of the first person rests on two claims: (i) the content of some of our thoughts is individuated anti-individualistically. Our mental states are causally related to our social environment. But (ii) the thesis of the privileged access (the way in which we approach our thoughts) is independent to the way in which mental states (other people's and most of mine) are individuated (so, the authority of first person in compatible with individualism and with anti-individualism[17]). If I am thinking that water is wet, I always reach the right content with this sentence or this belief, just because this is the thought I am thinking. In Burge's own words:

> We 'individuate' our thoughts, or discriminate them from others, by thinking those and not the others, self-ascriptively. Crudely put, our knowledge of our own thoughts is immediate, not discursive. Our epistemic right rests on this immediacy, as does our epistemic right to perceptual beliefs. For its justification, basic self-knowledge in no way needs supplementation from discursive investigations or comparisons. (1988b:72).

I cannot think the wrong thing. But if this story has to make any sense, it is clear that we need to distinguish two senses in which we can say, as Professor Burge does, that "[w]e know which thoughts we think" (1988b:69), two senses of *knowing our thoughts*, one weaker than the other. Otherwise the debate about the relationships between anti-individualism and basic self-knowledge seems to be incomprehensible. Burge is also aware of the ambiguity in the expression "knowing one's own thoughts", and in fact he says:

> One should not assimilate "knowing what one's thoughts are" in the sense of basic self-knowledge to "knowing what one's thoughts are" in the sense of being able to explicate them correctly—being able to delineate their constitutive relations to other thoughts. (1988b:78)

In the first sense, we have knowledge of a second-order thought, which probably is the Cartesian cogito: knowing that one is doubting, or thinking, or wondering, etc. This first case also provides an epistemological conception of the content of first-order thoughts. In the second sense of "knowing what one's thoughts are", we have knowledge of the content of first-order thoughts, a knowledge that is now aware of their enabling conditions and so of the social meanings and concepts involved.

Basic self-knowledge, in the sense in which Professor Burge uses the phrase, has a narrow scope. I have basic self-knowledge about my act of believing (I know that I *think* this) and also about my act of believing *this* self-ascriptively (I know that *I* think *this*). But, and this is

---

17 And the reason for this compatibility is that individualism and anti-individualism are theories of how we individuate our first order thoughts, and they do not say anything about second order thoughts which characterize basic self-knowledge.

one of our conclusions, this is not what is threatened by the consequences of externalism for a theory of mind, this is not the point in which externalism represents a problem to the epistemic privilege of the first person. As we see it, what was threatened by externalism and its consequences for the mind is our access to the content of first-order beliefs and the role of introspection in this access. Nevertheless, what Professor Burge makes compatible with externalism and anti-individualism is basic self-knowledge in the first of the two senses mentioned above: self-knowledge of a second-order thought (which also includes an epistemological—and so internal—access to the contents of first-order thoughts). Probably he is right in maintaining that Cartesian cogito is compatible with anti-individualism (we think he is), but this compatibility does not cancel the externalist's threat. In fact we think that the externalist's threat remains untouched.

Externalism, as a theory of meaning, and anti-individualism, as a theory of mind, overcome solipsism by shifting around the gap located by Cartesianism between the individual's mind and the rest of the world. But this gap, the gap that keeps us away from certainty, is not closed. It emerges between the subject and the content of her own first-order thoughts. Professor Burge's proposal circumvents the gap through second-order thoughts that inherit their enabling conditions from the first-order thoughts that are their objects. In this sense, he is right in claiming that the authority of the first person is not a sufficient condition for individualism, although externalism and anti-individualism diminish the first person authority to an almost trivial role.

3 Conclusion

Internalism is a single-factor theory of meaning, the theory of meaning that considers that meanings are ideas in the mind, and so the theory of mind related to it must be some sort of individualism: all that is relevant for individuating mental states has to be internal to the speaker's mind. Pure externalisms are other single-factor theories of meaning, theories of meaning that consider that meanings are not in the head, and, together with an account of meanings and concepts that make them dependent one of the others, the only theory of mind compatible with them is some sort of anti-individualism: what is relevant for individuating mental states cannot be internal to the speaker's mind. Professor Burge claims that authoritative basic self knowledge is compatible with an anti-individualistic individuation of mental states but this thesis requires a richer, many-sided, account of meanings and contents, which includes the aspect of an epistemic approach to them, independent of their ways of individuation. On one hand, we need to be able to reach some of our thoughts, and directly, non-discursively, ascribe them to each one of us, without needing to be aware of their enabling conditions. On the other hand, we need a picture of meaning that accounts for its social, objective, and non-internal, nature. We need the best part of each world. The epistemic arguments for internalism reassure us about our epistemic capacities, externalism explains the social nature of language. And a more complex, better articulated, picture might explain both: why we feel that we are in a privileged position relative to some of our thoughts and why we do not need to refute solipsism. Nevertheless, we cannot have everything at the same time about the same thing: when we are immediately certain, we are alone, and, as far as we are with others, our certainty must be discursive. The externalist's threat to the authority of first person, interpreted in a strong sense, still stands. We no longer have an internal, introspective, and reliable path to all aspects of our beliefs about the world, capable of founding a metaphysical system of certainties. Unfortunately, we cannot have the cake and eat it. We are certain about some of our second-order acts, but we do not have an internal access to all the features of the contents of our beliefs. Basic self-knowledge is then consistent with anti-individualism but anti-individualism corners it to a land emptied of much philosophical interest.

References

Burge, Tyler, 1979. "Individualism and the Mental", in T.E. Uehling, Jr., and Wettstein, H.K., eds., *Midwest Studies in Philosophy*, vol. IV, Minneapolis: University of Minnesota Press, pp. 73-121.

Burge, Tyler, 1986a. "Cartesian Error and the Objectivity of Perception" in P. Pettit (ed.), *Subject, Thought, and Context*, Oxford: Clarendon Press, pp. 117-136.

Burge, Tyler, 1986b. "Intellectual Norms and Foundation of Mind", *The Journal of Philosophy*, vol. 83, no. 12, pp.697-720.

Burge, Tyler, 1988a. "Perceptual Individualism and Authoritative Self-knowledge", in R. Grimm and D. Merrill (eds.), *Contents of Thought* (Tucson, Ariz., 1988).

Burge, Tyler, 1988b. "Individualism and Self-knowledge", *The Journal of Philosophy*, 85, pp. 649-63. Also in Cassam, Q. (ed.), *Self-Knowledge*, Oxford University Press, 1984.

Burge, Tyler, 1989. "Wherein is language social?". In Alexander George (ed.), *Reflections on Language*, Basil Blackwell, pp. 175-191.

Burge, Tyler, 1992. "Philosophy of Language and Mind: 1950–1990", *Philosophical Review*, vol. 101, no.1, pp.3-51.

Burge, Tyler, 1993a. "Concepts, Definitions, and Meaning", *The Metaphilosophy*, vol 24, no.4, pp.309-325.

Burge, Tyler, 1993b. "Content Preservation", *The Philosophical Review*, vol.4, pp.457-88.

Burge, Tyler, 1996. "Our Entitlement to Self-knowledge", in P. Ludlow and N. Martin (1998), *Externalism and Self-knowledge*. Stanford: CSLI.

Putnam, Hilary, 1970. "Is Semantics Possible?", in Stephen P. Schwartz (ed.): *Naming, Necessity, and Natural Kinds*. Cornell University Press, 1977.

Putnam, Hilary, 1973. "Meaning and Reference", in Stephen P. Schwartz (ed.) (1977).

Recanati, François, 1993. *Direct Reference. From language to thought*. Oxford, Blackwell.

7

Thought Experiments and Semantic Competence

Antoni Gomila Benejam

1 Introduction

I would like to take advantage of the coincidence of two circumstances, prof. Burge's visit and the celebration of the fourth centenary of Descartes' birth, to opportunistically raise the question of the epistemological value of thought experiments and of how a theory of concepts is to account for them. It is clear that thought experiments are key elements both in Descartes' and Burge's philosophical arguments and theories, that both resort to them and conclude from them important consequences. Thus, they join a tradition that values thought experiments for their contribution to conceptual change, to help modify old conceptions and to forge new ones, in philosophy as in science. To my view, a theory of concepts has to face the question of how this is possible—how is it that by mere reflection, new, sounder concepts develop. More so

Meaning, Basic Self-Knowledge and Mind: Essays on Tyler Burge.
María J. Frápolli and Esther Romero (eds.).
Copyright © 2003, CSLI Publications.

given its metaphilosophical implications, since it is the very methodological legitimacy of this philosophical practice that is at stake.

In so doing, I intend to enrich the "supposed" debate between Cartesian internalism, on the one hand, and semantic externalism, on the other—less simply sketched nowadays[1]—but taking a different tack, one which can shed light on the contemporary debt to Descartes. What I shall try to do is to show that Burge's methodological standpoint is congenial to Descartes', but that his externalism prevents him from being fully able to account for this aspect of his position.

When we turn to thought experiments, the work of Descartes still seems to be a landmark. For it looks as if the Cartesian dictum that "what is clearly and distinctly perceived is true", central to his method of analysis and synthesis, continues to play a distinguished role as a working assumption in how to interpret thought experiments: they are so designed as to make clear and distinct which taxonomic principles are involved in a concept, so that any incoherence, any incongruence, may be overcome. And so works Burge as well. Be it as it may, we need an account of how is this possible, how is it that thought experiments manage to prove fruitful.

The answer I shall develop consists in placing thought experiments within the range of semantic (or conceptual) competence. The idea is that semantic competence gives one an implicit grasp of the potential use of a concept and this potential use can be made explicit and tested by means of potential, counterfactual, scenarios. Thus they are useful in devising a conceptual explication even though the intuitions that they mobilize may not constitute an explicit conceptual explication. Moreover, they can contribute to focus on internal incoherence in a given way to understand a concept, that show up in such counterfactual scenarios, and in this way, to suggest a diagnosis of the problem and a way to fix it up.

It seems to me that Burge's externalist picture of semantic competence is not fully able to accommodate anything like this proposal, although it is possible to find in his writing elements congenial to this view. In divorcing what he sometimes calls "translational meaning" from "explicational meaning", and reducing semantic competence to "translational meaning", his picture misses the link between this two notions of meaning, and consequently lacks an account of how is it possible that the intuitions that the thought experiments elicit can yield a

---

[1]Burge himself has contributed to a view of externalism as opposed to Descartes' theory of ideas. See Burge (1986a, 1988b), even though he has recognized later the complexity of Descartes' conception, in Burge (1988a), p. 651, ft. 4

conceptual change. To conclude, I will suggest a way an externalist theory of concepts could be enriched so that a more adequate view of semantic competence would follow, one which may account for, and thus ground, the methodology of thought experiments.

2 Thought experiments

To get a feeling of how thought experiments work, let's start remembering a couple of them. Among the best well-known in science we can mention Galileo's thought experiment on falling bodies. It was designed to show an inconsistency in Aristotle's theory of motion. According to Aristotle, the heavier a body, the faster it will fall. This seems intuitively obvious: if we let fall this pencil and this leaf of paper, the pencil will reach the ground first. On the other hand, Aristotle also realized that when a faster body is linked to a slower one, the faster reduces its velocity. If we attach a tortoise to a rabbit, the rabbit cannot run as faster as before.

Galileo's insight was to realize that these two were consequences of Aristotle's view of motion, and to think of a situation in which they could come apart. This thought experiment consisted in a scenario in which a big stone is linked to a small one in free fall. According to the first principle, since the compound of the two stones is bigger than any of them separately, we should expect that it would fall faster. According to the second, though, we should expect that the compound would fall less fast than the big one alone. Now, it is not possible that the compound of the two stones fall at the same time faster and slower than the big stone alone. Conclusion: something must be wrong in the Aristotelian theory. Galileo's solution consisted in saying that both stones should fall with the same velocity. This move was possible by the separation of two magnitudes: mass from weight, and the introduction of rubbing to explain the factual appearances.

Galileo's works are full of thought experiments, and this is decisive to the epistemic respectability of thought experiments. He exemplifies their potential fruitfulness, thus casting doubt on the characteristically whig view of the origin of modern science, which identified empirical experimentation as the only way to advance science. Otherwise, thought experiments could have fallen in disrepute, under the influence of such notorious examples as the one on the existence of the vacuum. It was a discussion that took place just a century before Galileo, and was started by the Nominalist philosophers who opposed Aristotle's claim that vacuum was impossible. Thus, they claimed, if a water jar is sealed and exposed to the winter cold, it would freeze, leaving an empty space on top of the jar. Not so, the Aristotelians replied, because either the ice would give off steam, or the jar would implode. Well, the debate continued, but with all parties oblivious of the "small detail" that water expands, not contracts, when it freezes.

For us, the moral should be that thought experiments are not fully reliable, although sometimes prove useful, especially in theoretical physics (Einstein is another eminent name associated with them). Their success in contributing to a conceptual change depends on getting the facts right, and on focussing on scenarios not well dealt with by the established understanding of the concept in question. In such cases, the very thought experiment may lead to sounder concepts by making explicit the reason of the incoherence and suggesting naturally a way to overcome it (in Galileo's case, for instance, the problem lies in that in Aristotelian cosmology—a celestial and a sublunar world—free fall is not really possible, and hence Galileo's split of Aristotelian weight in mass and weight).

Something similar could be said of thought experiments in philosophy, and not just analytical philosophy. Philosophers have frequently resorted to thought experiments to develop arguments and theories. It is obliged to mention here as an example the several ones developed by prof. Burge himself, which have a common structure: they typically distinguish two distinct socio-linguistic communities and focus on one individual from one community with a physical (neurological) duplicate in the other, to show that which concepts can be attributed to both depend upon the community to which they respectively belong, irrespective of a mistaken or partial understanding of the concepts involved they may individually have (which they are assumed to share in virtue of their physical identity). Thus, it is concluded, which concepts one grasps is not determined by internal facts, but by social, external facts.

The importance of thought experiments has seldom been acknowledged in general. Moreover, it has been assumed that they work differently in science as in philosophy. Within analytical philosophy, for instance, they have been adopted as a customary methodological tool, a means for conceptual analysis, a form of uncovering a priori necessary truths—something considered unsuitable, of course, for science[2]. The recent cognitive turn in philosophy of science has paid more attention to them (Gooding, 1992; Nersessian, 1992; Norton, 1991; Sorensen, 1992), following up Kuhn (1977), but retaining this dichotomy between philosophical and scientific ones. To my view, however, they take advan-

---

[2]For an explicit defence of this view, see McGinn (1983).

tage of the same cognitive capacities, in particular, the capacity to explore hypothetical counterfactual possibilities, covered by our concepts because of their generality, though not hitherto encountered or non-encounterable, and to access our intuitions of what we should say, how they would apply, in these scenarios. In other words, it is a capacity to make explicit what is already implicit in our conceptual competence, to clarify the rule of their application.[3]

Since this sounds pretty individualistic and Cartesian—in fact, the occasional success of thought experiments is taken by Rationalists to support this view of knowledge (Brown, 1991)—I would like to turn to a brief examination of Descartes' view of ideas to clarify to what extent his views help us understand why thought experiments are sometimes fruitful and what is involved in semantic competence.

3   Descartes and semantic competence

Despite continuing interest in Descartes' metaphysical and epistemological views, even though often just to rebut them, there are other aspects in his thought worth as well of attention. I would like to focus here briefly on how his methodological requirement of clear and distinct ideas bear on thought experiments' dependency on semantic competence. Of course, methodology cannot be separated from metaphysics or epistemology in Descartes. It has been shown that his interest in metaphysics arose out of the need to found his new, non-Aristotelian, mechanic-geometrical, science. Nevertheless, it is possible for us to isolate an insight without buying the whole picture. What I am aiming at is that there is one such insight in his criterion of evidence, an insight that sheds light on the epistemic value of thought experiments, and that is unconsciously assumed in the current practice of analytical philosophers. Burge himself presupposes this insight in his thought experiments, even though, as I shall try to show, his own view of semantic competence does not allow him to fully account for it.

Of course, we are not going to find in Descartes a full-blown theory of thought experimentation. What we do find in his requirement of clear and distinct ideas is a rationale that fits the practice of thought experiments as the explicitation of our semantic competence.

First of all, we have to realize what is involved in a thought experiment. As the examples in the previous section show, they characteristically include a possible situation—or set of possible situa-

---

[3]I tried to develop a non-analytical view of thought experiments in philosophy in Gomila (1991).

tions—devised in terms of our current concepts, but where some anomaly occurs: something paradoxical, unexpected, unforeseen, contradictory. This is taken to suggest that something must be wrong with the assumed understanding of the concept or concepts that that situation was supposed to illustrate. In the most outstanding thought experiments, moreover, that very situation points to a diagnosis of the anomaly and suggests a way to overcome it, a way that amounts to a conceptual change (a conceptual split, or overlap, or re-definition, as we will see later on).

In the same vein, a discussion of them consists in trying to ascertain whether the possible situation devised is really possible, or whether it would really be like how it has been depicted, or some other features or changes would stand in such a counterfactual situation. But if the possibility is accepted and problematic, the conceptual reform will take ground. This is what makes thought experiments striking for the empiricists: that mere consideration of an imagined situation be relevant to the evaluation of our current concepts appears nonsense.

It is at this point that Descartes helps us to fill this gap. The filling is not straightforward, though, and it relies on a reading of Descartes' theory of ideas which I won't be able to develop here in detail.[4] Let's start with Descartes' definition of clarity and distinction:

> A clear perception I call that which is present and open to the attending mind; just as we say that those things are clearly seen by us which, being present to the regarding eye, move it sufficiently strongly and openly. But that perception is distinct which is not only clear but also is so precise and separated from all others that it plainly contains in itself nothing other than what is clear. (AT VIII, 45)

In different works, Descartes claims that one cannot be wrong as regards a clear and distinct idea. Now, to understand the epistemological strength of this criterion of truth, we must take into account the ambiguity of the term "idea", as Descartes himself emphasized in the Preface to the Meditations, in order to avoid a misunderstanding:

> [I]n this term *idea* there is here something equivocal, for it may either be taken materially, as an act of my understanding, (...) or it may be taken objectively, as the thing which is represented by this act. (AT VII, 8)

In contemporary terms, Descartes distinguishes two senses of "idea" just as we distinguish two senses of "thought": as a mental state, and as the content of the mental state. In fact, it is possible to find in Descartes the origins of this notion of "content", since ideas (second sense) is what ideas (first sense) contain. The problem is that, as has been

---

[4]Vd. Gomila (1996).

pointed out[5], Descartes is careless within the Meditations, to warn which sense he intends when he uses the term. Because of this, the criterion of evidence has been misread. Thus, if we understand the criterion of clear and distinct ideas in the first sense, that is, as mental states, it amounts to a statement of the view that the mind is transparent to itself, that it has access to its own states. This is Descartes' position, no doubt, but so stated lacks any epistemological bite to found our knowledge of the world. This requires the second reading of "idea" as content: it is as regards the contents of our thoughts that clarity and distinction guarantee truth. Clarity and distinction in an idea as representational content means that we get at what is essential in the content, that without which it cannot be conceived, that which necessarily constitutes its essence, its "true and eternal nature". As regards it, we can judge confidently.

As a matter of fact, this is the methodological procedure that Descartes follows all the time in the Meditations: in arriving at the conclusion that he could not doubt were he not to exist, or that God cannot be a deceiver, etc. he works through a modal reasoning about what is impossible and what is necessary, what can be conceived separately from anything else, and what necessarily go together with something else. As he says: "it is enough to be able to conceive clear and distinctly a thing without another, to be certain that one is different from the other, since at least in virtue of God's omnipotence, they can exist separately" (AT VII, 70).

It seems to me that this can shed light on the rationale of thought experiments: to design situations such that they show what the content of our concepts really is and whether they imply impossibilities or contradictions as they stand and so need modification or be made more precise. The reason is that our concepts, as Descartes' epistemological project puts to the foreground, are meant to apply to the world in general, and not to a restricted set of cases, the actual ones.

Of course, Descartes' project is much more ambitious than this: it not just aspires to exclude what generates contradiction or impossibility, but to grasp the principles of nature—in their mechanic-geometrical format, the one for which this reflexive method has any plausibility—and to do so with full certainty, warranted by God. Nevertheless, he makes clear what is involved in this sort of reflexive activity, as far as it goes; he provides a clear indication of its ground: semantic/conceptual competence; and clearly states its goal: to find out how things are, given how we conceive of them.

---

[5]Especially by Kenny (1968).

To see this, let's step back a little. The requirement of clear and distinct ideas presupposes the existence of obscure and confused ideas. In fact, although Descartes attributes the power to reach clear and distinct ideas to everybody in principle, he is well aware that it is barely exercised, as his Preface, for instance, reveals. This suggests that we must distinguish between "having an idea" as having a certain representational content, and "grasping its essence", which follows from a clear and distinct conception of it. In fact, Descartes is explicit about this distinction. Thus, on the one hand, we are immediately aware of our ideas; that we "have the idea" is revealed in that we understand the word that signify it:

> Idea is a word by which I understand the form of any thought, that form by the immediate awareness of which I am conscious of that said thought. Such that when I understand what I say, I cannot express anything with words without being true, in virtue of that, that I have with me the idea of the thing that my words signify. (AT VII, 129)

On the other hand, we can spell out this understanding, making explicit what was implicit in it, i.e., making it clear and distinct, acknowledging its essence. This is best stated in Meditation Fifth, where Descartes comes to the question of what can be known, beyond mine's and God's existence. Taking as example the idea of triangle, Descartes says:

> It is not necessary that I imagine a triangle, but if I ever do imagine a rectilinear figure composed of three angles, it will be absolutely necessary that I attribute to it everything that entails that its three angles equal to two right angles, and this attribution will be implicitly necessary, even though explicitly I may be unaware of it at the moment of considering the triangle. (AT VII, 115).

In other words, an effort to clarify and conceive separately, in itself, an idea is required to become aware not just of our understanding of it, but of what this understanding consists in. Thought experiments, and other sorts of reflexive techniques to find out what is essential to an entity or property, what goes necessarily with it—be it thinking and existence, or God and existence, or being a triangle and having the three angles equal to two right angles, or whatever—are possible in so far as they rely on an implicit understanding of these ideas. This understanding constitutes our semantic competence, our ability to use language meaningfully, but it needs depuration to reach clarity and distinction, so that it can ground epistemically warranted judgements.

It is clear that this essentialist view of concepts, pivotal to Descartes' epistemological project, is no longer acceptable, except for geometry, perhaps. As Burge himself has made explicit, contemporary confirmation holism and anti-individualism have forced changes in this view of definitions and essences, that challenge the claim to necessary a priori truths, as classical conceptual analysis aimed to (Burge, 1993). But it is the link between implicit understanding and clear and distinct ideas, or between semantic competence and thought experimentation, understood as a way to test the coherence of our concepts, that I find revealing in Descartes' work, and still of interest.

As a matter of fact, Burge comes very close to a view similar to Descartes' in "Individualism and Psychology" (Burge, 1986c). Answering some empiricist qualms about the relevance of thought experiments to "real" science, he says:

> The correct use of counterfactuals in thought experiments consists in exploring the reach and extent of the notions of class that have been developed before to deal with actual empirical cases. In counterfactual reasoning we assume an understanding of what our language expresses and explore its condition of application by considering how they apply to non real cases. (1986c, 32)

In fact, this is what Burge does in his thought experiments -as everybody else, I would add, following Descartes' insight that a conceptual contradiction involves an ontological impossibility, that consideration of conceptual possibilities is instrumental to conceptual clarification, or analysis. The difference, however, lies in how this "understanding of what our language expresses" is cashed out. As I shall try to show in the next section, Burge conceives this "understanding" in such a deflationary way, in terms of "effective communitarian use", that he lacks the resources to account for the capacity of thought experimentation to make it explicit. To put it paradoxically: if Burge's theory of concepts was true, it would lose its justification (the thought experiments which ground it would lose their import for lack of epistemic justification); and if the methodology of thought experiments is valid, his theory cannot be the whole truth.

4 Burge's view of semantic competence

It is clear that Burge, along with semantic externalism in general, rejects an essentialist view of semantic/conceptual competence, which I share. A constant moral of his thought experiments is that there is no need for necessary and sufficient conditions to have a concept, because of the important role that the linguistic context plays in individuating somebody's concepts, even if she is ignorant or mistaken about their references. In fact, a common feature in all thought experiments that support externalist conclusions is that the subject in the actual scenario lacks complete or correct knowledge of what the concept is about -be it that water is H2O or that arthritis just affects articulations. This down-playing of descriptive information for having a concept, and the corresponding emphasis on being at the right place at the right time, however, suggests a view of semantic/conceptual competence that amounts to conformity in actual use with social practice[6]. If this were so, if conceptual competence reduced to externalist conditions for concept possession, it would fall short of accounting for the kind of conceptual understanding deployed in thought experiments. Let me argue both points in turn.

In several papers, Burge introduces the distinction between "translational meaning" and "explicational meaning" as a way to clarify his externalism:

> I also distinguish between the concept associated with the word and the concept(s) associated with the entry. Call the former "the concept" and the latter "the conceptual explication". Finally, I distinguish between a type of meaning associated with the word, 'translational meaning', and the meaning associated with its entry, 'explicational meaning'. For our purposes, the explicational meaning is the semantical analogue of the conceptual explication. (Burge, 1989, 181)

In order to substantiate his conclusion that ignorance or error do not prevent conceptual attribution (nor self-attribution), he needs to distinguish what a subject believes about a class of things and that class of things her words refer to, in such a way that it is not necessary to have the right beliefs about the class in order to have the concept. In other words, it is not having the right "explicational meaning" which determines which "translational meaning" one grasps, but contextual factors as well as non-conceptual abilities.

> ... a word's explicational meaning and its translational meaning are, for purposes of characterizing the individual's idiolect, always interchangeable; and that the individual's conceptual explication always completely exhausts his or her concept. This view is incorrect. It is incorrect because the role that the referent plays in individuating the concept and translational meaning, and because of the role that non-explicational abilities play in the individual's application of the word and concept. (idem)

Thus, it is "translational meaning" what is involved in conceptual attribution (and self-attribution). Let's remember that in Burge's thought experiments this is done exclusively on the ground of a single proference. For instance, in the first thought experiment it was explicitly stated that the disposition to say "I have arthritis in my thigh" was never reinforced or extinguished up until the moment to visit the doctor. As he has made clear, what is required for conceptual attribution is a com-

---

[6]See Burge (1986b).

mitment to follow the linguistic practices of the linguistic community, as this is manifested in actual linguistic use. What "translational meaning" amounts to, though, is very little:

> The translational meaning of a word can be articulated through exact translation and sometimes through such trivial thoughts as my word 'tiger' applies to tigers, but need not be exhaustively expressible in other terms in an idiolect. (idem)

Consequently, this is all there is to semantic competence:

> I know that my word 'mercury' applies to mercury (if to anything) not by being able to provide an explication that distinguishes mercury from every conceivable twin mercury, but by being a competent user of the word, whose meaning and reference are grounded in this environment rather than in some environment where the meaning of the word form would be different." (Burge, 1988, 661, note 9)

Furthermore, Burge also rejects that this semantic competence implicitly contains a correct explication of the word's reference:

> But it would be a mistake to infer that I always already know the correct explication in some suppressed way." (1989, p. 183)

> It is a truism that to think one's thoughts, and thus to think cogito-like thoughts, one must understand what one is thinking well enough to think it. But it does not follow that such understanding carries with it an ability to explicate correctly one's thoughts or concepts via other thoughts or concepts; not does it carries an immunity to failures of explication. (1988, p. 662)

To sum up, then, there is a clear sense in which conceptual attribution is based on actual usage as the only way to ascertain semantic competence. In this sense, "translational meaning"—"understood" disquotational sentences—is all that there is to understanding. To my view, this picture, motivated by the reluctance to fall into an essentialist view of concepts, is nonetheless insatisfactory.

In the first place, it suggests an all-or-nothing conception of semantic competence and conceptual attribution. This is clear in the case of "arthritis in the thigh", where Burge justifies the attribution of the concept "arthritis" in virtue of a single proference that reveals a misunderstanding. But think now of this example: last month I heard in a radio programme of medical consultation a woman expressing her prosthratic pain and asking for help. Following Burge, we should attribute her the obviously 'de dicto' belief "I have pain in my prosthrate", since she tried to use the word standardly. In a sense, well, yes, but since it is male organ, and hence she cannot feel such a pain, there is something deeply misleading with this attribution, even if we assume Burge's point that we are just attributing "translational meaning".

The ignorance or error need not concern only one's conception of the concept, but may involve the non-explicational, perceptual, abilities involved. Think, for instance, of a Donnellan kind of case. The patient says: 'I feel the pain in my knee, just here', while pointing to her wrist. Following Burge, it looks that we should attribute the believe in pain in one's knee, thus attributing an understanding of the "translational meaning" of "knee", but again, this is contentious: does she really understand that 'knee' applies to knees?

This point appears clearer when we turn to little children, at the initial stages of language mastery. Even children of four call their teachers "mum", but it would be mistaken to claim that they believe that the teachers are their mums, or that they understand that "'mum" applies to mums'. What the example shows is that they do not understand it yet. Understanding comes in degrees, and this should be reflected in our attributive practices. In other words, semantic competence cannot be exclusively attributed on the grounds of actual linguistic usage, because linguistic usage can take place without (full) understanding. Otherwise we could find a gap between conceptual attribution from the third person and from the first person point of view, that is to say, following Burge, we could attribute a concept to somebody that would deny having it. (This is common in second language learning, where the speaker is aware that she does not quite understands what she says). The converse of these examples is also relevant: it happens when there occurs a mistake in a linguistic proference (a slip of the tongue, a malapropism, a tip of the tongue phenomenon): taken in itself it doesn't justify attribution of a deviated understanding.

I take it that it is clear that, understood Burge's way, semantic competence is clearly inadequate to account for thought experiments. For one thing, it doesn't give us a clue as to what would say a person such as the one in Burge's arthritis case, for instance, were she to feel a similar pain in a knee. She might well say that she suffered from a ligament break, were she to be mistaken on this as well. Therefore, "translational meaning" gives us no enough guidance as what to say in counterfactual circumstances, as thought experiments require.

It could be answered that it is not "translational meaning" that provides a ground for thought experiments, but "explicational meaning". As a matter of fact, Burge suggests that it provides another kind of understanding:

> I distinguish between a lexical item and the explication of its meaning that articulates what the individual would give, under some reflection, as his understanding of the word. (1989, 181)

Thus, we could say, one "understands" a word's "translational meaning" if one uses the word according to common usage; and one "understands" a word's "explicational meaning" if one is able to articulate her beliefs about its referent. Thought experiments, we said in the previous section, contribute to this articulation and its revision, by exposing any inconsistency or unforeseen possibility they may involve. Nevertheless, we also underlined that one of the goals of thought experiments is to improve one's conceptual make-up, to rearrange one's taxonomic principles, and in some outstanding cases -as Galileo's or Einstein's thought experiments-, to introduce new concepts, that is, new magnitudes, properties or entities, not just our conception of them. As Descartes made plain, the import of reflection is not just psychological, but ontological as well, whereby it has epistemological value. However, Burge's view of explication meaning make it difficult how its modification (via a thought experiment) may affect translational meaning.

It looks as if what is required is some connection between the two kinds of meaning for Burge to make sense of thought experiments. At this point, in fact, we could be accused of having been criticizing a strawman, because Burge, especially in "Wherein is language social?" (Burge, 1989), offers some hints in this respect. Thus, he suggests that "explicational meaning" is relevant to conceptual attribution, so that we should not only attend to actual linguistic usage but to the conceptions associated in fixing the "translational concept" attributed. For example:

> Accounting for a person's lexical entry or conceptual explication is relevant to determining the nature of a person's meaning or concept. But the two enterprises are not the same. (1989, 181)

Nevertheless, this relevance is not spelled out, and in fact, in his well-known thought experiments it plays no clear role, as I've tried to show. On the contrary, since their point is to show that despite a wrong conceptual explanation the subject has the concept. There is, though, something of a "via negativa", of saying what this connection is not, that purport to justify the former. Thus, conceptual explication does not determine or fix the concept—since contextual factors are involved. Moreover, as already quoted, a concept "need not be exhaustively expressible in other terms in an idiolect" (1989, 181); hence, a correct conceptual explanation may be missing in principle. We could sum up this part saying that a conceptual explication is not sufficient for having a concept. Given that the thought experiments assume that it is not necessary either, we have not advanced much in linking both kinds of meaning. It looks as if the conceptions associated with a concept may or may not exist, without thereby affecting the attribution of the concept.

The picture that results is one that keeps independent of each other the two kinds of meaning, of understanding, of semantic competence. It could be argued that in some cases—i.e., for experts—both sorts of understanding must be coincidentally related, as suggested, for instance, by Putnam, and his appeal to the division of linguistic labour and expert knowledge to fix the reference of natural kind terms. I'm not sure as regards how Burge feels about this view of the matter. It has some prima facie appeal as regards the explanation of thought experiments, since it is experts, o privileged minds, those that have a best understanding, that are able to design the most remarkable thought experiments (this, despite appearances, is supposed to be a compliment of prof. Burge).

Nevertheless, to my view, it is an unsatisfactory picture of semantic competence. It really suggests a twofold view of semantic competence: the semantic competence of lay people, and the Semantic Competence, thus, with capital letters, of the experts—which threatens to reintroduce an essentialist view of semantic competence. As our discussion has purported to show, concepts—and consequently, semantic competence—cannot be attributed just on the grounds of actual linguistic usage, of its conformity to standard usage. Some other aspects—perceptual abilities, ostensive naming and recognition, minimal conceptual understanding—are important as well, even though they do not amount to a "conceptual explication". On the other hand, the conceptual understanding elicited by the though experiment is not just idiosyncratic, affecting only the "explicational meaning" of the person doing the experiment, but is conceived of as relevant for the whole community, and contends a new collective use of the term (or new terms). This is also difficult as well to accommodate within Burge's framework. Let me briefly explore how we could make sense of these aspects.

5   A qualified externalism

What we need, it seems to me, is a conception of semantic competence that explores a middle ground between the one of the competent user of a language (as witnessed on a limited number of occasions) and the one of an expert theorist of the kind conceptualised. A view of semantic competence that keeps equilibrium among use, understanding and knowledge, instead of focussing exclusively on linguistic use. In this way we can satisfy what seems to be a reasonable constraint on a theory of concepts: that it attributes to a subject those concepts that she in fact understands.

A useful way to approach this issue is to ask: what are we attributing when we ascribe a concept to a subject? My point is that we do not just attribute a capacity to conform to social use of language, but a capacity to think thoughts with that concept as a constituent. This capacity involves, minimally, an explicational competence, being able to relate such thoughts to other thoughts one may think, to give some account of what they are about, and a referential competence, to point to what they are about, to reidentify different instances as of the same king. Of course, no commitment is made that these sub-competences be complete and correct, nor that they are fully reliable, nor that the concept reduces to, or is determined by, these underlying conceptions. How much competence is required to have the concept may vary from one kind of concept to another, from concepts for the "mesocosmos" to more theoretical ones, from common sense concepts to more technical, specialized ones. Thus, I'm not disputing the attributions that Burge proposes in his thought experiments, nor his idea that "the explicational meaning" does not determines the reference of the concept. My point is, rather, that this view of concept individuation needs supplementation to amount to a view of semantic/conceptual competence, to a view that may account for what is achieved in the thought experiments themselves.

If we view Burge's thought experiments as a way to make explicit our views of conceptual individuation, to point out the unacceptability of the standard individualist view because of the possibility pictured by the scenario in the thought experiments themselves, then we must view Burge as departing from an implicit conception, perhaps minimal, probably wrong, of the concept "concept individuation". Semantic competence cannot reduce to standard use of the word, but requires some minimal, implicit, shared, understanding, that can be made explicit through a thought experiment. And which can change, thus changing the concept, by means of a thought experiment if a tension is "clearly and distinctly" noticed. But Burge's split of meaning in two makes it difficult to understand how by reflecting on the explicational meaning, through a thought experiment, the translational meaning can be altered, redefined (as happens, for instance, with "meaning" in Burge's works).

I take it that it was the externalist effort to mark distances with Frege, and his idea that "sense" (which roughly corresponds to Burge's "explicational meaning") determines "reference", that brought about the thought that "sense" was no longer required for having a concept. But although believing that water is a colourless, odourless,... liquid that quenches thirst may not suffice for fixing the reference of "water", it contributes much more than just believing that water is a liquid, for instance, in that it makes more reliable the recognition of water when in presence of it. All the same with our perceptual capacities to reidentify the same as the same: they enrich our semantic competence, making likely that we apply "water" to water. Of course, this network of perceptual and cognitive capacities that ground our semantic competence do not play the same roles as Fregean senses: they may be idiosyncratic, individual, not public and abstract entities; and they may be in large part implicit, not verbalizable. But they ground, as Fregean senses, semantic competence and significance along communitarian use. They constitute the ground for the intuitions that are elicited in thought experiments, in making them explicit, which do not require having a correct unique conceptual explication of the concepts tested—rather the contrary.

Now, near the end of his 1989 paper, Burge says something very similar to this:

> Most empirically applicable concepts are fixed by three factors: by actual referents encountered through experience—one's own, one's fellows', or one's species ancestors', or indirectly through theory; by some rudimentary conceptualization of the examples—learned or innately possessed by virtually everyone who comes in contact with the terms; and by perceptual information, inferential capacities, and kind-forming abilities, that may be pre-conceptual. (1989, 187)

Although this is not yet fully clear on the point of the connection between "having a concept" and "having some conception about it", it seems to entail that some minimal conceptual understanding of the concept is required to ground a conceptual attribution. If Burge really thinks so, we couldn't agree more. Unfortunately, it seems to me that his thought experiments are understood to suggest a more deflationary view of semantic competence, a view which does not allow an understanding of thought experiments as grounded in semantic/conceptual competence. But as I said before, there may not be a unique way to deal with any incongruence that shows up in a thought experiment.

Thus, I would say that, contrary to the main strand of Burge's view, thought experiments help to make clear the connection between "having a concept" and "having the conception about it", in that by reflecting of one's conception about something, if this reflection is clear and distinct enough, the concept itself (referentially individuated) may change, in virtue of a change in the rule that guides its use. This is what happens to the concept of meaning with Burge's own thought experiments, as Einstein's thought experiments (the elevator, the train) changed the Newtonian concept of mass, or Galileo's changed the Aristotelian concept of weight. Conceptual change in general may happen in different ways: a single concept may become splitted in two (mass and weight), may become more narrow, in that its reference gets restricted (as happened with the concept of gene), or may become more broad (as happened with "mammal" when the whales were thought of as included in the class). It is also possible a more radical change which generates "incommensurability", when it is not possible to identify a stable class of reference for the previous and new concepts ("mass" in Newtonian and relativistic physics). As it is well known, conceptual change in science and philosophy is not an atomic process, something easy to happen; it rather depends on a whole bunch of evidences, and affects a whole bunch of concepts and beliefs.

6   Conclusion

In this paper, assuming the insights of externalism, I've tried to point out the inadequacy of prof. Burge's conception of conceptual/semantic competence through a detour by thought experiments and Descartes. In thought experiments we put on trial our conceptual understanding devising possibilities that make explicit the rules that guide our linguistic use. Burge assumes this methodology and thus is committed to a conception of semantic competence that goes beyond actual use. Nevertheless, his account sticks to the latter, if not always by word, by practice. I've tried to locate the reason for this option and to show how could be enriched without adopting essentialism.

I would like to close with a final mention of Descartes. I've used him as a rethorical aid but also out of dissatisfaction with current abuse of anything Cartesian—an attitude partially fostered by prof. Burge, though the lion's share of the responsibility goes to the faithful Wittgensteinians. My aim has been to point to an aspect in which we are heirs to Descartes, although I think that Descartes' inheritance consists not so much in particular doctrines but rather in a lively set of problems and arguments, and a style of dealing with them. Instead of confronting ourselves to Descartes, we should rather see ourselves as extending and advancing the philosophical framework he initiated.[7]

[7] I would like to thank the referees for a suggestion that avoided a simplistic reading of Burge—well, a more simplistic one, say—and to prof. Burge as well for his comments and clarifications. This research has been supported by the Ministry of Education of Spain, through the project PB95-0585.

References

Boghossian, P. 1989. Content and Self-Knowledge, *Philosophical Topics* 17: 5-26.

Brown, J.R. 1991. *The laboratory of the mind*, Routledge.

Burge, T. 1986a. Cartesian error and the Objectivity of Perception, in Subject, Thought and Context, P. Pettit & J. McDowell, eds. OUP.

———. 1986b. Intellectual Norms and Foundations of Mind, *Journal of Philosophy* 83: 697-720.

———. 1986c. Individualism and Psychology, *The Philosophical Review*, 95: 3-45.

———. 1988a. Individualism and Self-knowledge, *Journal of Philosophy* 85: 649-663.

———. 1988b. Perceptual Individualism and Authoritative Self-knowledge, in *Contents of Thought*, R. Grimm & D. Merrill, eds. Arizona U.P.

———. 1989. Wherein is language social?, in *Reflections on Chomsky*, A. George, ed. B. Blackwell.

———. 1993. Concepts, definitions and meaning. *Metaphilosophy* 24: 309-325.

Descartes, R. *Oeuvres de Descartes*. Ch. Adam & P. Tannery, eds. Paris, J. Vrin, 1964-1986, XI vol.

Giere, R. (ed.) 1992. *Cognitive models of science, Minnesota Studies in the Philosophy of Science*. Minnesota U.P.

Gomila, A. 1991. What is a thought experiment?, *Metaphilosophy*, 22: 84-92.

———. 1996. La teoría de las ideas de Descartes, *Teorema* XVI/1 (1996): 47-70.

Gooding, D. 1992. The procedural turn, in Giere (1992), 45-76.

Kenny, A. 1967. Descartes on ideas, in W. Doney, ed.: *Descartes*, New York, Anchor Books.

Kuhn, T. 1977. A function for thought experiments, in *The Essential Tension*, Chicago U.P.

McGinn, C. 1983. *The Character of Mind*, Oxford U.P.

Nersessian, N. 1992. How do scientists think? Capturing the dynamics of conceptual change in science, in Giere (1992), 3-44.

Sorensen, R. 1992. *Thought experiments*, Oxford U.P.

8

Externalism, Inclusion, and Knowledge of Content*

CARLOS J. MOYA

1 Introduction

In this paper I shall address the question whether self-knowledge is compatible with an externalist individuation of mental content. This question becomes pressing only in so far as self-knowledge is taken to be a genuine cognitive achievement. Not everybody accepts this. Some conceptions of self-knowledge interpret first-person statements about mental states as expressive, non-cognitive statements. Wittgensteinian

---

* Research for this paper has been funded by the Spanish Government's DGES as part of the project PB96-1091-C03-02. My thanks to this institution for its help and encouragement. I would also like to express my gratitude to Sven Bernecker, Tobies Grimaltos, Andreas Kemmerling and Nenad Miscevic for their help and comments on previous drafts of this paper.

Meaning, Basic Self-Knowledge and Mind:Essays on Tyler Burge.
María J. Frápolli and Esther Romero (eds.).

approaches take this line. On this perspective, the privilege of the first-person amounts to an entitlement to express mental states: linguistic statements replace more primitive, non-linguistic expressions. No cognitive achievement is involved here. Related positions view first-person avowability as constitutive of the human mind itself. Against these approaches, I take self-knowledge to be a genuinely cognitive achievement: it is correct, I think, to say that we usually know what we currently want, believe or intend. Against a Cartesian perspective, self-knowledge is neither incorrigible nor infallible. It is, however, direct, in the sense of non inferential, a priori, in the sense of not being based on empirical investigation of one's surroundings, and, in normal cases, presumptively true and endowed with prima facie special authority. Now the question is: Can we have self-knowledge, so understood, if we also accept externalism, i.e., if we accept that mental content is constitutively determined by factors distinct from and external to the subject's brain or body? My answer to this question will be affirmative. There are, as far as I know, two main lines of attack to compatibility between self-knowledge and externalism. According to one of them, compatibilism entails that a subject can know, a priori, substantial truths about the external world.[1] The other line rests on the possibility of a subject's being unwittingly switched between worlds (cf. Boghossian 1989, 1992, 1994). In this paper I shall consider only the latter, though I think that my proposal could also be shown to be successful against the former.[2] The philosophical interest of the question addressed here lies in the fact that both externalism and self-knowledge seem to be true and important doctrines about the human mind. Without externalism, we cannot make distinctions between thought contents (e.g., between water-thoughts and twater-thoughts) that are intuitively there, nor can we put forward certain intuitively correct semantic evaluations (e.g., that water-thoughts are false on Twin Earth). Besides, externalism contains the promise of a picture of the mind that could set us free from the traps of Cartesianism. Self-knowledge, in turn, is still more central to our conception of mentality. Lack of self-knowledge threatens responsible agency and critical rationality, as some authors have rightly stressed (cf. e.g. Bilgrami 1992, pp. 250-1 and Burge 1996). So, it would certainly be good news if we

---

[1] The original argument was first put forward in McKinsey 1991. See also Brown 1995. The argument is given a new version in Boghossian 1997. For replies to Boghossian's version see my 1998 and Brown 1999. For recent discussions of this line of argument see Brueckner 2000 and Falvey 2000.

[2] As I try to argue in my 1998 paper.

could have both externalism and self-knowledge. Let us see whether we can.

2   The Simple Argument

At first sight, there is at least a tension between the thesis that content is determined by external factors on which a subject has no special cognitive authority and the thesis that a subject has a special cognitive authority over this content. This tension can be given expression in what I shall call "the simple argument". The argument can be put as follows: if the contents of one's thoughts depend on factors over which one has no direct, a priori, authoritative knowledge, one cannot have direct, a priori, authoritative knowledge over those contents themselves (first premise); but the antecedent of this conditional is true if externalism is true (second premise); so, if externalism is true, one cannot have self-knowledge (conclusion). This argument is implicit in many incompatibilist authors (cf. Woodfield 1982, pp. vii-viii). But we can find it explicitly stated by Laurence Bonjour in a reference book, the *Blackwell Companion to Epistemology*. He writes:

> An objection to externalist accounts of content is that they seem unable to do justice to our ability to know the contents of our beliefs or thoughts 'from the inside', simply by reflection. If content is dependent on external factors pertaining to the environment, then knowledge of content should depend on knowledge of those factors—which will not in general be available to the person whose belief or thought is in question. (Bonjour 1992, p. 136).

That this text appears in this important reference book is a symptom that incompatibilism is gradually becoming the received opinion on this subject and that the simple argument for it seems convincing to many thinkers.

And, nevertheless, the simple argument does not prove the incompatibility thesis, for, even if the argument is valid, its first premise is arguably false. To see this, think that there is a dependence relation, maybe of a metaphysical character, between my existence and my parents' existence, so that I would not exist if my parents had not existed. However, I know that I exist in a direct, authoritative, a priori way, whereas my knowledge of my parents' existence is only empirical (cf. McKinsey 1991; see also Heil 1992, p. 163). By the way, this is why Descartes' argument from the certainty of the Cogito to the conclusion that the thinking self is independent of the body fails, as Arnauld already noticed (cf. Burge 1988, p. 651). It seems, then, that the first premise of the Simple Argument is false. At least, it cannot be true as a case of the general statement according to which if A depends upon B, one cannot have direct, a priori, authoritative knowledge of A if one does not have such a knowledge of B. The case of my parents' and my own existence is a counterexample to this statement. So, content might also be known in a direct, a priori, authoritative way even if it depends on external factors that cannot be known that way. If A depends upon B, it is not true, in general, that, in order to know A, I have first to know B. This holds as well when the dependence relation is constitutive or conceptual. There is such a relation between a certain figure's being a triangle and its internal angles' measuring 180 degrees. However, I can know in a direct, authoritative way that a certain figure is a triangle without knowing that its internal angles measure 180 degrees. We can conclude, then, that the simple argument does not prove that self-knowledge and externalism are incompatible. Incompatibilists must work harder in order to substantiate their claim.

3 The Inclusion Model

The failure of the Simple Argument does not dispel the feeling that there is a conflict or tension between self-knowledge and externalism. A positive account of how they are compatible would be welcome. The most widely accepted compatibilist account of self-knowledge is what Sven Bernecker has called "the inclusion theory of self-knowledge" (Bernecker 1996, p. 265) and I would prefer to call "the inclusion model" of self-knowledge. Advocates of this model include Tyler Burge, Donald Davidson and John Heil, among others.[3] As Sanford C. Goldberg has pointed out, this proposal exploits the fact that the same form of words used to express a thought (e. g. "it's raining") is also used to self-ascribe the thought (e. g. "I think: it's raining") (Goldberg 1997, pp. 211-212). The central idea of this model is that reflective awareness of a first-order thought (say, a reflective judgment that one has a certain thought) inherits or includes (whence the label "inclusion model") the content of the first-order thought itself. Burge writes:

> ... Knowledge [of one's own mental events] consists in a reflexive judgment which involves thinking a first-order thought that the judgment itself is about. The reflexive judgment simply inherits the content of the first-order thought." (Burge 1988, p. 656; cf. also Heil 1988, p. 246 and 1992, ch. 5).

On an externalist perspective, the individuation conditions of certain thoughts are partly external to the thinker; they consist in certain links

---

[3] For a recent defence of a refined version of this model see Gibbons 1996.

with some aspects of the environment or with a social linguistic community to which the thinker defers. These conditions enable me to have a thought with a certain content, even if I do not know or believe that these conditions obtain or even what they are. Now, when I reflexively ascribe that thought to myself, the content of this thought is simply included in my reflexive awareness, and the external conditions that partly determine the content of the first-order thought also contribute to determining the content of the reflexive or second-order thought. As Davidson points out:

> Showing that there is no conflict [between externalism and knowledge of content] is basically simple. It depends on realizing that whatever is responsible for the contents of our thoughts, whether known or not, is also responsible for the content of the thought that we have the thought" (Davidson, unpubl. ms, p. 35).

The inclusion model ensures that Cogito-like judgments are contextually self-verifying. Suppose, in effect, that external conditions partly determine, for the thought I express with "water quenches thirst", the content that water quenches thirst. I may not know that those conditions do in fact obtain or, for that matter, what they are, but if I am reflexively aware of this thought and I express this reflexive awareness with, say, "I am hereby judging that water quenches thirst", the content of the that-clause of this reflexive attitude is that water quenches thirst, that is, it is the content of the first-order thought itself. But if a corresponding episode happens on Twin-Earth, the thought that my Twin expresses with "water quenches thirst" has the content that twin water (twater) quenches thirst, and this is also the content of the that-clause of my Twin's reflexive attitude. So, on the inclusion model, Cogito-like judgments are reliably true in that they are contextually self-verifying. In this sense, a subject can be said to have authoritative knowledge over his thoughts' content, in spite of these thoughts' having external individuation conditions which the subject has no privileged knowledge of.

I think that the inclusion model is ultimately correct, but, as it stands, it is affected by some shortcomings. One problem is that it draws too heavily on an externalist, reliabilist view of justification (see, e. g., Bernecker 1998), for, on this model, justification of self-ascriptions rests on the existence of a mechanism (which the subject need not have cognitive access to) ensuring that the content of first-order thoughts is ipso facto included in self-ascriptions of those thoughts. This important reliabilist component links the inclusion model too closely to the fate of reliabilism itself. It also needs some more work of a general kind about the nature of external determination of meaning and content if it is to be able to meet the objections we are about to see. One major objection is that this model does not ensure what Boghossian has called the "transparency of content". I shall try to do part of the required additional work later in this paper. Let us now turn to Boghossian's objection.

4 Transparency of content: switching between worlds

Some philosophers feel that the inclusion model makes self-knowledge into a rather anaemic cognitive achievement, so much so that its entitlement to the dignity of knowledge could be justifiably questioned. Paul Boghossian, for one, acknowledges that accounts of self-knowledge on the lines of the inclusion model ensure that, at least in basic cases, a subject's reports of his current thought contents will always be true (Boghossian 1992, p. 15), but he complains that such accounts do not ensure that these thought contents are transparent for him. Boghossian construes the notion of transparency of content on the basis of Dummett's concept of transparency of meaning. According to Dummett, "... meaning is *transparent* in the sense that, if someone attaches a meaning to each of two words, he must know whether these meanings are the same" (quoted from Boghossian 1992, p. 16). Correspondingly, content is transparent to a subject only if he is able to know in a direct, a priori way whether the contents of two thoughts of his are the same or not. Boghossian grounds his contention that the inclusion model does not grant transparency of content on thought experiments in which we are asked to imagine that a subject is unwittingly transported, say, from Earth to Twin Earth and remains there for a fairly long time.[4] Let's call our inter-world traveller "Peter". Boghossian writes:

> How should we think about the semantics of Peter's thoughts? Well, one intuition that is shared by practically everyone who has thought about these cases is that, after a while (how long is unclear), tokens of 'water' in Peter's mentalese will cease to mean *water* and will come to mean *twater*. (Boghossian 1992, p. 18).

This intuition coheres especially well, according to Boghossian, with the following principle of content fixation which underlies standard Twin Earth cases: "The contents of thought tokens of a given syntactic type are determined by whatever environmental property is the typical cause of the perceptions that cause and sustain tokens of that type" (Boghossian 1992, p. 19). I shall dispute later both the intuition and the principle, but let us provisionally grant them for the sake of the argument. Consequences of this thought experiment for self-knowledge are quite

---

[4] This sort of thought experiment had been already devised by Burge: see Burge 1988, p. 652.

clear. Suppose, in effect, that, while still on Earth, in summer, Peter is thirsty and fills a glass with cold water while muttering: "Water will quench my thirst". Some years later, a similar episode takes place on Twin Earth and Peter mutters tokens of the same words, while remembering the analogous occasion we have referred to. Since his subjective experience has not been disrupted and, for all he knows, he has not travelled to another world, he will certainly judge that the token thought contents he has expressed on both occasions are of the same type. But, if externalism is true, they are not. So, content is not transparent for him. His comparative judgment about his thought contents is false. On this basis, Boghossian contends that Burge's self-verifying judgments do not amount to knowledge. He tries to show this as follows. Suppose that, after being on Twin Earth long enough, Peter is told that the switch has occurred, but not when it took place. We ask Peter: "Two years ago, were you thinking that water quenches thirst or that twater quenches thirst?" Peter will not know the answer. However, according to Burge's inclusion model, two years ago Peter knew what he was thinking in that he was able to reflexively self-ascribe a thought he expressed with the sentence "water quenches thirst". But now Peter acknowledges that he doesn't know what thought he was having two years ago. Why? According to Boghossian, there are two possible explanations: that Peter has forgotten or that he never knew. But memory failure should be excluded by stipulation, for "it is not as if thoughts with widely individuated contents might be easily known but difficult to remember. The only explanation, I venture to suggest, is not that he has forgotten but that he never knew. Burge's self-verifying judgments do not constitute genuine knowledge. What other reason is there for why our slowly transported thinker will not know tomorrow what he is said to know directly and authoritatively today?" (Boghossian 1989, p. 23). Therefore, externalism is not compatible with self-knowledge. This is, in rough terms, Boghossian's incompatibilist argument.

5 Does self-knowledge include transparency of content?

One possible way of countering Boghossian's incompatibilist argument is to hold that, appearances to the contrary notwithstanding, ordinary self-knowledge does not include transparency of content. This thesis has been defended by Kevin Falvey and Joseph Owens.[5] Falvey and Owens contend that, independently of externalism, we do not enjoy what they

---

[5] This view has also been defended by John Gibbons. See Gibbons 1996, p. 304. It is also present in Burge 1998.

call "introspective knowledge of comparative content". I take this knowledge to be equivalent to Boghossian's transparency of content, for it is characterized as follows:

> With respect to any two of his thoughts or beliefs, an individual can know authoritatively and directly (that is, without relying on inferences from his observed environment) whether or not they have the same content (Falvey and Owens 1994, pp. 109-110; cf. also Owens 1995).

They seem to endorse the inclusion model of self-knowledge, with its resulting self-verifying judgments, and, on this basis, they accept that we possess what they call "introspective knowledge of content", according to which "an individual knows the contents of his occurrent thoughts and beliefs authoritatively and directly (that is, without relying on inferences from observation of his environment)" (Falvey and Owens 1994, pp. 109-110).

Boghossian's objection is quite probably innocuous against introspective knowledge of content. So, an externalist might easily embrace compatibilism by limiting the scope of self-knowledge in this way. But I have the suspicion that this would be too cheap a victory against incompatibilism. For, on the one hand, Falvey and Owens defend his thesis that we do not enjoy comparative self-knowledge on the basis of examples involving pairs of synonymous and co-extensive terms (e. g. 'physician' and 'doctor', or 'cilantro' and 'coriander') that a subject does not know to be so. But these examples seem to me controversial and capable of receiving quite natural interpretations that do not entail that a subject lacks comparative self-knowledge. Suppose, for instance, that Andrew thinks that the thought he expresses with the words "Mary is a physician" is not the same as the thought he expresses with "Mary is a doctor". Suppose he thinks so because he believes that 'physician' and 'doctor' are not synonyms (let us suppose that he thinks that 'physician' is synonymous with 'physicist'). Only from an implausibly crude externalist perspective would someone be inclined to think that the subject is wrong about his two thoughts' being different. I tend to hold that Andrew's two thoughts are in fact different, that he is right in believing that they are and, therefore, that he has comparative self-knowledge. And, on the other hand, Boghossian's transparency requirement for self-knowledge seems to be well grounded on a reasonable requirement (a necessary condition) for knowledge in general. This requirement might be called "the principle of relevant alternatives". According to this principle, a subject cannot be said to know that a is an F, though it in fact is, if, in case a were a G, where being a G is a relevant alternative to being an F, this subject would still judge that a is an F. Knowledge requires the ability to discriminate between relevant alternatives. So, imagine, using the famous Putnamian example, that I cannot tell elms from beeches. Then, even if my judgments of the form "*a* is an elm" happen to be always true, I cannot be said to *know* that *a* is an elm, for, if *a* were a beech instead, where being a beech is a relevant alternative to being an elm, I would still judge that it was an elm. Note that this still holds even if I do not know about the existence of beeches. It is the existence of relevant alternatives, not my belief or knowledge that there are, what matters here for possession of knowledge. Now Peter, the inter-world traveller, does not seem to satisfy this requirement. He cannot discriminate between his water-thoughts and his twater-thoughts and the latter are, for him, relevant alternatives to the former. He does not know about the existence of these relevant alternatives, but, as I said, this does not change matters. In terms of the inclusion model, Peter's judgments about his thought contents happen to be true. When Peter is on Earth and reflexively mutters "I am judging that water quenches thirst", this judgment is true, for it has the content that water quenches thirst, but Peter does not *know* that his thought has this content, for, if it had the content that twater quenches thirst instead, he still would think, mistakenly, that it had the same content it now has.

This, if correct, restates Boghossian's incompatibilist argument against Falvey and Owens' response and makes things harder for compatibilists. They had better show that externalism is compatible with transparency of content if they want to show that it is compatible with self-knowledge.

6   Incompatibilism and memory

Other attempts to meet Boghossian's objection focus on the role memory plays in his argument. Let us extend a bit on this part of the argument. Recall that Peter, the inter-world traveller, interpreted in the light of the inclusion model and its corresponding self-verifying judgments, knows at t1 what he is thinking, but at t2, after being told about the switch, he does not know what he was thinking at t1. But Boghossian takes it to be a "platitude about memory and knowledge" that "if S knows that p at t1, and if at (some later time) t2, S remembers everything he knew at t1, then S knows that p at t2" (Boghossian 1989, p. 23). Now if S does *not* know that p at t2, then either he does not remember at t2 everything he knew at t1 or he did not know that p at t1. If, by assumption, we rule out memory failure, it seems we have to conclude that S did not know that p at t1. Ludlow has given this useful reconstruction of this part of Boghossian's incompatibilist argument: "(1)

If S forgets nothing, then what S knows at t1, S knows at t2, (2) S forgot nothing, (3) S does not know that P at t2; (4) therefore, S did not know that P at t1" (Ludlow 1995a, p. 157).

That the 'platitude' Boghossian states (which corresponds to premise (1) in Ludlow's reconstruction) is indeed a platitude has been put into question by some authors, such as Ludlow (1995b) and Goldberg (1997). Goldberg's remarks are especially interesting from the perspective of the present paper, for they point to an element that seems to be an integral part of Boghossian's argument, namely the relevant alternatives account of knowledge, in order to undermine Boghossian's supposed platitude. According to Goldberg (who acknowledges his debt to Falvey on this point),

> someone could know that *p* at *t1*, remember at *t2* everything she knew at *t1*, and yet fail to know that *p* at *t2*—even if she continues to believe that *p*, and *p* is true—for the very familiar reason that there might be *new evidence* encountered along the way that points to a relevant alternative she cannot exclude" (Goldberg 1997, p. 214).

Brueckner (1997) has also questioned premise (1) on a similar basis. He writes:

> To say that at t2, S has forgotten nothing that he knew at t1 is to say that at t2, remembers everything that he knew at t1. But it does not follow that that at t2, S knows everything that he knew at t1. This is because for some P that he knew at t1, he may remember at t2 that P while failing to know at t2 that P, say, because of some defeating information that he has learned between t1 and t2" (Brueckner 1997, p. 8).

In Boghossian's example, Peter has acquired new information (namely that he has been switched at some unknown time) that defeats his justification for believing that at t1 he was thinking that water quenches thirst. This, if correct, shows premise (1) to be false.

Is Boghossian's incompatibilist argument thereby defeated? I do not think so, for the argument can be restated without any essential appeal to memory. The conclusion that Peter does not know at t1 what he is thinking at t1, so that Burge's self-verifying judgments do not constitute knowledge, can be reached with no need of premise (1). Suppose, in effect, that Peter is told that he has suffered repeated switching between Earth and Twin Earth, but neither when the switches took place nor where he is now. In these circumstances, he will recognize that he does not know, right now, what he is thinking right now, because he does not know whether he is thinking that water quenches thirst or that twater quenches thirst.

The possibility that Boghossian's argument is restated without appealing to memory suggests that no criticism based on reflections on memory can aspire to a definitive rebuttal of Boghossian's incompatibilism. Goldberg has also tried to show that Boghossian's argument may dispose of an appeal to memory and be restated in terms of an ability to knowingly identify self-ascribed thoughts (Goldberg 1997, p. 215). Both Goldberg's and my own restatement of Boghossian's incompatibilist contentions without appeal to memory make use of the notion of discrimination between thought contents, a notion closely related to that of transparency of content and to the relevant alternatives account of knowledge. I have argued in favour of transparency of content as a necessary condition for self-knowledge in the previous section, against Falvey and Owens' denial of this condition. I want now to consider a possible objection to this condition, according to which it might seem implausibly strong to require of Peter, as far as he is fully unaware of his switching career, that he be able to knowingly identify his *water*-thoughts as *water*-thoughts and his *twater*-thoughts as *twater*-thoughts. This form of discrimination we might call "strong discrimination". I can agree that this requirement is too demanding. However, it is not implausible to require of Peter, if he is to have self-knowledge, at least that he does not take his *water*-thoughts and his *twater*-thoughts to be of the same type. We might call this "weak discrimination". Now, Peter does not satisfy even the weak discrimination condition. If he is unaware of the switching, he will certainly judge that a *water*-thought he expresses with 'water quenches thirst' is of the same type as a *twater*-thought he expresses with those same words, even if he is having those two thoughts in the specious present (provided both concepts are available to him). The inclusion model ensures that his self-ascriptions are true, but not, if the weak discrimination condition is correct, that they amount to knowledge.

In a recent paper (Burge 1998),[6] Burge has countered Boghossian's argument by distinguishing two ways in which memory can work, namely by discriminatory identification and by preservation. Preservative memory retains the content of past thinkings through causal links with them, preserving contents and attitudes without the subject's having to refer to or identify them, similarly to what happens with anaphoric uses of pronouns. So, by simply having a thought that Peter expresses with "I thought that water is wet", preservative memory, working properly, connects Peter's present thought to the remembered though, with the content and concepts that were in play at that earlier time.

---

[6] Some central ideas in this paper relate closely to those Burge had developed in his 1993 paper.

Burge holds, then, that discriminatory identification is not necessary in order to know what one is thinking. Besides, a strong reliabilist component is present in Burge's account of preservative memory, as is also in his understanding of present-tense self-knowledge. These two aspects may undermine the force of his response to Boghossian, if either reliabilism were shown to be wrong or if the ability to discriminate between relevant alternatives were to be a necessary condition for knowledge. I have argued in favour of the latter above. Suppose that Peter, being very thirsty on Twin Earth, thinks to himself "water will quench my thirst" and self-ascribes this thought, while also thinking "I thought the same thing two years ago". It is hard to accept that in these conditions, where the comparative thought is supposedly false, his plain self-ascription amounts to knowledge. But then it is hard (and arbitrary) to accept that, in order to have self-knowledge, the self-ascribed thought must not be accompanied by a corresponding comparative thought.

It would be good, then, to have compatibilism even accepting the discrimination condition. And it would also be good if compatibilism did not depend on strong reliabilist assumptions.

7   Switching cases: actual and possible

Another way of countering Boghossian's incompatibilist argument is to hold that the mere possibility of switching cases does not prove that we lack self-knowledge. Only actual switching cases would threaten self-knowledge. Ted Warfield (1992) has taken this line of response. He summarizes Boghossian's argument as follows (where "P" = "S's thought is about water" and "S" designates an individual in our world):

> P1. To know that P by introspection, S must be able to introspectively discriminate P from all relevant alternatives of P.
>
> P2. S cannot introspectively discriminate water thoughts from twater thoughts.
>
> P3. If the Switching case is actual, then twater thoughts are relevant alternatives of water thoughts.
>
> C1. S doesn't know that P by introspection" (Warfield 1992, p. 235)

Warfield holds, correctly, that this argument is not valid. All that follows from premises P1-P3 is the much weaker conclusion C1':

C1'. If the Switching case is actual, then S doesn't know that P by introspection.

In order to obtain C1 an additional premise, P*, would be needed:

P*. The Switching case is actual.

Boghossian's argument shows, at most, that, given externalism, it is not necessary that the contents of a subject's thoughts are knowable to him on the basis of introspection.

In a different paper, Warfield gives the following informal summary of his response to Boghossian:

> Boghossian argues that if externalism is true, an individual (called a Traveller) who is somehow transported back and forth between Earth and Twin Earth will not know the content of the thought she expresses with the sentence 'Water is wet'. Leaving aside the question of whether or not Travellers can have knowledge of the contents of their 'water' thoughts, I show in my (1992) that Boghossian's argument shows at most that *Travellers* do not know the contents of their thoughts; it does not show that we do not know the contents of our thoughts because Boghossian has not argued that we are Travellers" (Warfield 1995, p. 540).

Peter Ludlow (1995a) has tried to reply to Warfield. According to Ludlow, premise (P3) in Warfield's reconstruction of Boghossian's argument is unnecessarily strong in stating the conditions under which there are relevant alternatives to water thoughts. A weaker premise like (P3') would do as well:

(P3') If switching cases in general are prevalent, then there are relevant alternatives of water thoughts.

In order to show that (P3') is sufficient, Ludlow offers the following analogy. Suppose that counterfeit is frequent at coin shows. Thus, even if there is no counterfeit at a particular coin show, a subject cannot be said to know that a certain coin is authentic if he is not able to discriminate it from a false replica. The alternative that a particular coin is false is relevant even if, as it may happen, there are no false coins in this particular context.

But if (P3') is the right premise, then a premise weaker than P* would be sufficient to establish Boghossian's incompatibility thesis, something like (P**):

(P**) Switching cases, in general, are prevalent.

He tries to show that this premise is true by construing a Burge-style case in which a subject, Biff, moves back and forth between communities largely overlapped with respect to language (namely British English and American English speaking communities). Biff uses the term 'chicory' deferring successively to each community without noticing that this term has a different meaning in each. So, when Biff has a thought involving that term in England he is thinking one thing, but when a similar episode takes place in the United States, he is thinking something different. However, he does not know that he is having different thoughts. In order to substantiate (P**), Ludlow generalizes Biff's case by saying that "we routinely move between social groups and institutions, and in many cases shifts in the content of our thoughts will not be detected by us. (There is, it appears, a little of Biff in all of us)" (Ludlow 1995a, p. 48).

It is worth noting that, if the proposal we are going to make below is correct, externalism does not necessarily entail the consequence Ludlow wants to draw from this example. But let us grant provisionally this consequence for the sake of the argument. In my opinion, Warfield's requirement that Switching cases be actual is misguided, as, correspondingly, is Ludlow's attempt to defend Boghossian's argument by showing such cases to be prevalent. Warfield is probably right that, strictly speaking, Boghossian's argument does not establish that we actually lack self-knowledge. Only the actuality or at least the prevalence of Switching cases would have that general consequence. As Warfield points out, the right conclusion of Boghossian's argument is that, given externalism, it is possible that we lack self-knowledge. But this conclusion is devastating enough if we carefully reflect on what it involves. Since Switching situations are possible, whether or not they are actual or prevalent, and since subjects in those situations may be fully unaware that they are in them, Boghossian's argument does establish that, given externalism, self-knowledge is contingent on circumstances (such as an undetected change in our environment) we might not be aware or have any control of. Externalism entails the possibility of situations where a subject's being mistaken about the world leads to his being mistaken about what he is thinking. Owens explicitly acknowledges this when he writes: "Because of her lack of information about the world a subject may have mistaken beliefs about her beliefs" (Owens 1995, p. 265). But this is unacceptable, whether or not we are victims of Switching cases. If externalism entails that we may lack self-knowledge owing to our being mistaken about the world, then externalism conceals the threat of an epistemological havoc, for we could not know what we believe before knowing that our beliefs about the world are true, but we could not know that our beliefs about the world are true without knowing what it is that we believe. This circle would lead to complete epistemological darkness.

8 Towards a reasonable compatibilism

In the following sections I will try to elaborate the makings of a reasonable form of compatibilism. My strategy will be to short-circuit Boghossian's argument at a much earlier stage than do the attempts we have been reviewing. The failure of those attempts, I suspect, is due to the fact that they concede too much to the incompatibilist. I shall be questioning instead some assumptions that underlie Boghossian's argument and allow it to get off the ground.

What makes us worry about self-knowledge, I contend, is not externalism as such, that is, the general doctrine that our thought contents and concepts are individuated, in part, by external factors, but rather a particular, though widely extended construal of this doctrine. This particular construal, which might be called "causal externalism", is explicitly assumed in Boghossian's incompatibilist argument as well as (sometimes implicitly) in the attempts to counter it we have seen so far, and is illegitimately identified with externalism as such. The core of this construal, in Boghossian's presentation of it, is the principle of content fixation we referred to above. To recall, the principle is as follows, in Boghossian's own words: "... The contents of thought tokens of a given syntactic type are determined by whatever environmental property is the typical cause of the perceptions that cause and sustain tokens of that type" (Boghossian 1992, p. 19). Given this principle, a change in the typical causes of thought tokens of a given syntactic type will lead to a change in the content of those tokens. Now, since the change of typical causes may go undetected by a subject, as happens in Switching cases, the change in his thought contents will also go undetected by him, hence (given some plausible discrimination condition) he will lack self-knowledge with respect to those thoughts. This construal of externalism cannot but fall prey to Switching cases arguments. But nothing forces us to accept this construal. In fact, I think we should reject it and turn to a different, more plausible construal.

Recall that, according to Boghossian, our intuition about the semantics of Switching cases is that, after an indeterminate period on a twin environment, tokens of 'water' in the Travellers' mentalese change their meaning, with a change in the content of the corresponding thought tokens (cf. Boghossian 1992, p. 18). I want to challenge that intuition. Intuitions, as we know, constitute a shaky, problematic domain. In many cases it is rather unclear whether they are really independent of previous theoretical commitments or are unwittingly fueled by these commitments themselves. I guess that the intuition Boghossian refers to is fed by a commitment to a causal construal of externalism, so it cannot be used to validate this construal. Another problem with this intuition is that it is raised by such extreme examples as transworld unwitting travelling cases, and it is doubtful that our conceptual background is fit enough to resist the strain and to yield clear verdicts when confronted with such extraordinary scenarios. A final point is that the intuition and the principle of content fixation that, according to Boghossian, accounts for it rest on the unwarranted attribution to environmental factors of an unexplained, unanalyzed and, let me say, sort of magical power to gradually influence and eventually change, after an indeterminate period of exposure to them, a Traveller's thought contents.

Let me dispute the intuition and the principle that supposedly explains it by resorting to more mundane, more realistic switching cases, where a factor in a subject's environment changes without the subject's noticing the change. For the reason given, our intuitions about these cases are likely to be more reliable than those raised by extraordinary stages and can be then extended to the latter. Think of the following case. Suppose I have been longing to possess a three carats diamond and that, after strenuous financial efforts, my dream comes finally true. A wonderful diamond shines now inside a glass case in my sitting room. It is clear that the term 'diamond' in my mental attitudes and verbal expressions of them up to now means *diamond*. Unfortunately, an expert thief gets in my house and replaces my diamond by a false replica, a zircon piece, which I cannot distinguish from my longed for diamond. From then on, paraphrasing Boghossian's principle of content fixation, the environmental property that is the typical cause of the perceptions that cause and sustain my tokens of the syntactic type 'diamond' (cf. Boghossian 1992, p. 19) is the property of being a zircon piece, not the property of being a diamond. But do we really have the intuition that, after an indeterminate while, my tokens of 'diamond' have come to mean *zircon*? I definitely think we don't. My tokens of 'diamond' continue to mean *diamond* and I know they do. This Switching case has, no doubt, epistemological consequences, but these consequences do not affect self-knowledge. My belief that I possess a diamond is now false, as well as my belief that my desire to possess a diamond is now satisfied, but no doubt I know what these beliefs and desires are. If Boghossian's principle of content fixation were correct, my beliefs would now be true and my desire would be satisfied, for their content would have come to be about zircon, but this is surely wrong. My tokens of 'diamond' still mean *diamond* despite their being now typically caused by zircon.

A possible objection to this example[7] is that it differs in some important respects from the Switching examples that motivate Boghossian's argument. In particular, it might be held that, in my example, what might be keeping the meaning of 'diamond' constant is the conti-

---

[7] I owe this objection to Andreas Kemmerling.

nuity of the social community to which the subject defers and in which 'diamond' means *diamond*. In order to meet this objection, we can try to construct a case where the shift also affects the social community. One problem with this attempt is that the example becomes less realistic and the intuitions it raises might correspondingly be less reliable. Anyway, I will try to make the example as realistic as possible. Imagine, then, that the theft occurs shortly after I have moved to another country where still English is spoken, with the only difference, which I do not know about, that members of the new community use 'diamond' to mean what in the original community was meant by 'zircon' and conversely. Does this imply, given Burge's social externalism, that after living in the new community long enough the thoughts I express with tokens of 'diamond' turn into thoughts about zircon? Think that the experts of the new community, if they were to examine the mineral, would assent to my utterance "I possess a nice diamond" (though they might be slightly surprised to find that I am so proud of my zircon). Though this case is a bit more complicated, my intuition is definitely that my tokens of 'diamond' still mean *diamond*, not *zircon*. With 'diamond' I do not want to unconditionally mean whatever it is that my new community (or its experts) mean by 'diamond'; I only intend to mean that under the assumption that what they mean by 'diamond' is the same as that which is meant by that word in my original community. Since this assumption is false, I still defer to my old community for what concerns the meaning of 'diamond'. The original community keeps its preeminence over the new one. To see this, suppose that I get to know about the semantic difference. From then on, I would certainly tell members of my new community that I possess a wonderful zircon (provided I am still ignorant of the theft), thus changing the word to preserve the meaning. And I would be sadly surprised to be told that what I possess is a diamond, not a zircon, as sadly surprised, in fact, as if in my original community I had been told that I possess a zircon and not a diamond. This speaks clearly, I think, in favour of the view that, while ignorant of the semantic difference, the meaning of my tokens of 'diamond' has not shifted, nor has the content of the thoughts I express with tokens of that word. This intuition is consistent with Burge's stress on the importance of social communities in fixing thought contents; it only requires to accept that deference to the actual community one happens to live in need not be unconditional: a subject may defer to a different community, especially if this is the community where he grew up.

My suggestion is that something similar would apply to the case of our hero Peter, the inter-world traveller. Peter's tokens of 'water' on

Twin Earth continue to mean *water*, in spite of their being now typically
caused by twater. In view of our modified example, it will not do to say
that, after staying on Twin Earth long enough, Peter's deference to the
Twin Earthian community makes his tokens of 'water' mean *twater*. Peter is only deferent to his new community under the assumption that this
community is that in which he learned language and its meaning. Since
this assumption is not true, Peter still defers to his original Earthian
community, and his tokens of 'water' still mean *water*.

9 Normative externalism

Let me now try to explain the intuitions about realistic switching cases.
Someone might be tempted to think that the only possible theoretical
explanation of them is internalism. If this were so, then compatibilism
would have lost the battle. But this is not so. A plausible externalist
view of meaning and content fixation can also account for them. Let me
call the construal of externalism I favour "normative externalism".[8] We
can contrast normative externalism and causal externalism by noticing
their respective answers to the following question: Why do tokens of
'water' mean *water* on Earth and *twater* on Twin Earth? The answer of
causal externalism is, roughly, as follows: because Earthians' tokens of
'water' are typically caused by water, while Twin Earthians' tokens of
'water' are typically caused by twater. It is clear how this conception
leaves open the possibility of Switching cases. According to normative
externalism, in turn, the answer would be: because Earthians learn and
teach the meaning of 'water' in connection with paradigmatic samples
of water, while Twin Earthians learn and teach the meaning of 'water' in
connection with samples of a different substance, namely twater. On this
construal of externalism, our words' meaning depends on external conditions because certain bits of the external world are used as samples in
order to *define* those words, to give those words their meaning. The external sample becomes a norm for a correct use of the word. So, suppose
that, in using certain words in thought and talk, we implicitly rely on the
paradigmatic samples in connection with which we learned the meaning
of those words and that we defer, unless we have positive reasons for
doing otherwise, to the original community where we learned that meaning. This would allow for a high degree of constancy in our words' meaning and in the thoughts we express with them, a constancy they would

---

[8] Nenad Miscevic suggested to me the label "definitional externalism" for my position. His reasons will be apparent from what follows. Nothing really substantial hinges
on the label, but I still prefer "normative externalism".

not have if meaning depended just on the typical causes of tokenings of those words.

It seems clear to me that this construal of externalism is consistent with Burge's social externalism. In fact, given the emphasis it puts on the social interaction involved in the process of language learning and teaching, this construal is much easier to square with Burge's insights than the causal construal. Besides, normative externalism is not really far from Putnam's conception either. Remarks about paradigmatic samples can also be found in Putnam's "The meaning of 'meaning'". Normative externalism and causal externalism, unlike internalism, can account for our intuitions about Putnam's original Twin Earth thought experiments. But normative externalism and internalism, unlike causal externalism, explain our intuitions about realistic Switching cases. So, only normative externalism can account for both groups of intuitions, which clearly speaks in its favour. It explains why we tend to judge that tokens of 'diamond' do not come to mean *zircon* after being, from a certain moment on, typically caused by zircon. The meaning of 'diamond' is not fixed by typical causes of tokenings of that word, but by paradigmatic samples of diamonds, and this is why a change in those typical causes does not affect the word's meaning.

If we extend our intuitions about realistic cases to more extreme, inter-world switching cases, something quite similar can be said about Peter. Peter learnt the meaning of 'water' on Earth in connection with samples of water, so that, with respect to this meaning, he defers to the real nature of these samples (and to the Earthian community where they are used) in tokening the word in speech or in thought. Since, after his unwitting travelling to Twin Earth, no new process of learning takes place, his tokenings of the word retain their Earthian meaning. They still mean *water*, in spite of their being now typically caused by twater. Consequences of all this for self-knowledge should be clear by now. Peter retains his introspective knowledge of comparative content; his thought contents are, in Boghossian's terms, transparent for him. Peter's judgment is that the thought he expresses, when he is on Twin Earth, in tokening the sentence "water quenches thirst" has the same content as the thought he expressed on Earth, some time ago, by tokening that sentence. According to causal externalism, Peter is wrong on this account. But according to normative externalism, *he is right*. Some of Peter's beliefs are now false on Twin Earth, but his beliefs, even comparative, about the contents of those beliefs are still true. If all this is correct, the inclusion model of self-knowledge, completed with a normative construal of externalism, can successfully meet the Switching cases objection to compatibilism.

My proposal can temperate the crude externalist reliabilism that underlies the inclusion model, thus making the latter less vulnerable to shortcomings of the former. I think it is correct to say that self-ascriptions include the content of the first-order thought, but on my account this content does not get fixed in complete independence of the subject's intentions to keep faithful to certain content-giving practices and definitions. The real nature of water, for example, contributes to the meaning of 'water', as does in the causal version of externalism, but not outside a social interaction frame in which the subject who uses the word is knowingly involved. This allows my proposal to prevent a mere shift in the causal (or even social) environment from automatically producing a shift in meaning and content.

It might be objected that, according to my account, if Peter's unwitting travel to Twin Earth takes place while he is still learning the meaning of 'water', so that this learning continues on Twin Earth, his term 'water' will come to mean *water-or-twater*. I accept this. But I do not think it is a problem for my account, for something similar would have happened on Earth if water had turned out to be a collection of different substances, as is the case, e. g., with jade. Peter would retain comparative self-knowledge. I conclude, then, that, at least for what concerns the Switching cases objection, externalism, on a normative reading, and self-knowledge, even in its stronger, comparative form, are compatible.

References

Bernecker, S. 1996. Externalism and the Attitudinal Component of Self-Knowledge, *Nous* 30: 262-275.

Bernecker, S. 1998. Self-Knowledge and Closure, in P. Ludlow & N. Martin (eds.), *Externalism and Self-Knowledge*, CSLI Publications, Stanford, 333-49.

Bilgrami, A. 1992. *Belief and Meaning*, Blackwell, Oxford/Cambridge Mass.

Boghossian, P. A. 1989. Content and Self-Knowledge, *Philosophical Topics* 17: 5-26.

Boghossian, P. A. 1992. Externalism and Inference, in E. Villanueva (ed.), *Rationality in Epistemology*, Philosophical Issues 2, Ridgeview Publishing Company, Atascadero (California), 11-28.

Boghossian, P. A. 1994. The Transparency of Mental Content, *Philosophical Perspectives* 8: 33-50.

Boghossian, P. A. 1997. What an Externalist Can Know A Priori, *Proceedings of the Aristotelian Society* 97: 161-75. Reprinted in E. Villanueva (ed.), *Concepts, Philosophical Issues* 9, 1998.

Bonjour, L. 1992. Entry 'Externalism/internalism', in J. Dancy and E. Sosa (eds.), *A Companion to Epistemology*, Blackwell, Oxford, 133-136.

Brown, J. 1995. The Incompatibility of Anti-individualism and Privileged Access, *Analysis* 55: 149-156.

Brown, J. 1999. Boghossian on Externalism and Privileged Access, *Analysis* 59: 52-59.

Brueckner, A. 1997. Externalism and Memory, *Pacific Philosophical Quarterly* 78: 1-12.

Brueckner, A. 2000. Externalism and the A Prioricity of Self-Knowledge, *Analysis* 60: 132-136.

Burge, T. 1988. Individualism and Self-Knowledge, *Journal of Philosophy* 85: 649-663.

Burge, T. 1993. Content Preservation, *The Philosophical Review* 102: 457-488.

Burge, T. 1996. Our Entitlement to Self-Knowledge, *Proceedings of the Aristotelian Society* 91: 91-116.

Burge, T. 1998. Memory and Self-Knowledge, in P. Ludlow and N. Martin (eds.), *Externalism and Self-Knowledge*, CSLI Publications, Stanford, 351-70.

Davidson, D. unpubl. ms. Quoted in Boghossian 1994, p. 35.

Falvey, K. 2000. The Compatibility of Anti-Individualism and Privileged Access, *Analysis* 60: 137-42.

Falvey, K. and Owens, J. 1994. Externalism, Self-Knowledge, and Skepticism, *The Philosophical Review* 103: 107-137.

Gibbons, J. 1996. Externalism and Knowledge of Content, *The Philosophical Review* 105: 287-310.

Goldberg, S. C. 1997. Self-Ascription, Self-Knowledge, and the Memory Argument, *Analysis* 57: 211-219.

Heil, J. 1988. Privileged Access, *Mind* 97: 238-251.

Heil, J. 1992. *The Nature of True Minds*, Cambridge University Press, Cambridge.

Ludlow, P. 1995a. Externalism, Self-Knowledge, and the Prevalence of Slow Switching, *Analysis* 55: 45-49.

Ludlow, P. 1995b. Social Externalism, Self-Knowledge, and Memory, *Analysis* 55 (1995): 157-159.

Ludlow, P. and Martin, N. (eds.) 1998. *Externalism and Self-Knowledge*, CSLI Press, Stanford.

McKinsey, M. 1991. Anti-Individualism and Privileged Access, *Analysis* 51: 9-16.

Moya, C. J. 1998. Boghossian's Reductio of Compatibilism, in E. Villanueva (ed.), *Concepts. Philosophical Issues* 9: 243-251.

Moya, C. J. 1999. Self-Knowledge and Content Externalism, in J. Nida-Rümelin (ed.), *Rationality, Realism, Revision*, W. de Gruyter, Berlin/New York, 182-187.

Owens, J. 1995. Pierre and the Fundamental Assumption, *Mind and Language* 10: 250-273.

Warfield, T. 1992. Privileged Self-Knowledge and Externalism Are Compatible, *Analysis* 52: 232-237.

Warfield, T. 1995. Knowing the World and Knowing Our Minds, *Philosophy and Phenomenological Research* 55: 525-545.

Woodfield, A. 1982. 'Foreword' to *Thought and Object. Essays on Intentionality*, Clarendon Press, Oxford, v-xi.

9

Basic Self-Knowledge and Externalism[1]

DANIEL QUESADA

1 Introduction

There seems to be a conflict between the knowledge that we have of
many of our mental states and the view that those very mental states are
to be essentially characterized in terms of mind-independent objects and
properties. I will first state this conflict, outlining the standard answer
from the standpoint of defenders of both basic self-knowledge and externalism. I will then argue that there is a problem for the usual characterization of this kind of knowledge, and consider how it fares *vis-a-vis* the
standard answer. It will finally emerge that the problem points both to
the presence of an empirical element in our basic self-knowledge and to
a certain limitation consequent upon it.

---

[1] Research for this paper has been funded by the Spanish Ministry of Education,
through research projects PB94-0717 and PB97-0192, and by the Generalitat of Catalo-
nia, through research project SGR99- 417. I am thankful for criticism and comments
by Tyler Burge, Manuel García-Carpintero, Antoni Gomila, Tobías Grimaltos, Manuel
Liz and Manuel Pérez Otero at the conference (University of Granada 1996) where a
first version of the paper was presented. I thank also Bill Brewer for allowing me to
read unpublished material connected to the topics of this paper.

Meaning, Basic Self-Knowledge and Mind: Essays on Tyler Burge.
María J. Frápolli and Esther Romero (eds.).

2   The conflict and the standard answer

In many cases, we seem to know very well what we think, believe, desire, and fear. It is true also that there appear to be many wishes, beliefs and fears of ours that do not straightforwardly make manifest to us, whether this is due to our inclination to wishful thinking, to limitations in our rational abilities, or to other causes. But there is no doubt that I know that I wished to have a coffee just a few minutes ago, or that I believed the elements for preparing it were in the kitchen, or that I doubt that the coffee in the coffee-pack is pure Arabic, regartheless of what is stated on it, or that I am thinking right now that there is still a long way to go until this paper is finished. Let us follow Burge in calling *basic* self-knowledge to this kind of seemingly unproblematic knowledge that we appear to have about our beliefs, wishes, fears and thoughts.[2]

Now, the seemingly simple claim that we possess this kind of knowledge appears to be in conflict with the thesis that the very *identity* of our mental states depends on objects and properties present in our environment. Indeed, how could it be that we have such an unproblematic and rather extensive knowledge of our mental states—that is, knowledge of *which* are the beliefs, desires and wishes that we have or the thoughts we entertain—when it depends on the environment whether it is *this* or *that* belief, thought, etc., the very belief or thought that we have or entertain?[3] It just seems that this thesis, that implies external-

---

[2] I believe that the term, with this meaning, was first introduced in Burge (1988b), p. 649.

[3] Probably this issue appears in the literature first in Mathews (1988), a comment on Burge (1986). Mathews presents the issue as a candidate argument for individualism. Perhaps this is a good place to remind that, contrary to what is sometimes assumed, *individualism* is not the same as *internalism* (and that, accordingly, their opposites—respectively *anti-individualism* and *externalism*—also do not fully coincide). Indeed, internalism is a view *on intentionality*, that is, a view on *which kind* of objects the intentional objects of mental states are. Instead, individualism is a general view *on the individuation* of mental states, to the effect that their *identity* does not depend on the environment of the subject that has them. Thus, internalism is relatively a more basic issue in the philosophy of mind, while individualism has a rather metaphysical character. The inference from internalism to individualism requires subscribing to a *further* view (however easily may it be endorsed by an adherent to internalism, or indeed, by anybody), to wit: that appeal to intentional objects is required to individuate mental states. Instead, the converse inference (from individualism to internalism) seems not to require any further premise. The last point is most easily seen in the implication of the converse positions. If we accept anti-individualism we accept that, in general, the identity of mental states depends on the environment, and this seems not to be possible without holding that, in some cases at least, intentional objects are objects of the subject's environment, objects that do not depend on him or her for their

ism, just does not accord well with the simple idea that we have basic self-knowledge, since it seems that this knowledge is completely unproblematic in a way in which knowledge that somehow involves the environment cannot possible be.

Now, which the conflict exactly is depends on how we determine what I have been, to this point, deliberately vaguely describing as the "unproblematic character" of basic self-knowledge. Thus, to illustrate, in one authoritative formulation:

> Our problem is that of understanding how we can know some of our mental events in a direct, nonempirical manner, when those events depend for their identities on our relation to the environment. A person need not investigate the environment to know what his thoughts are. A person does have to investigate the environment to know what the environment is like. Does this not indicate that the mental events are what they are independently of the environment? (Burge 1988b, p. 650)

Here, basic self-knowledge is described as "direct" and "nonempirical", and the problem appears then to be that it would seem that we cannot have "direct" or "nonempirical" knowledge of anything at all that depends for its identity on the environment.

It is important that we notice that in this text *two different features* are used to qualify basic self-knowledge. It just might be that the conflict takes a different character with the different features that are putatively attributed to basic self-knowledge. That is, we must be fully aware that the conflict is one between proclaiming that we have a kind of self-knowledge with a certain feature, say *F,* on the one hand, and the fact that the very beliefs (or other mental states) about which we have such knowledge are said to have environment-dependent contents, on the other. For there are just three possible resolutions of the conflict: either, first, appearances notwithstanding we do not have such a kind of knowledge (self-knowledge with feature *F*); or, second, we have such a knowledge and externalism is false; or, finally, it turns out, on closer inspection, that there is no such a conflict. And—the point is—*which* of the three possibilities is defensible may vary for different *F*'s.

Now, is there really a conflict, when *F* is the property of *being direct*? That is, is there a conflict between the fact that our basic self-knowledge is *direct*, with anti-individualism or externalism? We will

---

existence, or, in other words, objective things. Thus, anti-individualism implies, without further ado, anti-internalism, that is, externalism. Now, these qualifications made, in view of the close relationships disclosed between anti-individualism and externalism, on the one hand, and their respective opposites, individualism and internalism, on the other, I will abide by the usual practice, and talk as if they were, respectively, identical theoretical views.

consider this question on the first place. To begin with, it is perhaps not altogether clear what 'direct' should mean in this context, but let us take it, for the sake of the argument, to mean 'without inference'—as I think it is indeed most reasonable to do.

To resolve this issue, we must find whether the kind of self-knowledge we are concerned with is non-inferential, and for this, we must first examine in close detail what this self-knowledge consists in. As it turns out, there are at least four kinds of cases in which it is correct to claim (basic) knowledge of one's own states.[4] The first kind consists of cases where the subject makes judgements whose content refer reflexively to those judgements themselves, like in (1) and (2):

(1) I judge, herewith, that there are physical entities.

(2) I am thinking (right now, herewith) that there are physical entities.

Certainly, we do not arrive to the content of these reflexive, second order judgments, by inference from first order judgements or thoughts. But neither seems there to be any conflict with the externalist view of content. I quote Burge on this point:

> Suppose that I think that I am engaging in a thought that there are physical objects. In thinking this, I have to engage in the very thought I am referring to and ascribing to myself. The reference to the content—expressed en the that-clause—cannot be carried out unless I actually engage in the thought. The intentional content mentioned in the that-clause is not merely an object of reference or cognition; it is part of the cognition itself. It is thought and thought about in the same act. *If background conditions are different enough so that I am thinking different thoughts, they will be different enough so that the objects of reference and self-ascription will also be different.* So no matter how my thoughts are affected, no matter how I am switched around, I will be correct in self-ascriptions of content that are correctly expressed in cogito-that-clause form. (Burge 1996, p. 96; my emphasis.)

The fact is then, that there must be, for the second-order thoughts or judgements to be produced at all, a "level-linking" that makes the following kind of counterfactuals true: Had the environment fulfilled conditions C, so that the content of the subject's first-order thoughts were different to the one that actually obtains, then her second-order thoughts and judgements (of Kind 0) would correspondingly have had a different content. The reason for the claim just made is that in such reflexive

---

[4] This taxonomy is worked out in Peacocke (1996), pp. 118-122, who belabors also the resolution of the conflict at issue for the cases not explicitly considered by Burge (who concentrated largely on *Kind 0* cases—see below).

judgements the same intentional content "is thought and thought about in the same act".

But, as anticipated, self-ascriptions of Kind 0 ("cogito-like reflexive judgements") are by no means the only kind of self-ascriptions that constitute basic self-knowledge. A further kind—*Kind 1*—comprises self-ascriptions made on the basis of memory, when we do take at face value what memory tells us. So, suppose somebody asks you who was the last muslim king of Granada, and then the name 'Boabdil' comes to your mind delivered, so to speak, by your memory, and suppose further that you think you can rely on your memory in this particular affair. Suppose further that you report what you believe in the following way:

(3) I believe that Boabdil was the last of the muslim kings of Granada.

As indicated, the example is supposed to work in such a way that your utterance of (3) is not to be interpreted as if you were giving voice to any hesitation on your part, but rather as a safe self-ascription of belief. In this kind of case, in which you report on your beliefs relying on memory, we find again reason—even if a different reason—to say that the content of the concepts in the self-ascription is the same as the content of the concepts in the belief so ascribed, precisely because it is a *report* what is at issue. In the report, the very concepts that constitute the belief are re-used or "redeployed". So that, we find again here necessarily—albeit for a different reason—that kind of level-linking that makes the kind of counterfactuals mentioned in connection with Kind 0 cases true. But appeal to memory is simply not inference; and thus, again, self-ascription is achieved in a direct—non-inferential—way.

Although I will spare the details, there is still reason to recognize the same level-link, and to claim also the truth of the corresponding counterfactuals in the remaining two kinds of cases. *Kind 2* cases are self-ascriptions arrived in a "just like that" way, so to speak, that is, without a conscious intermediate state of recollecting, but there is otherwise in them nothing essentially new that would require us to change the verdict we applied to the previous case. Finally, *Kind 3* comprises cases in which the self-ascription is at the same time the expression of a decision, or in which one works out the answer to the question whether one believes that p by working out the answer to the question whether p. Again, the corresponding self-ascriptions are arrived at without inference and we find reason to sustain the level-link and the counterfactuals (see Peacocke 1996, pp. 121-122 for details).

Thus, in all the cases considered, we proceed to self-ascribe thoughts and beliefs to ourselves without the need of inference of any

192 / DANIEL QUESADA

kind. And, if we accept—as I think we should—that we do have justification for those self-ascriptions,[5] we find that we have knowledge—indeed, self-knowledge—arrived at without inference. On the other hand, because of the fact that in issuing such self-ascriptions we basically re-use the concepts that make up the content of the belief, second-order beliefs or judgements coincide *so* in content with the first-order beliefs or other mental states self-ascribed *that* the content of self-ascriptions preserves whatever connection with the environment the first-order states might have. In this way, we reach an account of how the direct, non-inferential character of basic self-knowledge does not conflict with the environment-dependency of content.

3 The importance of understanding

So far, so good. But still, we should not be blamed if a feeling of insatisfaction remains. According to what it has been told so far, it would appear that there is no conflict whatsoever between basic self-knowledge and externalism, only because the self-ascribing beliefs that constitute such knowledge are, so to speak, *immunized* against changes in the environment. A change in the environment, even if it would perhaps alter the *content* of those beliefs, would not in any case affect their *truth*. Is this not a rather peculiar kind of dependency on the environment?

To see where the catch lies, it is convenient to turn to self-ascriptions with a demonstrative content, where the beliefs putatively self-ascribed are perceptual beliefs. Let us consider then a reflective Macbeth who reasons in the following way:

(A1) I believe that *that dagger* (in front of me) is blood-dirty.

(A2) If x believes that *that dagger* (in front of him) is blood-dirty, then the environment of *x* contains *that dagger* (the dagger in front of him).

(A3) My environment contains *that dagger* (the dagger in front of me).

Thus reflecting, Macbeth has arrived, it seems, validly to a false conclusion. Then, the premises cannot both be true. But the externalist cannot deny (A2); so, she must deny (A1). But, how can she? Does (A1) not express the very kind of self-ascription that we have found rea-

---

[5] I think that Burge and Peacock are right in that we are justified in our self-ascriptions of the kinds at issue, or "epistemically entitled" to them, or "epistemically warranted" to make them, as Burge says to emphasize that we need here a wider notion of justification.

son to say any subject can make without inference? Are we to deny that the reflective Macbeth has a belief that he is self-ascribing to him? Yes, it appears that we *must* do this.[6]

The fact is that the certification of self-ascriptions comes with a proviso about which I have so far been silent. Here is how Burge puts it:

> ... to self-ascribe thoughts in the way expressed by that-clauses, one has to understand the thoughts one is referring to well enough to think them (...) one *is* guaranteed that one ascribes something of which one has the ordinary understanding involved in using concepts and thinking thoughts. (Burge 1996, p. 96)

Although it is not logically implied by what Burge says in the second sentence of this text, the suggestion is that one *does not* ascribe something of which one lacks "ordinary understanding". I think this claim is unexceptionable.[7] Thus, *the truth of a (basic) self-ascription requires the (ordinary) understanding of the content of the that-clause in the self-ascription.* This will prove to be the crucial first step in removing the uneasiness that we felt above, which was caused by the apparent immunity of basic self-ascriptions.

We must now inquire on what this *understanding-requirement* amounts to, both in general and as applied to the case at hand. I should think that it is easy to agree in that, for understanding a content, what is minimally required from a subject is that he or she possesses the concepts that built up that content. Further, the externalist should accept that, for empirical concepts, possession of them involves their application to things in the environment. This, I think, does not necessarily require that the subject herself is able to apply them effectively to things in the environment, because there are empirical concepts for which she can delegate this task to experts, but she should at least be in a position to *know* that the concepts apply to objects in the environment, and, moreover, for many concepts—as for concepts of the properties that are manifest to the subject—she must be in a position to apply them knowledgeably to objects in the environment.

I will not argue here for the last claim, since I think it is widely accepted by externalists (see, e. gr. Peacocke 1992, pp. 7 and 108), and

---

[6] Notice that we may very well feel inclined to argue here from (¬A3) and (A2) to the conclusion (¬A1). Certainly, our reflective Macbeth would not be en a position to assert (¬A3), but this is what we know is true of him in the situation imagined. For more on this kind of arguing, see below.

[7] There is no doubt that this is fully endorsed by Burge. See his former (1988b) paper, where, in each example considered he insists that "the ability to think" the thought is a prerequisite for self-ascription (cf. pp. 654, 656, 661 and note 9 in that paper).

we are precisely investigating possible conflicts of externalism with basic self-knowledge. But I think that exactly the same applies to the case of *perceptual-demonstrative concepts* like *that dagger*. Possessing this concept, I suggest, involves the ability to use it to apply *to a particular dagger*, and indeed, to be in a position to know that a particular dagger is present. If this is true, then, our reflective Macbeth does not possess the demonstrative concept required for the ordinary understanding of the thought he would express as 'That dagger is blood-dirty'. And then, according to the understanding-requirement, he is barred to make a true self-ascription in the imagined situation; thus, (A1) is false.

The crucial premise in this argument is, of course, that possessing a perceptual-demonstrative concept requires the ability to apply it to a particular object (or to a particular object of a certain kind, when the demonstrative is "impure", as, indeed, the one expressed by 'this dagger' turns out to be), and, moreover, to be in a position to know that that particular object is present. It will suffice to argue for the first part of this claim, since it should be sufficient to establish lack of ordinary understanding in the case at hand.

My argument for this premise is, in outline, as follows. First, I take into account the fact that the claim that there are such things as perceptual-demonstrative concepts could be rejected by those "direct-reference theorists" of the Millian variety who would perhaps simply deny that a demonstrative clause like 'that dagger' expresses any concept (over and above, that is, the general concept expressed by 'dagger').[8] Against this, I simply appeal to the work of Evans and others, as having established that there is no such a thing as reference to an individual without some kind of mode of presentation—more precisely, a *singular* mode of presentation—of the individual at issue, and, moreover, that this includes thoughts expressed with the help of demonstratives (see especially Evans 1982, ch. 6). Perceptual-demonstrative concepts are then just the modes of presentation of objects in thoughts expressible in singular statements in which demonstrative expressions occur that refer to such objects. Once it is accepted that 'that dagger' can express a perceptual-demonstrative concept, we only need to remark that it is indeed a *singular* concept which is at issue, and so, that this concept is empty if it does not refer to anything. I think that denying this amounts simply to falling in a pretty straightforward form of internalism. Literally then, someone who undergoes some sort of mental activity which he could be inclined to express by saying 'that dagger is blood-dirty', as a singular

---

[8] Burge (1977) is a very good representative of the view that the relation between thought and individual objects is fundamentally non-conceptual.

statement, has *attempted* a thought, but has failed to engage in one at all, when the putative object is lacking.[9]

If this is correct, then only a person that perceives the relevant kind of object can engage in a thought of the relevant kind. That is, if Macbeth would not have been hallucinating a dagger, he would have expressed a truth, had he uttered (A1). As it supposedly happened, his self-ascription was false. What this means is that *it is not true, after all, that the truth of a self-ascription is immune to (radical) changes in the environment*; changes in the environment do not change the truth-value of a self-ascription *only when they are not radical enough to affect decisively the understanding of the thought self-ascribed.*

This, I think, is a conclusion fully generally valid. Examples involving perceptual demonstratives play only a helpful role in confronting us vividly—namely, through the unacceptable consequences (viz. (A3)) of certain self-ascription claims—with the need to complete the standard resolution of the conflict between externalism and basic self-knowledge as this resolution was presented in the previous section.

These considerations make it more urgent to stress a necessary qualification in the claim, sometimes made, that we are *infallible* in claims of self-knowledge. We are indeed infallible for those claims that concern thoughts that we understand; but because, as argued, basic understanding has, after all, a non-negligible dependence on the environment, we simply do not have an unrestricted infallibility.

In the last section, we turn to examine the alleged conflict between the *non-empirical* character of our basic self-knowledge and externalism.

4   Basic self-knowledge and the empirical

Locating the, so to speak, "recognizable effects" of the environment on basic self-knowledge in the *understanding* of the mental states self-ascribed, is also the key to dispel the puzzlement that inferences of the following kind initially are prone to provoke in us.[10]

---

[9] See Evans (1982), chapter 1, especially § 1.7, and also McDowell (1986), e. gr. pp. 142 and 156. Both, Evans and McDowell attribute this position to Frege himself, but I share with many the opinion that their view on this point is misguided.

[10] Similar inferences are used in Davies (1997) and Boghossian (1989, 1997) to discuss the putative conflict between externalism and basic self-knowledge. While Boghossian's discussion is more in the spirit of pressing problems *for externalism* (not for any kind of characterization of basic self-knowledge), Davis's is rather in the opposite spirit of finding the way out. As it will be seen, there seems to be no need of a principle like Davis's "Second Limitation Principle" to pull externalism out of this hole. The line here adopted follows the lead of Bill Brewer's reply to an earlier version of Davies

(B1) I believe that there are physical entities.

(B2) (For any *x*) if *x* believes that there are physical entities, then there are physical entities in *x*'s environment.

(B3) There are physical entities in my environment.

It seems that, if we are justified in asserting (B1), then, granted the externalist claim (B2), we are justified in asserting (B3). Now, accepting that any of us is justified in asserting (B1), we should inquire about the nature of this justification. It certainly seems that we do not need empirical evidence to claim (B1) justifiably. But then, assuming that the arguments for externalism are also non-empirical, it would turn out, it seems, that the justification for (B3) is fully non-empirical. Generalizing then, we would have, it seems, non-empirical justification for existence assertions to the effect that there are physical entities in our environment, and so that there is water, mercury or whatever. This just does not seem right. But then, it would seem as if an externalist would be forced to accept that we arrive at claims of type (B1) using *empirical* evidence.

In fact, the externalist is not so forced. Remember that a subject can have a *belief* about physical objects (or whatever) only if she is able to understand this belief, and that, in the case in which the belief is indeed about a physical object, this requires her *possession of the concept of a physical object*. And the externalist is only consequent when she claims that possession of the concept of a physical object requires that the subject is in a position to apply the concept to physical objects, for which in turn she must have *empirical information or evidence* about physical objects. Thus, in short, if it is true that the subject believes that there are physical objects in the environment, this can only be because she has empirical evidence about there being physical objects in the environment.

It follows from this that the inference from (B1) and (B2) to (B3) cannot be used to *establish* the existence of physical objects in anybody's environment, since the subject must already have empirical evidence for (B3)—that is, for the very existence of physical objects in the environment—in order even to *understand* the belief self-ascribed in the premise (B1).

---

paper at the 1996 meeting of the European Society for Philosophy and Psychology (Barcelona).

It does *not* follow from this, however, that we need empirical evidence *to justify a claim like (B1)*. The reason is that empirical evidence can figure in the process of coming to understand a belief-content without that evidence entering in the epistemic justification for believing this content (cf. Burge 1996 p. 94).

As Burge has repeatedly stressed, basic self-knowledge has a rather special character. It has been claimed (by Burge and others) that what is special about it is that it is *direct (non-inferential), non-empirical* and *infallible*. What we have found (following Burge and Peacocke) is that, because of the mechanism of "redeployment", that knowledge is indeed *direct*, but that this aspect of the matter by no means puts in jeopardy anti-individualism or externalism about mental states. Further, we have been reassured in accepting the *non-empirical* character of the justification for the beliefs that constitute such basic self-knowledge, by showing the fallacy in an argument that threatened it, and dispelling also the appearance of a conflict between the a-priority claim and externalism or anti-individualism. But finally, we have found that we should qualify the claim that basic self-knowledge has the third property mentioned above (*infallibility*). However, when we look at the reason for this, we understand both the essential compatibility of the special character of basic self-knowledge and the limits of this compatibility, since we come then to recognize wherein the dependency on the environment makes itself manifest.

References

Boghossian, P. 1989. Content and Self-Knowledge, *Philosophical Topics*, 17: 5-26.

Boghossian, P. 1997. What the Externalist Can Know A Priori, *Proceedings of the Aristotelian Society*, 97: 161-175.

Burge, T. 1977. Belief *De Re*, *Journal of Philosophy* 74: 338-362.

Burge, T. 1986: Cartesian Error and the Objectivity of Perception, in McDowell, J. and Pettit, P. (eds.), *Subject, Thought and Context*, Oxford: Oxford University Press. Also in Grimm, R.H. and Merrill, D.D. (eds.), *Contents of Thought*, Tucson: Arizona University Press, 1988.

Burge, T. 1988a. Reply: Authoritative Self-Knowledge and Perceptual Individualism, in Grimm, R.H. and Merrill, D.D. (eds.), *op. cit.*

Burge, T. 1988b. Individualism and Self-knowledge, *Journal of Philosophy*, 85: 649-663.

Burge, T. 1996. Our Entitlement to Self-Knowledge, *Proceedings of the Aristotelian Society*, 96: 91-116.

Davies, M. 1997. Externalism, Architecturalism and Epistemic Warrant, in Wright, C.J.G., Smith, B.C. and Macdonald, C. (eds.), *Knowing Our Own Minds: Essays on Self-Knowledge*, Oxford: Oxford University Press.

Evans, G. 1982. *The Varieties of Reference*, Oxford: Clarendon Press.

Matthews, R. J. 1988. Comments to T. Burge's 'Cartesian Error and the Objectivity of Perception', in Grimm, R.H. and Merrill, D.D. (eds.), *op. cit.*

McDowell, 1986. Singular Thought and the Extent of Inner Space, in McDowell, J. and Pettit, P. (eds.), *op. cit.*

Peacocke, C. 1992. *A Study of Concepts*, Cambridge, Mass.: MIT Press.

Peacocke, C. 1996. Entitlement, Self-Knowledge and Conceptual Redeployment, *Proceedings of the Aristotelian Society*, 96: 117-158.

10

Intentional States: Individuation, Explanation, and Supervenience

MANUEL LIZ

1 Individuation, explanation and supervenience

The philosophy of mind of the last years has overestimated the importance of anti-individualism. The topic of supervenience is one of the clearest examples where this has been so (other one would be self-knowledge). The recent philosophy of mind has exaggerated the consequences that a non-individualistic individuation and a non-individualistic explanation of intentional mental states can have in relation to their individualistic supervenience.

In a certain sense, the individualistic supervenience of the intentional is a very trivial thesis. It says only that something non-intentional must happen inside our bodies when we are thinking, and that different things must happen inside our bodies when we have different thoughts. In other words, there must be a function from (tokens of) intentional phenomena to (tokens of) non-intentional states inside our bodies, and that such a function cannot be "from-many-to-one". However, it is important to preserve the individualistic supervenience of the intentional even in that trivial sense. It may be that the claim of a supervenience of intentional states over certain non-intentional states of the individual's

Meaning, Basic Self-Knowledge and Mind: Essays on Tyler Burge.
María J. Frápolli and Esther Romero (eds.).
Copyright © 2003, CSLI Publications.

body offers no help in order to identify the intentional states we can attribute to the subject. And it may be that in order to explain them, for instance, by means of appropriate causal types, we always have to make reference to conditions of the individual's physical or social environments. Nevertheless, we need to preserve the individualistic supervenience of the intentional if we do not want our minds to become "pure mirrors" of our current environmental conditions, pure mirrors unable to record any internal trace and also unable to make any contribution on their own part.

Individuation, explanation, and supervenience are related in many ways. But they involve very different strategies to conceptualize and see reality. Furthermore, the epistemic achievements that can be obtained through these different ways to deal with any object may be not completely overlapping. In fact, we rarely have a perfect convergence among what is obtained through individuation, explanation and supervenience claims. This is particularly so in the case of special sciences like psychology. Very often this is not taken into account in the philosophical discussions about individualism. It is common to assume that a rejection of individualism concerning the individuation or the explanation of intentional states entails, more or less immediately, the failure of their individualistic supervenience.

1.1 A Doubtful Piece of Reasoning

To beging with, let us consider more closely the following piece of reasoning:

> (R) The intentional states of a subject cannot be individualistically supervenient on her non-intentional history because neither their individuation nor an adequate explanation of those intentional states can be individualistic.

This is just the kind of inference, which seems deeply doubtful. We shall try to show that very obvious remarks and distinctions concerning the individuation, explanation, and supervenience of intentional states can make clear the reasons why (R) cannot be a conclusive argument. We will argue that the conclusion of (R) does not conceptually follow from its premises. In other words, the non-individualistic supervenience of intentional states cannot be grounded in deductive reasons coming from their non-individualistic individuation or from their non-individualistic explanation.

More importantly, we will also argue that the non-individualistic supervenience of the intentional states cannot be grounded either in non-deductive reasons having to do with those premises. Even if the individuation and the explanation of intentional states is in fact non-individualistic, the ways in which these individuations and these explanations have to be made involve important individualistic compromises. And these compromises are able to make plausible, or at least are compatible with, the individualistic supervenience of the intentional states.

Usually, Burge's anti-individualistic arguments are interpreted as giving support to (R). The points we will make would count against such interpretations of Burge's anti-individualism, and they would suggest a serious reconsideration of its scope and significance.

1.2 The Conceptual Relationships Among Individuation, Explanation, and Supervenience

The individuation of intentional states has to do with the way tokens of intentional states are taken to be of the same or different types. This involves procedures to identify or determine whether or not a subject is in an intentional state of a certain kind. Individualism about the individuation of intentional states would maintain that these procedures never take into consideration anything outside the subject's limits. In Burge (1986:4), for instance, we can read the following characterization:

1) Individualistic Individuation
"According to individualism about the mind, the mental natures of all a person's or animal's mental states (and events) are such that there is no necessary or deep individuative relation between the individual's being in states of those kinds and the nature of the individual's physical or social environments"

Burge (1986:4) also distinguishes two other individualistic doctrines. We may call them, respectively, "individualistic explanation" and "individualistic supervenience". In Burge's own words:

2) Individualistic Explanation
"... an individual's being in any given intentional state (or being the subject of such an event) can be *explicated* by reference to states and events of the individual that are specifiable without using intentional vocabulary and without presupposing anything about the individual subject's social or physical environments."

3) Individualistic Supervenience
"... an individual's intentional states and events (types and tokens) could not be different from what they are, given the individual's physical, chemical, neural, or functional histories, where these histories are speci-

fied non-intentionally and in a way that is independent of physical or so-cial conditions outside the individual's body."

It is very important to differentiate with precision these three doctrines. Burge says that individualistic supervenience is entailed by individualistic explanation. We think that he is right. If it were possible for some intentional states to differ without any difference in the individualistic histories of the subjects, we could not have an individualistic explanation of those intentional states. Moreover, one of the best reasons to maintain the individualistic supervenience of the intentional would be the possibility of explaining it in an individualistic way. However, the entailment only goes in that direction. The third doctrine is weaker than the second one, and it cannot entail it. The second doctrine, i.e., individualistic explanation, emphasizes the explanatory dispensability of the environmental conditions. But the third doctrine, i.e., individualistic supervenience, does not mention anything about explanation. It simply makes a, let us say, local claim about what has to happen in the individualistic histories of the subjects when there are changes in their intentional lives.

There are many sorts of explanations and many sorts of explanatory interests. But, in any case, explanation is much more demanding than supervenience. And the individualistic explanation of the intentional phenomena also is much more demanding than their individualistic supervenience. With regard to any intentional phenomenon, one could maintain an individualistic supervenience thesis without being able to offer any individualistic explanation in the sense expressed by the second doctrine. Differences in the intentional states of the subjects could be taken as necessarily entailing differences in their non-intentional individualistic histories without these histories being able to offer any sufficient basis for an individualistic explanation of those intentional states.

Turning now to individuation, it is also clear that individualistic supervenience is entailed by individualistic individuation. If the individuation of intentional states is individualistic, then differences in the intentional states of a subject have to entail discernible differences inside her body and, hence, they have to entail individualistic differences. Again, one of the best reasons to maintain an individualistic supervenience of the intentional would be the possibility of individuating it in an individualistic way[1]. But, just as before, this entailment only goes in

---

[1] According to the above notions of individualistic individuation and individualistic supervenience, it is not so clear if we admit that a "purely intentional individualistic

one direction. Individualistic supervenience is weaker than individualistic individuation and cannot entail it.

Like explanation, individuation is much more demanding than supervenience. And the individualistic individuation of the intentional phenomena also is much more demanding than their individualistic supervenience. With respect to any intentional phenomenon, one could have reasons to maintain an individualistic supervenience without having any individualistic procedure able to determine whether or not the subject is in an intentional state of a certain kind. Differences in the intentional states of the subjects could be taken as necessarily entailing differences in their non-intentional individualistic histories without these histories being able to offer any available basis for an individualistic individuation of those intentional states.

Now, what about the relationships between individualistic individuation and individualistic explanation? To explain something in an individualistic way certainly entails being able to individuate it also in an individualistic way. If the explanation of intentional states does not presuppose anything about the subject's social or physical environments, then the individuation of these intentional states can be made without reference to anything outside the subject's limits. However, being able to individuate something does not entail the availability of explanations. Explanation requires much more than merely determining or identifying whether or not the subject is in an intentional state of a certain kind. Hence, even if individualistic explanation entails individualistic individuation, the converse does not hold.

It is time to go back to (R). Our previous analyses may help us to see clearly why (R) is not a conclusive argument. The relationships of conceptual entailment among individualistic individuation, individualistic explanation and individualistic supervenience would be restricted to what is shown in the following figure:

---

individuation" of intentional states can make sense (let us think of telepathy, for instance). Individualistic individuation entails individualistic supervenience only if individualistic individuation is made with reference to the individualistic histories of the subjects non-intentionally specified. In what follows, we will have in mind only the last kind of non-intentional individualistic individuation.

Individualistic Individuation

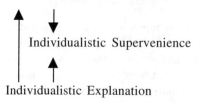

Individualistic Supervenience

Individualistic Explanation

As a general rule, to have the individualistic individuation of something entails its individualistic supervenience. And to have individualistic explanations of something also entails to have both its individualistic supervenience and the possibility to individuate it in an individualistic way. However, as we have said, the converses do not hold. Individuation, explanation, and supervenience claims call for different things. And this is the reason why (R) cannot be a conclusive argument. There is no argument against individualistic supervenience that can be grounded in deductive reasons coming either from non-individualistic explanation or from non-individualistic individuation. To think that there is such an argument would be fallacious.

So far, if this were correct, we would have very strong reasons to question the force of (R). Argument (R) cannot be conclusive. However, there would be another very important way to defend (R). The point is that argument (R) could have another different kind of argumentative force. One might say that (R) would not have to be taken as a deductive argument but only as an argument offering some sound reasons to reject individualistic supervenience. Under this interpretation of (R), the non-individualistic explanation or the non-individualistic individuation of intentional states could lead to their non-individualistic supervenience in a non-deductive sense.

In what follows, we are going to inquire whether this is so. We are going to assess whether the premises of (R) can have enough non-deductive force to put in doubt the individualistic supervenience of intentional states. Are the non-individualistic individuations and the non-individualistic explanations of the intentional states of a subject really made in such a way that they suggest the rejection of their individualistic supervenience? This will be our question. We will argue that they are not. The next two sections will try to show that the non-individualistic individuations and the non-individualistic explanations of the intentional states really involve substantial individualistic compromises able to make plausible, or at least able to be compatible with, their individualistic supervenience.

2 The long trip towards the individuation of the intentional states

First, let us concentrate on individuation. The individuation of intentional states is typically made through the truth of some peculiar sentences involving that-clauses, sentences like "She believes that she has arthritis in her thighs", "She desires that London is pretty", and so on. And the contents of the intentional states in question are intended to be described by those that-clauses.

Burge's anti-individualistic position with respect to individuation could be summarized as follows. The non-intentional individualistic histories of the subjects remaining constant, changes in the references of the terms embedded in the ascribed that-clauses entail changes in their meanings; these changes of meaning entail changes in the mental contents attributed and, finally, these changes in the mental contents attributed entail changes in the intentional states themselves. The conclusion is that the individuation of the intentional states would not be individualistic. It would not be individualistic because the individuation of the referential part of the oblique occurrences of the terms embedded in the that-clauses we employ to describe their contents would not be individualistic either.[2]

Through this long trip we have left aside many small details. Nonetheless, the accumulation of so many small details can become very important in order to put in doubt the lack of individualistic compromises in our individuatory procedures for intentional states. We have two crucial steps. The first one goes from the references of some oblique occurrences of the terms embedded in that-clauses to mental contents. The claim is that different references in these terms always entail different mental contents. The other step goes from the attributed mental contents to the intentional states themselves. And the claim is that different attributed mental contents always entail different intentional states. However, none of these two steps is easy to take.

2.1 From meanings to mental contents: the inertia of content

With respect to the first step, there are many cases where we cannot go simply from differences in the references of the terms embedded in certain that-clauses to the attribution of different mental contents. There is an important sense in which mental contents have to have a stronger inertial character than the literal meanings socially available to de-

---

[2] This line of argumentation with respect to individuation is made explicit, for instance, in Burge (1979) and Burge (1986).

scribe those mental contents. The sense in question has to do with the normative value the subjects have in many situations as reliable sources of information about themselves and the world. A variation of Burge's well known case about arthritis will serve us to illustrate that sense, and to show that we would have to be very cautious in that first step from meanings to mental contents.[3]

Suppose that I sincerely say "I have recurrent painful arthritis in my thigh". Let us assume that I know that arthritis has certain characteristic features a, b, and c, but that I do not know other features of arthritis, for instance that it cannot occur outside of joints. Having a, b, and c enough weight to make my thoughts be about arthritis, it could be said that I am wrong in what I am saying. My discrimination of my recurrent pain in the thigh as a case of arthritis are wrong. My experience is wrongly categorized as a case of arthritis. But it is categorized as arthritis. And even if I do not know that arthritis cannot occur outside of joints, there would be many circumstances in which I could have the true belief that I have arthritis! Now, imagine the following situation. My linguistic environment changes and the word "arthritis" acquires a new meaning. In the new environment, the word "arthritis" refers to a disease that having features a, b, and c, among others, can also occur in the thighs. Being things as such, let us explore the point of view of a good doctor who knows, in the new situation, what arthritis really is, and who does not dispose of any other means to identify my disease but through my honest reports. What would the doctor have to conclude when I sincerely say, "I have recurrent painful arthritis in my thigh"?

It would seem to be a very bad clinical policy for such a doctor to immediately conclude from what I sincerely say that I have a tendency to suffer arthritis in my thigh and to initiate a preventive treatment. For even if, in fact, my experiences was a case of arthritis such as that disease is now conceived, a good doctor would have to be very cautious and not to take my description in a literal sense. A good doctor cannot merely rely on literal meanings, on the social meanings that are available in her linguistic community. She has to discover how my experience is understood. For one reason: my experience could have been wrongly categorized in relation to some other meaning, and it could be only a mere coincidence that my recurrent pain in the thigh was in fact a case of arthritis such as that disease is now conceived.

---

[3] We will assume the commonplace view that differences in the reference of the terms embedded in that-clauses entail differences of meaning. And that the hard problems come with the projection of these meanings into the intentional states of the subjects as being their contents.

In order to state this point with precision, let us introduce a bit of notation:

A: I honestly say, "I have recurrent painful arthritis in my thigh".

B: I have recurrent painful arthritis-2 (The disease called "arthritis" in the new situation).

C: I have learned to use the word "arthritis" in an environment where "arthritis" means arthritis-1 (The disease called "arthritis" in the old situation).

D: I have learned to use the word "arthritis" in an environment where "arthritis" means arthritis-2.

In order to exclude mere casual coincidences in the diagnosis of my disease, it seems that a good doctor would have to interpret my reports assuming the truth of the following correlation between conditional probabilities:

Prob(B/A,D)>Prob(B/A,C).

A good doctor would have to consider my report reliable, and my discrimination of pain in my thigh as a reliable one, only under the supposition that I have learned to use the word "arthritis" in an environment where "arthritis" means arthritis-2 and not arthritis-1. In other words, even if, in fact, I have arthritis-2, if I have learned to use the word "arthritis" in an environment where "arthritis" means arthritis-1, then it could be only a mere coincidence that my honest report "I have recurrent painful arthritis in my thigh" interpreted according to the new meaning gives the doctor the right information about my recurrent pain in the thigh.

The assumptions behind this model for the reliability of a sincere report would be:

1) That when a subject learns to use a word like "arthritis" in a certain environment, he has to display a greater relevant number of successes than errors in the use of that word in that environment,

2) that the specific environment in which the subject has learned to use the word "arthritis" is perhaps not the same as the environment in which the doctor makes her diagnosis, and

3) that the closer the first environment is to the second one, the more reliable the sincere reports of the subject have to be taken from the perspective of the doctor.

This is the relevant model to adopt when the reliability of my report is important. And from this model, changes in the available literal meanings of certain words would not entail a change in the contents of my thoughts but changes in the individuatory and descriptive tools that would be appropriate to employ in order to individuate my mental contents. When there is a change of meaning because there has been a change of environment, there is certainly a problem of individuation concerning my mental contents. But this problem arises only because communication goes through the social meanings that are available. So, in order to individuate and describe the contents of my thoughts when in the new environment I sincerely say "I have arthritis in my thigh", it would be confusing to employ sentential expressions with the same that-clauses as the ones that should be employed to describe the mental contents of a subject who has learned to use the word "arthritis" in the new environment.

We can generalize the above results saying that the best way to individuate the contents of a subject's thoughts would always consist in trying to follow the strategy of a good doctor: 1) we would have to find out whether the meanings employed in an oblique description of those contents are or are not the meanings which are partially known by the subject, and 2) we would have to mention in the that-clauses only those terms whose meaning could remain constant in spite of the changes made in the physical and social environments of the subject. The important point is that according to this strategy, differences in the available literal meaning of the terms involved in the that-clauses do not lead to differences in the attributed mental contents. Rather, they call for different that-clauses in the description of the contents. We assume for the mental contents some kind of inertial character with respect to environmental changes. Furthermore, we attempt the that-clauses which identify these contents contain only words whose meaning can be taken as remaining constant through those changes.

In any case, that linguistic practice in the attribution of contents through mentalistic idioms would show that it is a mistake not to consider in many cases as fundamental that the partial understanding the subjects have of some words really can be a partial understanding of very different meanings. Suppose, for instance, that arthritis-2 is a disease that has to display some feature d when my thigh is affected by it. And suppose that the doctor is asking me, "Do you know that if you have arthritis in your thigh, then your disease has to display feature d?". Only under the assumption that I have learned to use the word "arthritis" in an environment where "arthritis" means arthritis-2, my partial ignorance about feature d could be surpassed by my general reliability about the possibility that in fact I have arthritis-2 when I say "I have recurrent painful arthritis in my thigh". And a good doctor has to be able to tell when it is justified to make such an assumption.

There are revealing similarities between the way a good doctor would attribute contents in cases as the one we have just discussed and the way we usually individuate the contents of an old text by means of that-clauses. Suppose that in an old text we find the word "arthritis" in a sentence that we can literally translate in English as "She had recurrent painful arthritis in her thigh". Suppose, further, that the meaning of "arthritis" has changed over time and that in our linguistic community that word refers to one specific disease that also can occur in the thigh. Being things as such, we would have to be very cautious. We cannot immediately individuate the content of the sentence in the old text through the description "The text says that she had recurrent painful arthritis in her thigh". Here, literal meanings, i.e. the social meanings that are available in our linguistic community, do not serve to individuate the content of the text. The content of the text has to be obtained applying what we have called the good doctor's strategy. We assume the inertial character of some kind of contents and, if we have reasons to suspect that there have been relevant changes of meaning, we try to obtain those inertial contents. In analogy with this example, we could say that what a good doctor would have to discover in the case above discussed is whether or not I am myself like an "old text".

Now, let us consider another situation where content shows that inertial character. It is a radical one. In this case, the subject is a distinguished epistemic authority in the matters in question. The subject, for instance, knows perfectly what kind of substance aluminum is. When such a subject is involved in a situation of teaching what aluminum is to a numerous group of other subjects, her environmental conditions change. But, we would not say that because her environmental conditions change, the contents of her thoughts are changed too. The aim of the teaching activity is simply to change the environmental situation of ignorance about aluminum. And even though the teaching situation were placed in a "Twin Earth" without any trace of aluminum, and even though the thoughts of the audience could not be at all thoughts about aluminum before the teaching activity, the thoughts of the teacher would be thoughts about aluminum. And her aim would be to change the minds of the audience transmitting those contents through the activity of teaching.

The individuation of mental contents is normative. And the normative reason that in all these cases undermines the step from changes in the available literal meanings to changes in mental content, giving to some contents the sort of inertial character we have stressed, is the attribution of some kind of reliability. Beyond possible changes in their social or physical environmental conditions, we assume that the mental contents and the reports of normal subjects are reliable sources of information about themselves and about the world. Surely, the subjects with the help of terms that they have learned to use but that they do not completely understand have categorized that information. This is what makes them more or less reliable. In any case, what we try to identify and describe through what we have called the good doctor's strategy is just that "understanding". Because we assume that it is only through that "understanding" that we get the intended kind of reliability.[4]

We do not know exactly how far these remarks can affect to the individuation of the contents of all of our intentional states[5]. In any case,

---

[4] At this point, one could ask whether that reliability claim is in fact true. If that claim were true, then "twins" not only would have to constitute rare exceptions in any environment (as, by the way, Fodor has recently maintained—See Fodor, 1995). If they would appear in front of us, we ought not to trust them. No "twin" could be a reliable source of information for us! To be a "twin" is to be a non reliable source of information. And to be a reliable source of information entails not to be a "twin". I have to make clear, however, that even though I would claim myself close to that position, I do not wish to argue for it here. The crucial point of my purpose is that sometimes we attribute contents as if that claim were true. Whenever we apply what we have called the good doctor's strategy, we assume the truth of that reliabilistic claim and we try to act according to probabilistic relations of the kind Prob(B/A,D)>Prob(B/A,C). And when we attribute mental contents this way, changes in the available literal meanings do not directly entail changes in mental content.

[5] Discussing the scope of his anti-individualistic arguments, Burge (1979:IIa) says: "I prefer to leave open precisely how far one can generalize the argument. But I think it has a very wide scope. The argument can get under way in any case where it is intuitively possible to attribute a mental state or event whose content involves a notion that the subject incompletely understands. As will become clear, this possibility is the key to the thought experiment." If I am right, Burge's anti-individualistic thought experiments and arguments based on individuation would need something more. They

when the inertial character of content can be seen as playing a relevant role in the individuation of the mental content of certain intentional state, i.e. when we are interested in obtaining reliable information from the subjects and we follow something like the good doctor's strategy, it is very difficult to reject with respect to those inertial contents certain kinds of individualistic supervenience. The inertial character of content makes it very difficult to reject certain individualistic supervenience in which variations of inertial contents have to entail variations in the individualistic histories of the subjects. The price to pay if we reject such individualistic supervenience for inertial contents is very high. We would lose the opportunity to take the subjects as reliable sources of information about themselves and about the world.

Curiously, we can find in the non-individualistic individuation of mental contents sound reasons for the individualistic supervenience of certain mental contents, sound reasons having to do with reliability. A complete rejection of the individualistic supervenience of the inertial contents of my thoughts would entail to reject that we can imagine many situations in which I am able to be, as individual, a reliable source of information about the world and myself. In fact, however, we can imagine a very wide spectrum of such situations. And that counterfactual force is able to give support to the above kind of individualistic supervenience.

If I am a reliable source of information about myself and the world under some set of inertial contents, then it is plausible to claim the supervenience thesis that these inertial contents could not be different given my non-intentional individualistic story. Those inertial contents have to be seen as something, let us say, "written", in some way or other, in my non-intentional individualistic story. And even though I can be "read" in many other ways, I am a reliable source of information only when I am "read" under that set of inertial contents. In a similar sense, a complete rejection in the case of an old text of the individualistic supervenience of its inertial contents would entail to forget that if we merely attribute literal meanings to its words, we can lose what the text is trying to say us. And, in a similar but extreme sense, to reject in the teaching case that a subject with the same individualistic history as our expert would have to have thoughts about aluminum would entail imagining situations in which the subject is not really the epistemic authority about aluminum that she was supposed to be.

---

would need to discard in the counterfactual situations what we have called the good doctor's strategy as an individuatory procedure.

Let us close this section describing another analogy that will help to make more clear what we are trying to point out. Suppose I want to know the values of some magnitudes in a certain kind of complicated device. In order to do that, suppose that I only have access to information about how the levels of some liquids are distributed in several tubes. Each tube has a set of marks and the liquids go up and down. The individuation of the values of the magnitudes is very indirect. It has to be done through applying some measure system onto these marks. And I use the measure systems available to me. I could use other measure systems. Other subjects in other environments would use other ones. Suppose that there were no agreement among the values obtained through those various procedures, i.e. that we are faced with non-equivalent results. In that situation, the individuatory procedures for the values of the magnitudes in question would have, in fact, a great non-individualistic character. However, there would be a privileged measure system (or better, an equivalent class of measure systems), the measure system used to make the original marks on the tubes. Up to a point, some marks could have been placed in the wrong places. Also, some of them could have been erased, and so on. But that privileged measure system (or the class of measure systems equivalent to it) is the only one that would be able to offer reliable information about the values of the magnitudes in the device. The information obtained with the measure system I am using could be relevant for many practical and theoretical purposes, certainly. And exactly the same could be said of the measure systems used by other subjects. But, if we want to be sure that this relevance is not the result of mere casual coincidences, we will have to follow what was called the good doctor's strategy. The measure system we were looking for through the good doctor's strategy would be the one that, having a strong inertial character over many possible changes in the environmental conditions of individuation, offers the most reliable reading of the values of the magnitudes. And even if, in fact, we do not have one but various non-equivalent measure systems, it is plausible to maintain the individualistic supervenience claim that, with reference to that privileged measure system, different values of the magnitudes would have to entail individualistic differences in the device.

In that sense, the non-individualistic individuation of mental contents could be at least compatible with certain individualist supervenience. If the intentional states of a subject are a reliable source of information about herself and about the world, then there must be certain kind of privileged meanings with which the contents of these intentional states have to be "measured". And those privileged meanings are the meanings that the good doctor's strategy always tries to determine. The subject can make wrong categorizations according to these meanings because she may have only a partial understanding of them. But they are the only meanings that can make her mental contents a reliable source of information. Of course, the good doctor's strategy may be seen as a non-individualistic procedure of individuation. However, the assumed inertia of the contents attributed through that strategy would make it plausible to claim the individualistic supervenience of those contents.

2.2 From mental contents to intentional states: the contribution of attitudes

The step from meanings to mental contents is a great leap full of serious risks and compromises. We have seen how some of these compromises are perfectly compatible with certain individualistic supervenience for mental contents (for those contents having the sort of inertial character we have pointed out). Now, let us examine the other step going this time from mental contents to intentional states. We will find in this step the possibility of important individualistic compromises able to give support to a certain kind of individualistic supervenience for the intentional states themselves.

The non-individualistic move from mental contents to intentional states assumes that different attributed mental contents always entail different intentional states. However, that conclusion only follows under certain assumptions about attitudes. If one adopts a, let us say, superficial conception of attitudes according to which they have to be understood as some sort of mere "boxes" (the "box" of beliefs, the "box" of desires, the "box" of memory, etc.) without any other structure with respect to their contents but the one derived from being the functional places where these contents come to be located, then it is clear that different mental contents immediately entail different intentional states. However, if attitudes are understood in a more structured or complex way, i.e. if we try to give some robust sense to the relational aspect of propositional attitudes, then there could be sound reasons to maintain that differences in content do not have to entail differences in the intentional states necessarily.[6]

---

[6] Curiously, the idea of giving a robust sense to the relational aspect of propositional attitudes may end up leading to a vindication of some sort of "non-relational" analisis of those propositional attitudes. Up to a certain extent, attitudes would have to fuse with their contents. This is exactly what I will suggest. From this point of view,

Let us think of a purely dispositional conception of attitudes according to which to believe that one has arthritis in the thigh, for instance, is to have certain dispositions to act as if it were true that one has arthritis in the thigh. In that case, the dispositions to act as if it were true that one has arthritis in the thigh could become exactly the same as the dispositions to act as if it were true that one has in the thigh the counterpart of arthritis in some appropriate "twin" situation. So, even if from the point of view of their contents both beliefs were to count as different beliefs, from the point of view of the peculiar contribution of the attitude of belief in each case, i.e., from the different bases on which the dispositions to act as if it were true that what is believed are configured, we could be faced with one and the same belief.

Even though we reject that pure dispositional account of attitudes, the moral we can draw from that extreme case is clear. The nonintentional individualistic histories of the subjects remaining constant, not every difference in the contents of our intentional states would have to entail differences in the intentional states themselves. Some of these differences in content could entail differences in the intentional states, but others could also be associated with exactly the same intentional state. It would depend on how the attitudinal parts of the intentional states contribute in each case to configure and structure the intentional states themselves[7]. Hence, even if we are prepared to take the first step from meanings to mental contents, and we accept that changes in the meaning of oblique occurrences of the terms embedded in that-clauses do in fact entail changes in the attributed contents, the second step from different mental contents to different intentional states could be blocked by the contribution of attitudes.

If attitudes are really conceived in that robust way, i.e., as contributing decisively to configure and structure the intentional states themselves, then it becomes possible for different mental contents not to have to entail different intentional states. And the contribution of attitudes become necessary even when different mental contents lead to different intentional states. There would be no situation in which the different mental contents alone can do all the work. From this perspec-

---

the important problem would not be whether or not attitudes and contents are able to maintain structuring relationships, but to what extent and in what ways they do.

[7] The use of ill-defined expressions like "thoughts about aluminum", "arthritis thoughts", "the thought of the individual in the counterfactual environment", etc., tends to make the step from mental contents to intentional states too much simple and direct. The problem we are pointing out arises when we ask what kind of specific thoughts we are speaking about.

tive, the same intentional state could incorporate very different contents. And intentional states could not be different only because their contents are different. Also, there would have to be differences in the ways these contents are related with, and are incorporated into, the subject's attitudes.[8]

Let us systematize the situation with the help of a matrix. In this matrix, S represents "the same mental content", or "the same contribution of the attitude", or "the same resulting intentional state"; and D represents "a different mental content", or "a different contribution of the attitude", or "a different resulting intentional state".

Mental Con- tent	Contribution of the Attitude	Resulting Inten- tional State	Row
S	S	S	1
S	S	D	2
S	D	S	3
S	D	D	4
D	S	S	5
D	S	D	6
D	D	S	7
D	D	D	8

Possibilities in rows 2 and 5 have to be discarded from the start. In 2, there would be no explanation of the fact that we could have different intentional states coming from the same mental content and the same contribution of the attitude. In 5, there would be no explanation of the fact that we could have the same intentional state coming from different mental contents and the same contribution of the attitude.

Of the remaining six possibilities, what we have called a superficial conception of attitudes would only accept the possibilities represented in rows 1 and 6. It is assumed that the same content always has to entail the same resulting intentional state and that different contents always have to entail different resulting intentional states. Here, there is no other available option. The contribution of the attitude has to remain

---

[8] Certain interesting proposals close to that robust conception of attitudes can be found in Chisholm (1981) and Lewis (1983).

constant through any variation of content. In other words, for each attitude, there is one and only one possible contribution.

On the other hand, it is clear that a purely dispositional conception of attitudes would reject the possibility represented in 6. As we have said, there could not be different resulting intentional states only because their contents are different. If the contents are different, the contribution of the attitude has to be different also. With different contents and different contributions of the attitude, we could obtain the same resulting intentional states or different ones. Hence, a purely dispositional conception of attitudes would admit the possibilities expressed in rows 1, 7 and 8. In 7, we would have cases like the one discussed above. Different contents lead to the same intentional state through different contributions of the attitude. The disposition to act as if it were true that one has arthritis in the thigh, for instance, could be just the same as the dispositions to act as if it were true that one has in the thigh the counterpart of arthritis in some appropriate "twin" situation. In 8, we would have cases in which different contents would lead to different intentional states through different contributions of the attitude. For instance, the disposition to act as if it were true that one has arthritis in the thigh would be different that the disposition to act as if it were true that one has a headache.

But, even though we reject such purely dispositional accounts, any robust relational conception of attitudes would have to accept these possibilities. Moreover, together with 1, 7 and 8, it would be also possible to defend the possibilities represented in rows 3 and 4. That is, it would be possible to defend that the same content could lead to the same intentional state through different contributions of the attitude. Also that the same content could lead to different intentional states through different contributions of the attitude.

It is at this point where, even though mental contents were not individualistically supervenient, certain individualistic supervenience for the intentional states themselves appears again to be plausible. There must be certain individualistic supervenience from the perspective of the procedures of individuation that are required to do justice to a robust relational conception of attitudes. For if contents alone cannot differentiate intentional states without a different contribution of the attitudes, and if the attitudinal part of intentional states is individualistically supervenient, as it is reasonable to concede, then the only way different mental contents could entail different intentional states would have to pass through the individualistic physical, chemical, neural, or functional make-up and history of the subject.[9]

3 Making room for individualistic compromises in the explanation of intentional states

The contribution of the attitudinal part of intentional states not only affects their individuation. It not only makes plausible that intentional states (or some intentional states, or some important parts of some intentional states) can be individualistically supervenient even if their contents are not. It also makes plausible the individualistic character of some psychological *explanations* and, in this way, the individualistic character of some supervenience relations. It is presumable that the explanations of the peculiar ways attitudes can contribute to configure and structure the intentional states would have to be full of individualistic compromises. And those individualistic compromises could also give support to certain individualistic supervenience claims.

Consequently, a robust relational conception of attitudes could give support to the individualistic supervenience of intentional states in two ways: through individualistic compromises present in the individuatory procedures required and through individualistic compromises present in the explanatory recourses that it would be appropriate to employ. However, we will not push this point here. The route towards an individualistic supervenience we shall take in this section would appeal directly to individualistic compromises in the non-individualistic explanations of the intentional states that can be offered by a superficial conception of

---

[9] It could be argued that if mental contents and attitudes, in fact, are able to maintain these structuring relationships, then there may be problems with the individualistic supervenience of the inertial contents such as was presented in the previous section. This is true, and it is an important point. However, assuming that mental contents are never isolated in our minds and, hence, that the individualistic supervenience of inertial contents has to entail that we cannot have the same resulting intentional state from different inertial contents, that individualistic supervenience of inertial contents would only be in serious danger if different inertial contents really could collapse into the same resulting intentional state through different contributions of the attitude (row 7 in our matrix). However, it is plausible to argue that the more inertial character have a set of contents for a subject (in other words, the more reliable such subject is under those contents), the less possible such a possibility becomes and the more possible the possibility that different contents yield different resulting intentional states through different contribution of the attitude (i.e., row 8 in our matrix). In any case, with the help of a robust relational conception of attitudes, one could defend the individualistic supervenience of the intentional states without being engaged in the individualistic supervenience of any privileged kind of inertial mental contents.

the attitudes. Therefore, even if what we have called a robust conception of attitudes is rejected, there would be independent reasons, directly based on explanation, for maintaining the individualistic supervenience of intentional states.

Let us begin by noting an important difference concerning psychological explanations. That a subject's being in any given intentional state is explained in a non-individualistic way is one thing; but another very different thing is that these explanations do not presuppose individualistic explanations of the fact that the subject can be in that intentional state so explicated. Here, there is a modal difference in the respective explananda which is crucial. In relation to that difference, what we are going to argue is, first, that complete non-individualistic explanations of the intentional states of a subject really would presuppose individualistic explanations of the subject's capacities to develop a certain distinguishable cognitive life and, second, that these presupposed individualistic explanations would make plausible, or at least are compatible with, the individualistic supervenience of the subject's intentional states.

A direct way to appreciate the importance of the difference between explananda we have just noted is through the following text of Burge (1979:I)

> For *contextually relevant purposes*, we might count a thought that the glass contains some water as "the same thought" as a thought that the glass contains some thirst-quenching liquid, particularly if we have no reason to attribute either content as opposed to the other, and distinctions between them are contextually irrelevant.

> (...)

> We sometimes count distinctions in content irrelevant for purposes of a given attribution, particularly where our evidence for the precise content of a person or animal's attitude is skimpy. Different contents may contextually identify (what amount to) the "same attitude". I have indicated that *even in these contexts*, I think it best, strictly speaking, to construe distinct contents as describing different mental states or events that are merely equivalent for the purposes at hand."

> (...)

> For any distinct contents, there will be imaginable contexts of attribution in which, even in the loosest, most informal ways of speaking, those contents would be said to describe different mental states or events. This is virtually a consequence of the *theoretical role of contents*, discussed earlier.

> (Emphases are added here)

Previously in the same text (i.e., Burge, 1979:I), we can find the following two theoretical reasons to discard those contextually relevant identifications of "the same" attitude and to construe any distinct contents as describing different mental states:

> One reason for doing so is that the person himself is *capable* of having different attitudes described by the different content-clauses, even if these differences are irrelevant in a particular context.

> A second reason is that the counterpart components of the that-clauses allude to *distinguishable elements in people's cognitive lives.*

(Again, emphases are added here)

Now, let us assume the two theoretical reasons offered by Burge. The question we want to ask is the following one: What would we say if we know that some subjects are not capable of having the different attitudes described by different content-clauses, or if we know that some of those contents cannot allude to distinguishable elements of their cognitive lives?

We believe the answer to that question would be straightforward. Simply, let us think about cases of non-standard subjects: Animals, children, psychologically handicapped people, and so on. Here, we could not say that we count two different contents as amounting to the same intentional state merely for contextual or pragmatical purposes. They would have to be counted as amounting to the same intentional state also for theoretical purposes. They have to be counted as the same intentional state from the point of view of certain individualistic explanations and individualistic theories about the psychological capacities and the distinguishable elements of the cognitive lives of such subjects.

The immediate conclusion appears to be that, at least for non-standard subjects, not every imaginable context of attribution would be relevant to describe a different intentional state by means of a different content-clause. There can be contexts of attribution which are very irrelevant, even completely irrelevant. And the relevant contexts of attribution would have to be fixed from an individualistic point of view. In other words, non-individualistic explanations of the subject's being in any given intentional state presuppose individualistic explanations of the capability of the subject to be in such a state.

Moreover, because it is the business of psychology not only to separate standard from non-standard psychological subjects, but also to separate standard from non-standard psychological processes, standard from non-standard psychological states, so on and so on, that first conclusion would lead to a more general one. Without a detailed individualistic explanation of the subject's psychological capacities and of the subject's distinguishable cognitive elements involved in each one of her different intentional states, complete non-individualistic explanations of those intentional states are not possible.

In fact, it may be that such complete explanations of the intentional states always have to remain outside the scope of the explanatory interests of psychology. However, even without these complete explanations, the need to presuppose the existence of all those psychological capacities and distinguishable cognitive elements in the subjects has important consequences with respect to the metaphysical issue of supervenience. It makes plausible the maintenance of the individualistic supervenience claim that the intentional states of a subject could not be different from what they are, given the subject's physical, chemical, neural, or functional make-up and history.

It is worthy of notice that, finally, the two theoretical reasons given by Burge to construe any distinct attributed contents as describing different intentional states are just two reasons able to give support to certain individualistic supervenience claims, for there is no way to make sense of the psychological capacities and the distinguishable cognitive elements mentioned in those reasons without supposing that they have a certain individualistic character.

4 Meanings, causal types, and supervenience *claims*

To summarize: Non-individualistic individuations and non-individualistic explanations of intentional states could force us to reject their individualistic supervenience. This is a true empirical statement. But, as we have seen, it is also true that there is no conceptual entailment between, on the one hand, non-individualistic individuation or non-individualistic explanation and, on the other hand, non-individualistic supervenience. Moreover, we have seen that there are important individualistic compromises both in the non-individualistic individuation of intentional states and in their non-individualistic explanation, and that these individualistic compromises are able to make empirically plausible, or at least are able to be compatible with, some kinds of individualistic superveniences.

If the meanings we use to individuate the contents of our intentional states really were "in our head" or if it were possible to find "in our head" appropriate ingredients to explain our being in such intentional states, for instance, suitable causal types, then the individualistic supervenience of both mental contents and intentional states would hold very easily. What I have tried to show in this paper is that even if those individuative meanings are not "in our head" and even if the appropriate explanatory causal types are not "in our head" either, some kinds of individualistic supervenience theses also could be maintained.

I have argued for three kinds of individualistic supervenience claims. In the first place, I have argued for the individualistic supervenience of certain mental contents: the inertial contents able to preserve the reliability of the intentional states of the subjects as important sources of information about themselves and their environment. Even though our procedures of individuation of mental contents are non-individualistic, to the extent they are sensitive to that reliability, as it happens when we try to apply the good doctor's strategy, there may be individualistic supervenience relations. In the second place, I have argued for the individualistic supervenience of the intentional states in virtue of the contribution of their attitudinal parts to configure and structure them. And this could be argued both in relation to the individuation of intentional states and in relation to the need of individualistic explanations concerning those contributions. In the third place, I have argued that non-individualistic explanations of intentional states also presuppose the existence of psychological capacities and distinguishable cognitive elements, and that this can offer new and independent reasons for the individualistic supervenience of intentional states.

In the paper, I have not discussed the details of a satisfactory formulation of the concept of supervenience, neither the merits of such a concept in order to achieve a better understanding of the notion of determination or dependence[10]. In any case, for my purposes it has been enough to use the following ideas about supervenience:

1) That what we get if the intentional is really individualistically supervenient on the subjects is the minimal but important thesis that there is something in the individualistic histories of the subjects that must change if their intentional life changes,

2) that to state such individualistic supervenience does not necessarily lead to any epistemic achievement of the sort provided by individuation or explanation, and

3) that, nevertheless, it is possible to have empirical reasons able to support the individualistic supervenience of the intentional.

---

[10] For a critical analysis of the notion of supervenience, see Kim (1993) and, more recently, Kim (1998).

Certainly, supervenience claims can be related in many ways with individuation and with explanation. And the convergence among the epistemic achievements that can be obtained through these different perspectives would be very economical and desirable, especially, when these three resorts are individualistic and make reference to causal types. The search for a causal and endogenous identification, explanation, and complete understanding of the systems and of their behavior is present everywhere in our culture[11]. However, our actual epistemic and scientific situation is a very different one. We rarely have a perfect convergence among individuation, explanation and supervenience. In most cases, we want to preserve certain individualistic supervenience, being our individuatory procedures and our explanations neither individualistic nor purely causal, and being, in general, our individuatory procedures even much less individualistic and much less causal than our explanations.

This is a typical situation with respect to the majority of properties mentioned in our special sciences. This is exactly what happens in the case of the intentional. With respect to the intentional we are really in a very pluralistic position. On the one hand, we have individuatory procedures which are neither individualistic nor causal. The individuation of intentional states appears to be unavoidably semantical and, because of that, neither individualistic nor causal. The main way of attributing intentional states to a subject goes through the adscription of ordinary mentalistic sentential expressions containing that-clauses, and through a determination of the meaning of oblique occurrences of the terms embedded in these that-clauses. On the other hand, our best available explanations are causal but non-individualistic. The explanation of the intentional intends to be ultimately causal. But, it is very difficult to see how it could be individualistic. As Burge himself has noted in several places[12], relevant and explanatory causal types in psychology usually involve crucial references to external conditions. Furthermore, there is the relevant fact that, at least for the moment, we do not have any way to arrange and systematize the intentional which is both individualistic and causal. In that context, the supervenience claims we have argued

---

[11] It is not only, for instance, a curiosity of Fodor's "methodological solipsism" programme. It has been present in our culture since philosophy and science focused on the notion of "*substance*" as what can exist by itself and can be known by itself.

[12] Specifically in Burge (1986) and Burge (1989). In Burge (1982:117), he also notes "The arguments of 'Individualism and the Mental' suggest that virtually no propositional attitudes can be explicated in individualistic terms."

for would make a very important point which is individualistic but not necessarily causal.

In a certain sense, the point made by those individualistic supervenience claims is trivial. It consists simply of saying that something must happen in our bodies when we are thinking, and that different things must happen in our bodies when we have different thoughts. And by itself, this statement offers no help in order to identify mental contents and intentional states, or to explain them by means of appropriate causal types. However, there is another sense in which the point made by our individualistic supervenience claims is a very important one. Our languages, as every other social institution, configure our minds. And the non-linguistic reality itself also does that. But, our minds are not "pure mirrors" of our current environmental conditions. Our minds are not pure mirrors that reflect reality without any internal trace or without any contribution on their own part. And individualistic supervenience claims try to strengthen that idea.

References

Burge, T. 1979. "Individualism and the Mental", *Midwest Studies in Philosophy*, 4.

Burge, T. 1982. "Other Bodies", in Andrew Woodfield (Ed.) *Thought and Object*, Oxford, Clarendon Press, 1982:97-120.

Burge, T. 1986. "Individualism and Psychology", *The Philosophical Review*, XCV, 1:3-45.

Burge, T. 1989. "Individuation and Causation in Psychology", *Pacific Philosophical Journal*, vol. 70.

Chisholm, R. 1981. *First Person*, Minneapolis, Univ. of Minnesota Press.

Fodor, J. 1995. *The Elm and the Expert*, Cambridge, The MIT Press.

Kim, J. 1993. *Supervenience and Mind*, Cambridge, Cambridge Univ. Press.

Kim, J. 1998. *Mind in a Physical World*, Cambridge, MIT Pres.

Lewis, D. 1983. "Attitudes *De Dicto* and *De Re*", in his *Philosophical Papers*, vol. 1, New York, Oxford Univ. Press.

11

Individualism, Internalism, and Wide Supervenience

STUART SILVERS

"Individualism" is the term Tyler Burge (1979, 1986) uses to character-ize the Cartesian tradition in psychology that explaining mental proper-ties requires nothing external to the mind-brain of the individual having the properties in question. Jerry Fodor's (1980, 1987) calls his version "methodological solipsism." Burge's sustained critique of and external-ist (or non-individualist) alternative to individualism pose a serious di-lemma regarding the appropriate explanatory framework for a scientific psychology. Rob Wilson (1995) takes a detailed look at the diverse range of issues surrounding the individualist-non-individualist contro-versy. The key to his analysis is a diagnosis of what he argues is a shared misconception of mental causation. The confusion centers on two quite different notions of mental causation, internal and intrinsic, the conflation of which leads both individualists and their opponents into a morass of seemingly irreconcilable issues. He proposes a way out by keeping properly separate the factors that impinge on Burge's distinction between causation and taxonomy. In the following I examine Wilson's (Burgian) proposal to see what light it sheds on mental causation, and in particular, on the idea of the individual as *agent*. I begin with agency and supervenience.

Meaning, Basic Self-Knowledge and Mind: Essays on Tyler Burge.
María J. Frápolli and Esther Romero (eds.).
Copyright © 2003, CSLI Publications.

Agency requires mental causation. In particular, agency requires the kind of mental causation that enables us to explain action as falling under the causal control of an agent's mental states. The causation in question requires that both the behavior to be explained (explanandum) and the mental state (explanans) be individuated or taxonomized such that the causal properties referred to in the explanans connect in the appropriate (or relevant) way to the effect properties in the explanandum. For example, we explain why A reaches for the phone because (she believes that) it's ringing and wants to answer the call. To say that A reaches for the phone describes A's behavior as an *action* and thus in terms of the content descriptions of A's beliefs and desires. A believes that the phone is ringing and desires to answer the call because she's also curious about the caller. The debate between individualism and non-individualism is about the ingredients of an adequate explanation for actions, explanation of behavior under the causal control of an agent's mental states. To understand the parameters of this debate it is important to be clear (as possible) on the concept of *supervenience*. Supervenience is a dependence relation between two sets of properties where one determines or anchors the other. Thus if F and G are two sets of properties, G supervenes on F when there are no possible circumstances where F properties differ from G properties. Biological properties, therefore, supervene (but are not reducible to physical properties) because, even though biological properties are not physical properties, there can be no two states involving the same physical properties that differ in their biological properties. This is merely to say that there are no two distinct situations where the facts of biology differ but the facts of physics do not.

The individualist argues that constraints on the concept of causation dictate that only bio-physical features of the agent, specifically the agent's brain, figure in behavioral explanation. In contrast, non-individualists acknowledge the causal role of relational and historical features relevant to an adequate explanation of an agent's behavior. The latter features may be viewed as *situational* in the sense that they are not properties of the agent's brain but are properties of the historical, social, context situating the agent relative to that context. In the jargon with which we have become familiar, the individualist explanations of action acknowledge only properties that *supervene* on the brain states of the agent; this is the thesis of *narrow supervenience*. Non-individualistic explanations recognize as relevant, properties beyond those of the agent's brain states, namely, contextual or situational properties; this is the thesis of *wide supervenience*.

An abiding truth (or at least an article of physicalist faith) is that all causation is *local*. The idea of local causation is that causal consequences are events brought about by conditions sufficient for their occurrence *and* to which such consequences are (counterfactually) linked directly or indirectly. In the indirect case, *directly* linked mediating events are present. Since all parties to the wide-narrow debate agree that causation is *local*, explanations that incorporate non-local features are suspect. However, the acknowledgment that causation is local appears to pose a problem for externalists like Burge because explanations that refer to features of an agent's environment or anything that does not supervene on the agent's bio-physical, cognitive-productive system, are said to invoke mysterious mechanism of causation. In particular, the (apparent) problem is that Burge's (wide supervenience) view seems to commit externalism to a notion of sufficient causation lacking the required local linkage. Wilson illustrates the problem with two well-known cases of molecular duplicates (physically identical individuals) in different mental states.

Block's (1986) *action at a distance* objection involves an Earth-Twin Earth thought-experiment about a tour bus with passengers of which half are Earthlings and half Twin Earthlings but among whom there are no relevant genetic or skin surface stimulus differences. These are the locally sufficient conditions, so that whatever supervenes on these physiological conditions, results in the same psychological state. However, since both populations typically use "water" indifferently despite the fact that Earth's water and Twin-Earth's water are chemically distinct, members of each half differ with respect to their water attitudes. For example, because of the differences in Earth water and Twin Earth water, Earthling thoughts about water are different from Twin Earthlings' thoughts about Twin-Earth water. Notwithstanding their molecular identity, the mental states of Earthlings and Twin Earthlings are different. Block maintains,

> An analysis of variance would have to attribute a large component of variance to differences in a factor that does not cause any differences in proteins, synaptic connections, or any other physiochemical feature of the body, as do differences in genes and surface stimulations. This would amount to a kind of action at a distance... (p. 625)

In considering psychological differences in doppelgangers Oscar and Oscar$_2$ Fodor (1987) argues that "... psychological taxonomy is taxonomy *by* causal powers." (p. 40) He denies that there is "some mechanism which can connect the causal powers of Oscar's mental states with the character of his linguistic affiliation *without affecting his physiological constitution.* (p. 40) The conclusion of this "*argument from crazy causation*" in Wilson's reformulation is, "To deny individualism is to be committed to 'crazy causal mechanisms', that is, psychological mechanisms that don't supervene on physical mechanisms." (p. 141) He summarizes the objections to non-individualism: "Taxonomizing psychological states by their wide content violates supervenience in that it allows the psychological states of two individuals to differ even though there need be no efficacious states precisely because they do not causally effect the intrinsic properties of individuals. Hence, psychological taxonomies that violate supervenience do not individuate types of psychological states that are causally efficacious." (p. 142)

Burge, however, distinguishes importantly between causation and taxonomy and Wilson employs the distinction to show that relational properties, those that do not supervene on brain states are important to causal explanation. Using it, he seeks to rectify the individualist's conception of causal mystery by reconfiguring the parameters of the debate and thus absolve Burge from the individualist indictment of suborning causal chaos. Wilson argues that Burge's distinction, properly analyzed, can overcome individualist causal scruples. As we've seen, the objection to the kind of mental causation that agency presupposes stems from the acknowledgment that causation is local. The burden of Wilson's reconstruction of Burge's distinction between taxonomy and causation is to show "that properties and events whose instantiation doesn't supervene on the intrinsic physical properties of a given entity can make a causal difference to the behavior of that entity only by affecting properties that do so supervene." (p. 142) The question is whether distinguishing between "making a causal difference" and "making a difference" is (to invert James' cliché) to cite a distinction without a difference.

The argument for non-individualism emphasizes the importance of a taxonomy of behavior that serves the purposes of psychological explanation, for example, as in explaining why the agent reaches for the phone. This requirement is satisfied by what individualists call a wide, non-locally causal taxonomy, and it depends crucially on the distinction between two conceptions of mental state. The two conceptions are of mental states as internal to individuals and as intrinsic to individuals. Intrinsic states are those essential to an individual; internal states are those that are locatable within an individual's physical boundaries. Wilson calls attention to what amounts to a four-fold scheme for mental states of the individual whose states they (purportedly) are. An individual can be parceled out into states that are either intrinsic or extrinsic and internal or external. (For example, sensory-motor events are both intrinsic and internal to an individual; a pocket calculator or agenda would be intrinsic and external; your appendix is both extrinsic and internal to you as an individual; and almost anything at all is both extrinsic and external.) The distinction supports Burge's (1979, 1986) causation-taxonomy distinction by showing how non-causally efficacious features such as historical and relational properties "can make a difference to the causal *explanations* that one offers." (Wilson, p. 143) The intrinsic properties of an entity are those on which local causal factors supervene. Thus two intrinsically identical particles move at different velocities "because they are located in magnetic fields of different strengths." (p. 143) The relational property "being located" does not supervene on the particles' intrinsic properties but it does affect their behavior (velocity) differentially. In other words, the relational facts of their different locations do not supervene on the particles' intrinsic properties but they do "causally explain the differential behavior. Historical properties are no different here." (p. 143)

The comparison that Wilson urges is, I think, a bit invidious. It seems clear that the different *locations* play a causal role in the different velocities and thus in the explanation of the difference. It's the physical forces that impact on the mass and charge of the particles that result in their differential behavior. Being located in region r figures manifestly in causal explanations of a particle's behavior. The particles and their behavior are spatially located as physical causation requires, regardless of the intrinsic properties of the particles in the sense that any particle with the same properties would be similarly impacted by causal forces. The particles' velocities are measurably different because of the measurable difference in physical impact at the two different locations. Historical properties seem to be of an entirely different order.[1] Historical properties have the impact they have because of their content, the interpreted meaning of some set of contextually defined and bounded events. Historical properties are thus *intentional* and different qualita-

---

[1] Historical properties, whatever else they are conceived to be, are relational to, and differentially relevant to, one's temporal career. Not everything in ones past is a historical property of it. There have to be what I call *situation* linkages (to be spelled out in a sequel) between a thing individuated in a particular way and the properties in the thing's career that impinged on its course of development. For example, the historical properties relevant to the development of the strokes of the great tennis player Arthur Ashe are not the same as those historically relevant to his requiring by-pass heart surgery and tragic transfusion with HIV contaminated blood. Notice that here such historical properties need not be external to the thing. In biologically individuated creatures the genetic code is both historical and intrinsic to the organism. In this respect social and other intuitively external, environmental features of a thing are distinctly non-supervenient on its intrinsic properties.

tively from the properties of spatial location that differentiate the particles. The principled distinction that Wilson argues may withstand my rejection of his example. However that may be, the intrinsic and internal properties dichotomy is motivated by the twofold wish to retain the letter of local causation (and thus avoid action at a distance and crazy causation) and preserve the spirit of (causal) explanations that refer to causally efficacious features beyond the physical boundaries of the agent. In short, the distinction between intrinsic and internal properties is designed to allow the non-individualist to have it both ways: preservation of causal integrity and interest-relevant explanatory strength.

The contrast allows for the denial of individualism without denying local causation, that is, without subscribing to action at a distance or crazy causation. For example, in psychology, the causal theory of reference with its wide taxonomy explains the content of mental representations. Wide taxonomy assimilates an individual's various environments to her psychology. The non-individualist can, by respecting the distinction between causation and taxonomy, adhere to local causation by broadening the base upon which causal factors supervene. But what remains to be accounted for is the relevance of broad-based properties to the explanations in terms of local causes. To this end Wilson elaborates Burge's distinction between factors that make a difference with respect to causal efficacy and factors making a causal difference with respect to the choice of taxonomy in causal explanations.

Wilson argues that individualists vacillate between the two quite different concepts of the mental and that their equivocation explains why individualists are forced to treat historical and relational properties as causally irrelevant to mental state taxonomy. He brings important insights to bear on the debate between individualists and non-individualists and correspondingly between local and non-local causation. However, the distinction, for all its intuitive appeal, fails to support his argument.

To illustrate the internal-intrinsic distinction, consider, as Wilson does, Davidson's (1987) sunburn. On the intrinsic conception of sunburn its cause can be either internal (skin inflammation) or external (relation of skin to sun). On the intrinsic conception the relevant distinction is between appropriate *descriptions* of the internal condition. That condition is properly a "sunburn" only if it has the right causal history, whereas "inflammation" is an ahistorical, non-relational description. The internal-intrinsic dichotomy supports the claim that individualists are caught in the grip of causal localism and thus conflates the two conceptions of mental states. The accusation depends on the viability of the internal-intrinsic distinction. The argument is that debate between individualists and non-individualists is not about the nature of causation but about taxonomic policy, in particular the taxonomy of mental states. Individualism's policy is *no taxonomy without local causation*. On the intrinsic conception, of mental states, "...individualism is a constraint on the types of *descriptions* that can be offered of the mental causes of behavior." (p. 151) For individualists local causation is decisive. For as Fodor states,

> When individuation is by causal powers, questions of individuation and causation don't divide in the way that Burge wants them to....You can have contextual individuation if you insist on it. But you can't have it for free. Etiology suffers. (Fodor, 1987, pp. 41-42)

Burge's (1979, 1986) non-individualism does not dispense with local causation, rather it advocates a supervenience base for taxonomizing mental states that respects the internal-external distinction but is neutral with respect to the intrinsic-extrinsic dichotomy. This allows for the diagnostic analysis of the individualist's equivocal inference from local causation to individualism. Although causal localism trivially entails intrinsic individualism, from the facts about how causal mechanisms work (by bumps) nothing follows about the proper *policy* for taxonomizing psychological kinds. It's this illicit inference that blocks individualism's route from narrow supervenience to mental causation. The individualist's answer to the normative question of which policy of taxonomy best suits psychology is, accordingly, marred by the flaw in the inference from local causation to individualism.

The non-individualist alternative starts from the idea of a wide, if not global, supervenience base for mental states and recommends the route between the horns of the individualist's dilemma: opt either for causally sound scientific psychology or for crazy folk psychological mental causation. That is, we either give up mentality and agency or give up (local) causation. Fodor is adamant,

> We abandon this (localism) principle at our peril; mind-brain supervenience (/identity) is our only plausible account of how mental states could have the causal powers that they do have...In the case of the behavioral consequences of the attitudes, it requires us to individuate them in ways that violate the commonsense taxonomy. So be it. (1987, p. 44)[2]

The point that Wilson argues is that non-individualism shouldn't reject individualism for there is something right about it. Individualism's

---

[2] This is odd for Fodor to admit given his disputes with eliminativists and his own project of converting folk psychology into scientific psychology without loss of intentional content.

flaw lies in its scope; the inference supports a conclusion about mental state causation but not the one individualism wants. To examine the argument carefully let us examine the premises to determine if they can bear the weight that Wilson's thesis requires.

The first premise in Wilson"s argument is that individualism adopts an intrinsic conception of mental states. Support for this premise derives from two sources. One is that the intrinsic properties of a thing are essential to its identity; thus the properties of mass and charge of the two particles are intrinsic because they are essential to being those particles. The other source is the idea of the scientific integrity of local causation.

The next premise is,

> Individualists and non-individualists agree that mental states are in the head, but disagree about whether the *kinds* recognized by psychology must be individuated purely in terms of the intrinsic properties of individuals. (p. 152).

There are serious challenges to this assertion. The obvious ones are from those who adopt the Putnam-Burge view of mental state content as individuated by the satisfaction of external truth conditions. More recent disavowals of mental states being in the head (McGinn 1989, Davies 1997, Silvers MS) even view the cognitive mechanisms implicated in having and acquiring belief content as external to the physical boundaries of the individual whose belief it is. In particular, the idea of the extended mind is the Clark and Chalmers (1998) model of cognitively active externalism. They describe as passive the Putnam-Burge externalist view of meaning, that the truth-conditions of thoughts 'just ain't in the head' in so far as the external conditions that individuate mental state content are "distal and historical." In their view the cognitive passivity of such features can play no causal role in cognitive processing for, as they argue, if you were (once again) unwittingly beamed to Twin Earth, your water-thoughts would still be about water despite being causally prompted by XYZ. The Clark and Chalmers thesis is that cognitive operations cannot be circumscribed by the physical boundaries of the cognitive system, in particular, not by the physical boundaries of the brain. Human organisms and their external environments form "coupled systems" for which "cognitive processes ain't (all) in the head."

Wilson's own wide computationalism seems to be a counterexample to the internalist premise. Wide computationalism also denies that the cognitive phenomena studied by empirical psychology are adequately captured by the methodology of individualistic computationalism. Assuming that cognition is computational,

The states (and the processes that are the transitions between such states) over which a computational psychology quantifies need not be individualistic because the cognitive system to which they belong could be a wide computational system. That is, the corresponding cognitive system could transcend the boundary of the individual and include parts of that individual's environment. (pp. 65-66)

In cognitive systems so conceived, the computational states "would not supervene on the intrinsic states of the individual...the resulting computational psychology would involve essential reference to the environment beyond the individual." (p. 66) The suggestion implicit in this passage seems to be that intrinsic and thus essential properties of an individual extend beyond its physical limits. So, while mental states are claimed to be internal, that is, locatable within the scope of an individual's *physical integrity*, intrinsic properties, properties essential to the individual's identity are not. Interestingly, this result comports as well with Cartesianism as with non-individualism since on Descartes' view, an individual's essential properties are not physical at all.

Wilson's third premise is that individualists base their policy of narrow taxonomy for mental states on the scientific imperative of local causation. The quotations from Fodor amply support this contention. Premise four is that localism trivially entails intrinsic internalism.

The fifth premise asserts that individualists slide from what localism gives them, (that intrinsic properties of mental states are brain states and thus internal to the individual), to the taxonomic policy that links intrinsic factors to scientifically relevant properties of the individual in whom those states are instantiated. This is the core of Wilson's analysis of what he takes to be the individualist's misconception of the relevant factors in the debate about narrow-wide supervenience bases.

According to premise six internal individualism is defined in terms of the properties of those individual in whom the mental states are instantiated. In contrast, it is neutral on what intrinsically mental properties are. So from correctly viewing mental states as internal, because they are "in the head", individualism, as claimed in the fifth premise, slides into inferring wrongly that mental states requires local, that is, internal causes. Taking a mental state as internal to the individual who instantiates it implies nothing about how to taxonomize it. In particular, you can't infer "that only descriptions of local causal factors supervening on the intrinsic physical states of individuals may be used for taxonomy in psychology." (p. 154) Thus the sixth premise, which is an intermediate result vis-à-vis Wilson's thesis, depends on premise five.

The conclusion is that the mystery of wide content causal efficacy (crazy causation) dissolves when the slide between the internal and intrinsic versions of individualism is blocked or at least re-routed. If we assume that Wilson's diagnosis is correct it does open the way for what looks to be a reasonable compromise. Regarding the internal, extrinsic combination he states,

> First, it enables someone who denies individualism to explain what is *right* about the individualist's conception of mental states, and to do so in a way that makes it clear how to make sense of mental causation: Individualists are right that mental states are internal states. Second, it provides the basis for seeing what's wrong with the individualist's claim that one needs individualism to make sense of mental causation: Individualists are wrong in thinking of mental states as *intrinsic* states. (p. 153)

I have already indicated that the second premise is weak based on my own 'empirical' survey. There is a growing number of philosophers and cognitive psychologists for whom the internal-external dichotomy does not coincide with the analysis of mental state content.[3] Wilson's argument is, of course, a priori and thus not directly subject to my merely empirical objection. He can always reply that given his arguments everyone *should* accept his distinction and he offers us an argument as to why it's a good idea to do so. In my view, however, it is precisely the nature of the objections that brings into question the very concept of *individual* that, according to Wilson, both individualists and non-individualists accept.

The claim is that there is reason for "non-individualists (to) accept the view that mental states are in the head, that is, that the denial of individualism is compatible with the *internal* conception of mental states." (p.152) The reason is that once we understand the implications of the internal-intrinsic distinction for deciding on the dimensions of the supervenience base for mental causation, we come to see that the idea of mental states being (properly) in the head is as natural as our original (that is, Fregean or pre-Putnam) intuitions. Need we be concerned that on this internalist conception, restoring mental states to inside the head of the individual who entertains them, there lurks an unwelcome residual Cartesianism? A worry of this kind would be most compelling from the 'language of thought' point of viewing attitude states propositionally, as 'Mentalese' sentences that are neurally instantiated in one's brain. This one time prevalent view has been seriously diminished by arguments that it is a biologically unrealistic model of mental processing and competing neurocomputational alternatives have called into question the explanatory strength of the language of thought hypothesis. Wilson's non-LOT approach, however, focuses on "states of *believing,*

---

[3] Merlin Donald, 1991; see my 1994 for critique.

rather than on *beliefs as* mental entities...(as) a way of understanding the internal of the mental..." (p. 153)

You thus believe that p "in virtue of (your) instantiating" the belief state that p. We are to understand the "in virtue of" relation not as causal but as conceptual or logical. I assume this means that my instantiating the belief that p makes it my belief that p in the same way that JFK's assassination made Jacqueline Kennedy a widow or that something instantiates a rectangle in virtue of it instantiating a square. For surely JFK's death didn't cause Jackie's becoming a widow any more than being a square doesn't cause being a rectangle. Wilson's explanation of this conceptual connection is that,

> On this view, believing is a state of a particular individual because it is that individual in whom that state is instantiated. This is how we ought to understand the idea that beliefs are in the head; believing is literally in the mind of the believer...This view weakens the grip of the reifying, locational metaphor by making it natural to see individuals as in states of believing, rather than those beliefs as in the individual. (p. 153)

It is hard to see how this move "weakens the grip of the reifying, locational metaphor..." since the "beliefs are in the head," albeit that we should understand the idea of beliefs not as propositional entities but as mental events, believings. Presumably being in the state of believing that p is substantively distinct from being in the state of believing that q in virtue of whatever distinguishes p and q. If so, this still leaves us with the believing events being content individuated. Moreover, the focus on states of believing means that an agent's only beliefs are occurrent. This should be good for the local cause part of Wilson's account of mental causation. For while he concentrates on 'bottom-up' internal causation, which has mental states as computational consequences of underlying causal processes, there is also the 'top-down' aspect of behavioral consequences of mental causes. Obviously, agency requires an analysis of the former that doesn't disable the latter. How should we understand that when I believe that p I am in the 'believing that p state?' I am presumably not in that state when I am, for a host of reasons, not attending to that p. For after all, if it is some latent or dispositional state of *believing* that is causally responsible for the ensuing behavior, that is, a state not consciously occurrent in the agent, then it is unclear that the agent's behavior is an action in the proprietary sense of being behavior under the agent's causal control. Plausibly, it is occurrent belief that is *agent-causally* implicated in the performance action. This issue is far from clear cut. Cases where an agent's purported action is argued on indirect evidence to be a causal consequence *of* nonconscious dispositions, or standing, as opposed to occurrent beliefs, may be taken as *reductios* of the agency ascription. So it looks like we need to understand *being in a state of believing that p* as being in the occurrent state of believing that p. Of course, you can be in a state that may be called 'believing that p' when not *consciously* attending to that p; for example, when you drive through an intersection controlled by a traffic light that at the moment is green. It would be disingenuous to deny that your success in driving through the intersection unscathed was independent of your attending to the color of the traffic signal. On the contrary, it seems perfectly correct to say, as might be the case, that you did not *consciously* attend to the color of the signal. Your system of cognitive processing *accessed* the information appropriately without the (dubious?) benefit of conscious attention. Even so, in their theory of the extended mind, Clark and Chalmers (1998) say that to hold "that the only true beliefs are occurrent beliefs...would be an extreme view." (p. 16) Robust empirical data support the sophisticated folk psychological view that intentionally driven behavior can be and is causally provoked by cognitive processes to which individuals have no conscious access.[4]

There is, furthermore, a troublesome ambiguity in Wilson's account. On the one hand, his view is, as we have seen, smoothly compatible with the extended mind concept that cognitive operations are not circumscribed by the physical limits of the cognizer (more on this below). If mental events such as believings are "literally in the mind of the believer" but need not be located within the physical dimensions of the believer's head, then it unclear what we are to understand when we are advised to understand "the idea that beliefs are in the head" because, on this account, minds transcend physical heads. This particular ambiguity is fostered by one that is still more profound. Intrinsic properties of an individual are, as noted, *sine qua non*, they are essential to the individual qua taxonomy. Wilson seems to be vulnerable to sliding from the idea of physically intrinsic properties of an individual that are *sine qua non* for the physically instantiated individual, to the psychologically (or mentally) intrinsic properties of the individual person or agent. If believings are literally in the mind of the believing individual and internal to it, we need to understand the connection between the intrinsic properties of the individual in both senses.

It looks like Wilson's proposal must presuppose the idea of *an individual* for his conceptual understanding of the "in virtue of" expression. Consider that the believing state is in me if I instantiate it. At the same time I am also in the believing state because I instantiate it. That's

---

[4] The text-book case is the experimental study by Lackner and Garrett.

certainly as true as squareness instantiating rectangularity and alas, as equally informative. The analogy with the sunburn case makes this clear. The inflammatory condition happens to be my sunburn (and not yours), since it is internal to me (and not you). Clark and Chalmers (1998), Donald (1991), Dennett (1991), and Wilson himself, among others, have raised serious questions about what it is to be, and a *fortiori*, what it is like to be, the instantiator or subject of mental states. This is especially critical for the concept of mental causation that subserves an individual's agency. The point is we can make sense of the internality of my sunburn to me since I am the experiential subject of the skin inflammation, even if I am anesthetized. The inflamed epithelial tissue is connected in all the appropriate ways to the nervous system that hooks me and my usual experiences to the sensory system originating the signals that occupy me. Moreover the signals occupy me in a way with which others not so connected can only sympathize. Mental events such as believings, however, seem to be of a very different order. For you and I both can and frequently do very easily instantiate the same states of believing. This is, of course, a fundamental principle of functionalism. And unless one is prepared to say that to instantiate a believing is internal to me in the same way that it is for me to instantiate my inflammation, which seems intuitively quite different, Wilson's notion of a belief being internal to an individual has little explanatory force. For while we conceive of states of believing in terms of their causal roles in the production of behavior, states of inflamed epithelial tissue have identifiable physical properties other than their causal role in my reaching for the skin lotion.

To spell this out we need to consider that Wilson ascribes to both individualists and non-individualists the "clear notion of what sort of entity they mean by 'individual': It is something like an *organism* or *agent*. More specifically, individuals are presumed to be both *physically integrated* and *psychologically independent*."(p. 18) The analysis of these shared concepts, physical (or perhaps biological[5]) integrity and psychological autonomy, is designed to satisfy the intuitive phenomenological criteria of continuous self-identity and meaning that individual persons ascribe to themselves. Assuming the plausibility of the integrity and autonomy theses, it would seem to follow that, in the search for the appropriate supervenience base for mental causation, an individual is the 'natural' ground. Accordingly, Wilson (pp. 66-67) quotes Gabriel Segal:

---

[5] Compare Flanagan, 1991, 1992, 1996 who, in virtue of his neo-Darwinian approach, favors the idea of the biological integrity of individual agents.

The supervenience base of a representation s content is some larger system in which the representation is embedded. This could be: the whole creature plus its environment, the whole creature,, the largest module in which the representation occurs, a sub-sub-processor of that module, a sub-sub-sub-sub Individualism is the thesis that the representational states of a system are determined by intrinsic properties of that system. It seems likely that whole subjects (or whole brains) make up large, integrated, computational systems. Whole subject plus embedding environment do not make up integrated, computational systems. That is one reason why individualists draw the line where they do: the whole subject is the largest acceptable candidate for the supervenience base because it is the largest integrated system available. (Segal 1991: 492, in the original)

Wide computationalism repudiates this view. "She (the wide computationalist) rejects the claim that the 'whole subject', the individual, is the largest integrated physical system available for computational, psychological explanation." (p. 67) There is in all this what seems to be a systematic ambiguity about what kind of entity counts as an individual. This is critical if we are to understand what it is for a belief state to be *internal* in virtue of that individual's instantiating it. One crucial aspect of the replacement of the narrow (individualist) supervenience with wide (non-individualist) supervenience base is that both the individual agent's physical integrity (or boundedness as McGinn, 1989, characterizes it) and psychological autonomy are less clearly delineated. But, since according to Wilson, both individualists and non-individualists agree on the integrity and autonomy of individuals while wide computationalists deny it, the latter idea of an individual seems to recede into obscurity. What is required of wide computationalism and cohort extended mind views, such as those of Clark and Chalmers (1997) and Donald (1991), is a characterization of the appropriately focal subject of mental states that does justice to our intuitions of ourselves as naturally causal efficacious agents in the world and unique subjects of subjects of experience.[6] Indeed, one notably undesirable consequence of Wilson's replacement thesis is that it undermines the coherence of the distinction between individuals as physically integrated, psychologically autonomous agents and non-individuals lacking one or the other of these properties.

The policy of how we should individuate mental states for psychological explanation depends on the normative question of how we should

---

[6] See Flanagan, 1992 for a detailed, optimistic discussion.

individuate individuals.[7] This is obviously important for any story of mental causation to make sense. In an ecumenical spirit, one might even suggest wide computationalism and other theories of an extended mind provide the machinery that makes the scientific world (and scientific world-view) safe for communitarianism. Non-individualists suspect the inference from causal localism to intrinsic individualism because nothing in the causal thesis implies taxonomic policy. May we not be equally suspicious of the non-individualists inference from the psychologically explanatory relevance of the wide supervenience base (historical and relational properties) to a taxonomic miscellany (or hodge-podge) of psychological kinds? A third alternative (Stich, 1996) is to consider that if these are the two irreconcilable corners that we have reasoned ourselves into, then perhaps we should reject them both and try to figure out how our intuitions led us this far astray.

There's a lot at stake, as Fodor warns; nothing less than the scientific status of psychology. Taxonomy is a pervasive and irresistible practice. Practices are relational, as Fodor would say, with a vengeance. We taxonomize in all sorts of ways for all sorts of purposes. Frequently our taxonomizing occurs to us, but not by us, as when we vacillate perceptually between the familiar duck-rabbit line drawings. Unless you're a radical constructivist as well as a non-individualist the inference from practices to natural kinds is not available to you without lots of serious work.[8] It is precisely this inclination to infer that seduces (or suborns) one into taxonomizing for the purpose of explanation and then into inferring that the taxonomized kinds are natural, and therefore causal be-

---

[7] To his credit, Wilson does not eschew this question. He addresses it in the final page of his book where he distinguishes individualism in social science methodology, in evolutionary biology, and liberal political theory. Coming as a kind of postscript at the end of a closely argued examination of an abstruse debate, his remarks are brief but provocative. He promises to attend to the deep problems of individualism in "normative political theory" in future work. With Cartesian *Psychology and Physical Minds* as an indication we may look forward to a thoughtful analysis of the individuailst-communitarian controversy.

[8] A sloganesque way of putting this point is to say that explanatory practices don't track truth or natural kinds. Early on in his book Wilson proposes a "revisability model" of explanation that allows for the various sorts of adjustments we make in our explanatory practices to calibrate them to the evidence nature yields. I formulate my view of this problem in terms of what I call the mortgage or *deficit-spending* model in which we take out a sizable loan against our cognitive capacity to improve our cognitive capacity to correctly carve nature at its joints. Kitcher's (1993) thesis is a rich resource in this area.

cause, as everyone agrees, only instantiations of natural kinds figure in causal relations.[9]

References

Block, N. 1986. Advertisement for a semantics for psychology. In P. French, T. Uehling Jr., and H. Wettstein, (eds.) *Midwest Studies in Philosophy Vol. 10: Studies in the Philosophy of Mind.* Minneapolis, University of Minnesota Press.

Burge, T. 1986. Individualism and psychology. *Philosophical Review.* 95: 3-45.

Burge, T. 1979. Individualism and the mental. In P. French, T Uehling, Jr., and H Wettstein (eds.), *Midwest Studies in Philosophy*, Vol. 4, *Metaphysics*, Minneapolis, University of Minnesota Press.

Clark, A. and Chalmers, D. 1998. The extended mind. *Analysis*, Vol. 58, No. 1: 7-19.

Dennett, D. 1991. *Consciousness Explained.* New York, Little Brown

Donald, M. 1991. *The Origins of Modern Mind.* Cambridge MA. Harvard University Press.

Flanagan, O. 1996. *Self-Expressions.* New York, Oxford University Press.

Flanagan, O. 1992. *Consciousness Reconsidered.* Cambridge, MA, MIT Press.

Flanagan, O. 1991. *The Science of the Mind.* Cambridge, MA, MIT Press.

Fodor, J.A. 1994. *The Elm and the Expert.* Cambridge, MA. MIT Press.

Fodor, J.A. 1987. *Psychosemantics.* Cambridge, MA. MIT Press.

Kitcher, Ph. 1993. The *Advancement of Science.* Oxford, Oxfords university Press.

Kitcher, Ph. 1989. Explanatory unification and the causal structure of the world. In, Ph. Kitcher and W. Salmon, (eds.), *Scientific Explanation*, Minneapolis, University of Minnesota Press, 410-505.

Lackner, J and Garrett, M. 1973. Resolving ambiguity: Effects of biasing context in the unattended ear. *Cognition*, 1: 359-372.

McGinn, C. 1989. *Mental Content.* Cambridge, MA, Blackwell.

Putnam, H. 1975. "The meaning of "meaning." In K. Gunderson (ed.), *Language, Mind, and Knowledge.* Minneapolis, University of Minnesota Press.

Salmon, W. 1984. *Scientific Explanation and the Causal Structure of the World.* Princeton, Princeton University Press.

---

[9] The history of science is replete with this sort of rational misadventure. To call it anything other than rational would be deplorable intellectual snobbism. Surely there are cases that merit a psychological rather than a logic evaluation in terms of the rationality of such practices, astrology and creation science qualify here. (Cf. Ph. Kitcher, 1 993)

Segal, G. 1991. Defense of a reasonable individualism. *Mind* 100: 485~94.

Silvers, S. 1994. Review of M. Donald, *The Origins* of *Modern Mind*. *Journal of the History of the Behavioral Sciences*. Vol. 29 (3): 422-427.

Silvers, S. MS. Externalizing externalism: exorcising perceptual content.

Stich, S.P. 1996. *Deconstructing the Mind*. London, Oxford University Press.

Wilson, R. 1995. *Cartesian Psychology and Physical Minds*. Cambridge, Cambridge University Press.

12

Replies from Tyler Burge

TYLER BURGE

Appreciation

I would like to thank Juan Acero and other faculty members at the University of Granada for organizing the conference in May of 1996. I thank them for their hard work, hospitality, philosophical acumen, and philosophical good spiritedness. I thank the other participants in the conference and all the contributors to this volume, including some who were not at the conference. I appreciate their attention to my work and their making possible a philosophical exchange that I hope will be of philosophical value and interest. I specially thank the editors, Maria Jose Frápolli and Esther Romero, for taking the trouble to edit the volume. Finally, I want to say what a special time the week in Granada was for me. The city itself is one of the gems of the civilized world. The sheer loveliness of its layout and the wealth and diversity of its cultural-historical treasures, crowned by the hauntingly beautiful Alhambra, underwrite the traditional saying: "it would be a misfortune indeed to be blind in Granada". One must count oneself fortunate to be able to

Meaning, Basic Self-Knowledge and Mind: Essays on Tyler Burge.
María J. Frápolli and Esther Romero (eds.).
Copyright © 2003, CSLI Publications.

combine philosophical exploration with inspiration from such an example of the positive potential of the human spirit.

1 Reply to Christopher Gauker, "Social Externalism and Linguistic Communication"

Christopher Gauker's ambitious paper attacks what he calls the "expressive theory of communication". He believes that I am committed to such a theory, or at any rate to a pernicious consequence of such a theory. He challenges me to explain myself.

The theory that he attacks receives a number of formulations–not all of them equivalent. I find the following formulations in the paper:

(i) The primary function of language is to enable speakers to convey the contents of their beliefs [elsewhere replaced by "thoughts"] to hearers.

(ii) People use words as they do because the primary function of language is to enable them to convey the contents of their beliefs to hearers.

(iii) Informative uses of language are those in which a speaker conveys the content of a thought to a hearer.

(iv) People use [sometimes replaced by "choose"] the words that they do because they intend to convey the content of their beliefs to hearers.

(i) is presented as the definition of "expressivism". I want to comment briefly on my attitudes toward these various theses.

I do not hold (i) because I find the issue over the "primary" function of language both vague and hard to adjudicate, and because I have no commitment about what use or function is primary, or whether there is a single primary function. I do think that conveying thoughts, including prominently beliefs, is one important use and function of language.

(ii) has the same liability, but adds the extremely over-general attempt to explain people's use of words in terms of this function. I think that people's statements are frequently an expression, or at least a partial expression or an indication, of their beliefs. I think that sometimes statements express the speaker's belief exactly, and sometimes a hearer understands what the belief is by understanding the language. I also think that commonly speakers' word uses or utterances can be explained in terms of antecedent psychological states, including thoughts, beliefs, and wants. I would find the generalization in (ii) uncomfortably schematic at best.

I do not use the term "informative use", and so am not sure what to say about (iii). As noted, I think that on some occasions, uses of language convey all or part of the speaker's thought in such a way that a hearer comes to entertain the thought (or some aspect of the thought).

I reject (iv) not only for the reasons that I do not accept (i) and (ii) but because of the prominence it gives to the meta-level intention to convey one's beliefs. We frequently have such intentions. Nonetheless, as against what appears to be Grice's view, I believe that language can be used informatively, conveying thoughts, without any such meta-level intentions. I think, for example, that children commonly make statements without forming such meta-level intentions, and perhaps even without having concepts of—much less beliefs about—their own beliefs.

Gauker's primary animus seems to be against some notion of mental content—the representational content of mental states or events—that is common to all these formulations. He presents the following reductio:

> Suppose, for reductio ad absurdum, that there is such a thing as content in the expressivist's proprietary sense. The expressivist holds that people use words the way they do because the primary function of language is to enable speakers to convey the contents of their beliefs to hearers. Burge's social externalism states that what it is for a persons' thought to have the content it has is explicable only in terms of the way words are used in the linguistic community. But that means that the expressivist's explanation of the way words are used leads in circles. So it is not a good explanation.

I can imagine views that this reductio might apply to. I think that it does not yield an objection to my own views. I do not accept either of the key steps. I do not hold the expressivist view, as I have just explained. And my social externalism, or anti-individualism, does not state what the argument says it does. This latter is perhaps best explained by centering discussion on the terms "content", "explicable", and "explanation". I begin with these last two.

The argument uses "because", "explicable", and "explanation" without gloss. What sorts of enterprises are indicated by these words? The enterprise involved in my social anti-individualist thought experiments is what one might call explication or elucidation. Through reflecting on cases, I attempted to find patterns and principles that give insight into the nature and individuation conditions of linguistic acts and mental states and events. I am primarily interested in the nature of mental states and events. The natures or basic kinds of most mental states and events are marked by what sort of attitude the state or event is--whether it is a belief, intention, want, or the like--and its representational content. I will say more about representational content below. The key point here is that representational content helps type, or mark the kind of, mental states and events. It does so in a way that indicates a propositional structure and the intentionality of the state. So elements in a propositional representational content refer or predicate. And the propositional content itself is normally true or false. So the explicational enterprise is to find very general conditions that bear on the kind or nature of a mental state or event, where the kind or nature fits it into an inferential and representational structure.

Gauker seems to understand this enterprise as "defining" a kind of content, "making sense" of a notion of content, "analyzing" content, or giving an account of what content "consists in", or elsewhere as "giving a serious theory" of content. I do not see myself as doing any of these things. I doubt that any of these enterprises is necessary or fruitful. I think that representational content is a fundamental notion–fundamental both to common sense psychology, to empirical cognitive psychology, and to epistemic and semantical enterprises. The explanatory and semantical enterprises are empirically well established. The epistemic enterprise is basic to the evaluation of an important dimension of human and animal life. The notion of representational content does not need analysis. It is not likely to be the object, or subject matter, of a theory. Rather, it is a primitive notion in these explanatory and evaluational enterprises. There are different sub-species of representational content, as I shall indicate below. None of them are the subject matter of the enterprises of analysis, definition, or theory. Although explication is central to one task of philosophy, it is a looser affair. It connects a notion (or what it refers to) with other important notions. When things go right, explication uncovers broad but fundamental principles presupposed in the individuation of kinds invoked by common sense and scientific psychology, semantics, and epistemology. These are principles necessarily associated with the nature of the kinds.

My thought experiments do not indicate that representational content is explicable only in terms of the way words are used in a linguistic community. So the third step of the reductio is mistaken, both about what my publically stated view has been and about what I believe the truth to be. Representational content is explicated through its connections to various other things besides communal linguistic use. What propositional representational content a mental state or event has depends on its inferential relations to contents of other mental states, on its connection to action, reaction, and perception, on non-representational (for example, causal) as well as representational relations that mental states of that type bear to entities in the environment, on relations to the individuals' own idiolectic uses of words, to qualitative states, and perhaps sometimes to neural states.

Within an explication, there are reciprocal relations among many of the important notions. Inferences depend on representational content, and vice-versa. In some cases representational content of a mental state depends on the representational content of uses of words. Uses of words depend for their meaning on connections to the content of mental states. None of these reciprocal relations are circular because definition and analysis are not at issue. The relations are deep, in some cases necessary, connections between a variety of different factors. Representation is possible only within a nexus of relations among such factors.

Explication, in the sense just developed, is not explanation in the sense in which events are explained. It is this latter notion of explanation that seems to appear in the second step of the reductio ("because") and in the conclusion. How are particular uses of words on particular occasions explained? A person's statements and utterances can be explained in psychological terms. I agree with Gauker that uses of words (where "uses" are taken either to have a definite content or to abstract from their linguistic content) are not all to be explained in terms of the individual's reasons. Some uses have more primitive psychological antecedents. The psychological terms used in such explanations may invoke tacit linguistic competencies, action sets, immediate reactions, and perceptions, as well as beliefs, wants, intentions (not necessarily meta-level intentions about conveying beliefs). These explanations often do appeal, however, to mental states or events with propositional representational content. The explanations of utterances or uses are sometimes in terms of their antecedent psychological (including propositional attitude) causes.

As indicated, I do not accept the second or third steps of the reductio. I do accept that psychological explanations of particular linguistic acts are possible, and that there is no bar in principle to there being counter-factual supporting generalizations that can be used in such explanations. I think that propositional attitudes invoked in such explanations are typed partly in terms of their representational content.[1]

The fact that some of an individual's propositional attitudes have the content that they do partly because of the connection between the attitudes of those types and types linguistic acts by the individual and others simply does not undermine the viability of such explanations. Such explanations are not of linguistic use in general, any more than

---

[1] Gauker's apparent rejection of empirically well-entrenched patterns of psychological explanation and generalization in the last pages of his paper seems to me very thin, and out of touch with empirical knowledge in these areas. His suggested surrogates seem to me equally thin.

they are of propositional attitude content in general. They appeal to particular psychological states to explain particular psychological and linguistic events. Many of these states are typed or individuated partly in terms of representational content. They are what they are only because of their connections to other states and kinds within a complex network which includes both linguistic and mentalistic factors.

Since the psychological state types are constrained by a multitude of factors beyond particular relations to others' uses, and since the others' uses are commonly constrained by yet further factors, it is simply a misunderstanding to think that the whole scheme of explanation collapses into a circle because of generic reciprocal relations between linguistic use and the representational content of mental states. Linguistic use itself must be partly typed in terms of representational content which is not free of relations to psychological states with such content.

There are passages in Gauker's paper that make me wonder whether he is attacking some special conception of representational content that I do not hold. Of course, my conception is certainly not committed to the idea that all representational content is what it is in complete independence of linguistic uses and abilities. But further, I allow that some thinking may be thinking outloud, so that representational mental content is sometimes indistinguishable from linguistic content. As will emerge, I reject Sellars' view that language is the only or primary model for thought. Yet I see no reason in principle to deny that overt speech is sometimes "part of a larger train of thought" the rest of which is hidden from immediate inspection from external observers.[2] When Gauker invokes such ideas, I wonder whether his animus is just against a bad theory of the relation of "expression" between word forms and representational content.

Similarly, Gauker's claim that there are different "notions" or "senses" of content and his talk of the expressivist's "proprietary" sense of content seem foreign to me. There is a generic notion of representational content that plays a role in different enterprises–explanatory, semantic, epistemic.[3] I do not believe in any notion of content whose sole or proprietary use is to explain linguistic utterances, or successful communication of thought. I believe that the most broadly interesting sub-species of representational content marks or type-individuates propositional mental states and events. In my writings, however, I have

---

[2] This is not to say that I accept that there is always, or that there must be, an inner language of thought in Fodor's sense. I simply leave that open.

[3] By "semantic" I do not mean necessarily semantics for language. I mean any account of representation, including reference, truth, truth-of.

indicated that representational content can be individuated so as to mark or type-individuate linguistic kinds–meanings of sentences or utterances of a communal language, meanings of sentences or utterances in idiolects. And indeed, different types of communal or idiolectic meaning.[4] These are not in general the same representational kinds as kinds of mental states and events. In none of these cases do reciprocal relations between thought and language undermine kind-individuation in terms of representational content or psychological explanation of linguistic acts that invokes such kinds.

What makes me believe that Gauker intends his attack to undermine a notion of representational content that I do make use of are his claim that animals lack propositional content and his claim that thought is "not a kind of thing". The former claim is intended, I think, to prevent the notion of content from being explicable in terms that go beyond uses of language. The latter appears to be intended to show that linguistic "use" is the solid and fundamental idea, and that talk of thought is a misleading way of talking of contextual "responses" and "interpretations".

I do not accept either of these claims. There is very substantial empirical evidence, increasingly sophisticated over the last two or three decades, that non-linguistic animals (certainly including non-human primates) have propositional attitudes, involving simple patterns of reasoning, perceptual belief, and so on. Talk of non-propositional imagistic "thought" plays only a subsidiary role in explanations of the empirical evidence. Moreover, as I have indicated, the explication of the representational content of mental states cites connections to non-linguistic factors that go beyond the fact that non-linguistic animals have propositional attitudes.

The second claim does no better with cognitive psychology than with common sense. The best schemes of explanation that we have are in terms of propositional attitudes. Contextualist deflation of notions like propositional attitude or thought seem to me to have no strong argumentative or intuitive support, and considerable empirical liability.

---

[4] Tyler Burge, "Intellectual Norms and Foundations of Mind," *The Journal of Philosophy* 83 (1986), pp. 697-720; "Wherein Is Language Social?" in Alexander George ed., *Reflections on* Chomsky (London: Basil Blackwell, 1989); reprinted in *The Role of Content in Logic, Language, and Mind*, Anderson and Owens eds. (Stanford Ca., CSLI, 1990); and in *Modern Philosophy of Language*, Baghramian ed., (London, J.M. Dent, 1998); and "Frege on Sense and Linguistic Meaning," in *The Analytic Tradition*, Bell and Cooper, eds., (London: Basil Blackwell, 1990)

I think that the most important application of the thought experiments that center on social inter-dependency is to the nature of concept mastery and propositional thought. Those thought experiments are not fundamentally about the proper interpretation of a person's words. The thought experiments can be run entirely on what a person thinks and could think, given certain circumstances.[5] The thought experiments are certainly also relevant to interpreting a person's words. I see no sound basis for thinking that one must exclude one of these applications in favor of the other.

2 Reply to Tobies Grimaltos, "Terms and Content"

There are some remarks in the introduction to this interesting paper that are not central to the point of the paper, but which I wish to express differences on. The claims that meanings are not in the head and that extension is not determined by intension are taken to be fundamental externalist claims. I think neither claim is central to externalism, and I do not propound either claim. Putnam's claim that meanings are not in the head is either false or very misleading. Meanings are certainly not in the environment. They are either abstract, and so not anywhere, or they are in the mind or brain. Moreover, I think that except in the case of indexical and demonstrative terms, intensions (or senses or meanings) do determine extensions. The concepts *arthritis* and *water*, or the senses of the terms, do determine the extensions in the sense that there is a function from the concept (sense, meaning) to the extension. It is

---

5   Tyler Burge, "Other Bodies," Andrew Woodfield, editor, *Thought and Object* (London, Oxford University Press, 1982); reprinted in *The Twin Earth Chronicles*, Pessin, ed., (New York, M.E. Sharpe, 1996); and in *Problems in Mind: Readings in Contemporary Philosophy of Mind,* Crumley ed. (Mountain View California, Mayfield Publishing Company, 2000). Cf. also "Wherein is Language Social?", *op. cit.* I include in this note remarks about two other characterizations of my views by Gauker that I do not accept. These involve the criticism, near the end of the paper, of my discussions of interlocution or testimony. I do not see what it would mean to examine our epistemological practice "from the outside" or "stand outside the practice of language", so I find this characterization of what I am trying to do inaccurate. More substantively, Gauker's claim that the acceptance principle in "Content Preservation" "will not entitle us to believe anything until we know what counts as a stronger reason not to do so" is based on a misunderstanding. The entitlement is in place (given appropriate comprehension) in the absence of a reason not to accept what one is told. It does not depend on one's knowing anything about reasons or stronger reasons. The rest of his discussion of my views in this area seems to me too hasty to be productive.

only by mistaking such terms for indexical terms that Putnam thought otherwise.[6]

The main thesis of Tobies Grimaltos' paper is that "the meaning of the terms we use in thinking or in expressing a thought does not always determine (not even partially) the content of the thought we have". I have accepted this thesis from early on. Into all of the thought experiments have been built provisions for failures of minimal understanding and for intentionally opting out of a communal usage. There are, of course, also uses of language that are not meant to express thought, but rather have some more practical focus.[7] Similarly, if some mechanism of speech distorts the expression of the individual's competence, then attribution of thought must allow for the distortion. If an individual uses words without understanding them at all, or engages in some tongue slip or malapropism, then the usual meaning of the words actually uttered contributes nothing to the person's thought. Similarly, if the individual's intentions and practice block any dependence on normal communal meaning, then that meaning does not constitute or contribute to the thought expressed by the individual.

Grimaltos attributes to me the intuition that we use our terms deferentially to the community we are living in. "So the expression token "has to refer to whatever that expression type refers to on Twin Earth...." This is somewhat misleading about what my view is. Commonly we use our terms deferentially or so as to depend on others. Then commonly (given minimal understanding) our terms share reference with those we defer to. Deference need not be a conscious commitment; it can be implicit in reliance on others. Deference does not always suffice to make usage dependent. One could defer to someone (perhaps on newly arriving on switched earth unawares) who does not speak one's language at all. Or one could defer even though one's abilities and practice do not conform to deference. Deference is more a symptom of a norm-eliciting dependence on others in one's own usage. Normal social intercourse leads to social dependence whether or not one has an attitude of deference. As noted, such dependence can be blocked, if the individual's intention or practice runs contrary to such deferential dependence. I emphasize the importance of considering individual cases rather than inferring from some general principle to some general conclusion about how any case must be treated. Principles are best discovered by mapping a variety of cases.

---

6 These points are explained in "Other Bodies", *op. cit.*

7 Cf. for example, my "Belief De Re", *The Journal of Philosophy* 74 (1977), pp. 338-362.

I think that Grimaltos is right that the characterization of externalism quoted from Boghossian is mistaken. He is right that contents of mental states (and meanings of terms) are determined by patterns of usage not by tokens. He is right that there is some role for intention in determining the content or meaning of any particular token utterance. I also think that much of what Grimaltos writes about referential and deferential (attributive) uses is right.[8] We can indeed refer to water while using a term that semantically means or refers to twater. It seems to me, however, that the cases discussed contain complexities that need to be kept track of.

In the first place, there are difficulties about understanding principles governing linguistic change. If an individual is switched unawares to twin earth for a long time, the individual's language will change. But it is not clear that the individual will lose the old words and meanings. He has memories and abilities that were fashioned when he was on earth, and these are, presumably not lost. Does this fact bear on the interpretation of his language after the switch? If it does, as it seems it might, then a more complex story is needed than Grimaltos offers. I shall lay these complexities aside in what follows.

In the second place, there are difficulties in understanding mental attributions. Although the speaker's present intentions may sometimes affect the individual's occurrent thoughts in the way Grimaltos says, there will remain a background of deferential attitudes–or at any rate, social dependencies. In fact, there will be deference through memory to the old community, and deference through current practice to the new community. Neither type of deference need be lost even in contexts in which referential attitudes and intentions are dominant. So even when an individual on switched-earth uses the switched-earth term "water", thinks *de re* through memory of (earthian) water, and thinks of it as water, there remain a set of beliefs that are expressed by what he says in the switched-earth language. He believes that twater (or else some amalgam of water and twater) was chilly in the river he swam in years ago (on earth). These are standing states, as distinct from occurrent thoughts. But inasmuch as they are occurrently expressed in language, and inasmuch as the relevant deferential abilities are thus exercised—even though they are not the focal thoughts in the individual's consciousness—it seems to me that such standing states are brought to

---

[8] I have discussed similar cases, from a different angle in "Memory and Self-Knowledge" in *Externalism and Self-Knowledge*, Ludlow and Martin eds., (Stanford, California, CSLI Publications, 1998). Some of what I say in the following is similar to remarks in that publication.

occurrent exercise. Thus it seems to me that in most of the "referential" cases Grimaltos discusses, there will be a pair of standing beliefs, and a pair of occurrent thoughts, not simply an occurrent linguistic expression interpreted one way and an occurrent thought interpreted another. Thus it seems to me that the primacy of the "referential" thoughts in the cases Grimaltos discusses must be characterized in a more subtle way.

As Grimaltos recommends, it is important in understanding occurrent thoughts to consider whether deferential attitudes or referential attitudes are dominant. Both sorts of attitudes will normally be present at the same time. An individual's mental states will often be dependent on both. As I have suggested, I think that the individual's language may itself not be neatly separated from these background abilities.

I think that the discussion of fortnights in section 5 has some insights. It can matter to one's understanding of a particular case whether the individual is thinking primarily of fortnights as a specific period of days or whether one is thinking of fortnight mainly deferentially, with a relatively uncertain sense of how many days a fortnight is. On the other hand, I think that it is very rare that "fortnight" and "twelve days" or "fortnight" and "fourteen days" are completely synonymous in an individual's idiolect, in such a way that one is simply an abbreviation for another. There will commonly be different skills marked by the different words, different patterns of deference to others, different types of inferential potential, different degrees of competence. Where there are such differences, the identity thought expressed by the two expressions in the individual's idiolect will commonly *not* be of the form "a = a" or "$(x)(Fx \leftrightarrow Fx)$".

The discussion of Grimaltos' displayed formulas 1) and 2) is misleadingly formulated. Although 2) uses words in a that-clause, hence in English, the word forms are intended to be understood as a Twin-Earthian would understand them. Moreover, if there is an inference from 1) to 2) it is hardly plausible that the beliefs are the same. Grimaltos says they are "not, in a sense, different". The reasons given for this claim are not convincing. The reason given is that the individual believes the identity that a twin-fortnight is twelve days with certainty, and excludes any possibility of the contrary. I believe that a person can treat two expressions as exactly synonymous. Doing so, however, takes more than having absolute certainty in the identity. I believe that 2 + 2 = 4 with absolute certainty, but "2 + 2" and "4" are not synonymous for me.

I cannot follow the discussion under Grimaltos' displayed formulas 1') and 2') since the key notions of proposition, content, and belief content are not explained. I agree that the mere fact that the expression "fortnight" means fourteen days in the community in which the individual finds himself does not make a person's belief, expressed in terms of "fortnight", refer to a period of fourteen days. On the other hand, I do not think that merely having a specific period of days in mind when one uses a term like "fortnight"—using the term "referentially" in Grimaltos' sense—absolves one from beliefs involving the concept normally expressed by the term. The deferential attitudes will still be in place.

I believe that the account of self-knowledge offered in the last section of Grimaltos' paper is subject to many of the same considerations just sketched. Moreover, I believe that authoritative self-knowledge is just as compatible with anti-individualism (or externalism) in cases where thoughts involve deferential attitudes as it is in cases where thoughts involve "referential" use in Grimaltos' sense. So I do not see the need for the proposed account. Still, I think that Grimaltos has elicited an interesting and worthwhile elaboration of the original referential/attributive distinction.

3 Reply to Jorge Rodriguez Marqueze, "On Orthodox and Heterodox Externalisms"

I am not an expert on the work of either Bilgrami or McCulloch. So I will remark on issues mainly as they touch my own views.

I find Jorge Rodriguez Marqueze's characterization of "orthodox" externalisms so general that I am unsure what to count. Putnam's views in the "Meaning of 'Meaning'" are counted. I have argued elsewhere these views are not instances of externalism (or anti-individualism) about the mind at all.[9] I doubt the orthodoxy of McCulloch's view as well, at least as Marqueze represents it in two-factor canonical form. I do not understand the minus sign in the canonical form. Of course, the referent must be distinguished from mental states, mental contents, and social practices. But any view that tries to factor the referent of general terms or concepts out from a "practice", so as to attempt to understand the practice independently of the referent would miss much of the force and point of anti-individualism (or externalism). Similarly, for mental states and contents. Perhaps Marqueze and McCulloch do not understand the canonical form in this way.

The Frege cases do require that representational content be differentiated from the referent or from what is represented. I think it quite mistaken, however, to think, as Marqueze and Bilgrami apparently do, that

---

[9] Tyler Burge, "Other Bodies", *op. cit.*

the Twin Earth Cases require that content be kept the same on Earth and Twin Earth. Two arguments are presented. Neither argument is spelled out. I have criticized both types of argument elsewhere.[10] There is no response to the criticisms in the present paper.

The first argument holds that supposed differences in content between twins in the Twin Earth water case are irrelevant to explaining their respective behavior or action. From this premise, it is concluded that the psychological states and contents should be the same. I think that there are two reasons why this argument fails.

One is that the premise is mistaken. Behavior is described in a multitude of different ways for purposes of psychological explanation. One of the ways includes explaining successes with respect to the individual's environment. Success is relative to the individual's functions, beliefs, and wants. These in turn are type-individuated in ways that depend on the nature of the environment. So action and behavior are sometimes typed in terms of the kinds that are present in the environment. Science fiction alternative environments that do not exist but would be indiscernible to the individuals are irrelevant for describing behavior from this point of view. It is mistaken to think that psychological explanation will always categorize action and behavior in such a way as to count the action and behavior of the twins the same.

The second reason why the argument fails is that it assumes that if behavior is the same, psychological states and contents must be the same. There is no argument for this assumption. It may depend on taking the point of psychology or of attitude-attribution to be that of explaining behavior. This would be a backwards characterization of psychology. The point of psychology is to explain mental states and mental events. Both common sense and actual psychological explanation presuppose environmentally centered individuation of mental states and events. So the idea that psychology must form explanations that treat the twins the same is out of step with the actual practice of psychology. The idea tries to fashion a context and point for psychology that comes in too late. The psychological states of the twins are different. Psycho-

---

[10] Tyler Burge, "Individualism and Psychology," *The Philosophical Review* 95 (1986), pp. 3-45. reprinted in Stuart Silvers, editor, *Representation* (Dordrecht: D. Reidel, 1989); in *The Philosophy of Science*, Boyd, Gasper, Trout eds. (Cambridge, Mass., MIT Press, 1991); in *Philosophy of Psychology: Debates on Psychological Explanation* MacDonald and MacDonald eds. (Oxford, Blackwells, 1995); in *Readings in Philosophy and Cognitive Science*, Goldman ed. (Cambridge, Mass., MIT Press, 1994) and in *Language and Mind: Contemporary Readings in Philosophy and Cognitive Science*, Losonsky and Geirsson eds. (Oxford, Blackwells, 1995); and "Individuation and Causation in Psychology," *Pacific Philosophical Quarterly* 70 (1989), pp. 303-322.

logical explanation cannot and does not contravene this fact. It explains behavior in terms of the psychological states that people in fact have. It is obvious that the individual on Twin Earth cannot have water thoughts, and obvious that the individual on Earth can.

The second argument is that the twins have the same causal powers because they would "react" the same way in the same contexts. So psychology should treat them identically. This argument fails for the same sorts of reasons that the first argument failed. First, causal power is specified in a variety of ways. These ways include powers specified in terms of psychological states. The psychological states of the twins differ. So some of their causal powers differ. These are powers specified in ways relevant to the particular environments that explain their psychological states. Causal power individuation is not prior to psychological state individuation in psychology. Psychological states are individuated in common sense and psychology in ways that distinguish between relevant body-twins. I am sympathetic with McCulloch's remark that this second argument begs the question by assuming that the mind is self-contained with respect to changes in environment between Earth and Twin Earth. I would add that the assimilation of environments to "contexts" fails to appreciate a key insight of anti-individualism or externalism—namely that there is a fundamental difference between the environment that enters into the explanation of psychological kinds, and various local contexts that an individual might be in, given that the psychological kinds are already in place.

Marqueze develops a twin-earth case that he deems harmful to McCulloch. I am not in a position to assess this criticism. I think that it is not harmful to my own view—on either interpretation of Marqueze's switching case. On the first interpretation, the person who switches between America and Ireland unwittingly acquires two concepts, expressed by a single word-form. Marqueze holds that the individual then "lacks self-knowledge about her own substance-concepts". By this he appears to mean simply that the individual has two concepts and does not realize that she has two. He regards such a result as leaving any view committed to it impaled on the third horn of Bilgrami's trilemma.

I think that this result cannot be taken to be an unattractive one without further argument. It is extremely misleading to count this as the subject's "lack of self-knowledge of his own contents". I have discussed at some length the difference between ordinary knowledge of one's contents in ordinary self-attributions that count as knowledge of one's mental states and events, on one hand, and an ability to explicate and individuate one's concepts in a global way (so as to deal with all contingencies), on the other.[11] I believe that individuals have no special first-person authority in the latter case. Concepts type abilities in ways that are sensitive to a variety of factors, including environmental factors. We have no special first-person authority to discern differences among all possible concepts that mark such abilities. In special cases, our ability to distinguish concepts may fail, while they mark relevantly different psychological or mental abilities. I believe that Marqueze tends to assume that self-knowledge tracks psychological explanation (and investigations of concept identity) more closely than it does.

On the second interpretation of Marqueze's case, the person who switches between America and Ireland is using a non-substance concept, like the concept of jade. This seems to me the more plausible interpretation. This interpretation yields the result that one can think that something is a substance word and be mistaken. This result seems to me true. Many Greeks thought that air, earth, and fire where substance words or concepts. They were mistaken. Marqueze protests that on this view the speaker's intentions would be irrelevant to what the word meant or what concept it expressed. I do not see that this follows.

There are several interesting remarks by Marqueze about special contexts in which an environment is very poor or very rich in kinds. I believe that they are worth pondering.

4   Reply to Steven Davis, "Arguments for Externalism"

I agree with most of Steven Davis' discussion of Donnellan's response to the thought experiments by Putnam and myself.[12] Most of my remarks will be supplementary.

Much of Davis' discussion revolves around the question of semantical rules that are supposed to be in the mind or head of the individual.

---

[11] For example in Tyler Burge, "Individualism and Self-Knowledge," *The Journal of Philosophy* 11 (1988), pp. 649-663; reprinted in *Self-Knowledge* Cassam ed. (Oxford: Oxford Press, 1994); in *The Twin Earth Chronicles* Pessin and Goldberg eds. (New York, M.E.Sharpe, New York, 1996; in *Externalism and Self-Knowledge*, Ludlow and Martin eds. (Stanford, Ca.; CSLI Stanford University, 1998); and in *Knowledge: Readings in Contemporary Epistemology* Dretske and Bernecker eds., (Oxford, Oxford University Press, 2000); also my "Cartesian Error and the Objectivity of Perception," McDowell and Pettit, eds., *Subject, Thought, and Context* (New York: Oxford University Press, 1986); reprinted in *Contents of Thought*, Grimm and Merrill, eds., (Tucson, Arizona, University of Arizona Press, 1987); and my "Reply: Authoritative Self-Knowledge and Perceptual Individualism," in *Contents of Thought ibid.*

[12] Cf. my "The Thought Experiments: Reply to Donnellan" in *Reflections and Replies: Essays on the Philosophy of Tyler Burge* (Cambridge, Mass., MIT Press, forthcoming), where I make some of the same points that Davis independently makes.

The idea that Donnellan proposes, which is a simple version of an idea that has been proposed many times by others, is that a concept like water has as a semantical rule something like:

> (10a) Apply "water" [or the concept water] to the liquid, and any liquid similar to it, in our lakes and rivers.

I want to make several points about this type of proposal.

First, in agreement with Davis, even granting the presence of a single such rule in twins in the relevant thought experiments, the sameness of rule does not suffice to make the meaning of the term, or the nature of the concept, the same. The rule is indexical and the term/concept is not. The rule is at best a reference fixer, not a determiner of representational content.[13] Thus the representational (or intentional) content that is the concept and that the term (in one sense) expresses is not captured by any such rule.

Second, the rule is much too simple to be general. One need not be acquainted with lakes and rivers, or even with water, to have a concept of water.[14] This problem may seem to be a matter of detail. But following out the problem of specifying even a reference-fixing rule brings out a number of important considerations.

The standards governing the "similarity" that the rule invokes are not in general known to individuals. Nor must they be "implicitly" represented in the individual. Relevant considerations that bear on individuation may emerge only from new empirical discovery. The paradigms themselves provide some of the factors relevant to projecting to new cases. This is true at various levels. Whether a term or concept is a natural kind concept need not be known to the individual. As I note in my reply to Marqueze, earth, air, fire, and water were thought to be on a par by many Greeks, but only one is a natural kind. It is not obvious that all Greeks (or indeed all modern individuals who have the relevant terms or concepts) have a definite concept of a natural kind. Their terms can, and almost surely did, apply more or less exactly to natural kinds. Moreover, standards for what counts as a relevant natural kind

---

[13] This point amounts to the first of Davis' three criticisms of Donnellan's account of Putnam's thought experiments. I do not accept the second of Davis' criticisms. In indexical cases, sameness of content in Kaplan's sense—which differs, of course, from my notion of representational content—is not in general necessary for sameness of psychological state. The key point is the first one–that the relevant states are not indexical. I agree with the third of Davis' criticisms of Donnellan, as will next emerge.

[14] Of course, water is so salient in our lives that we are inevitably perceptual acquainted with it, but someone could have gotten such a concept by reading, by interlocution, or by theorizing together with the exercise of imagination.

need not be known or implicitly represented in advance. The chemical theory that specifies the kind relevant to water was not available until long past when people were talking and thinking about water (and not thinking about possible look-alikes, such as XYZ).

What counts as a relevant similarity is not in general available to the individual who uses a term or concept. What counts as similar is partly dependent on discovery and on the potential for interaction between individuals and environment. The rules governing how an individual's term or concept applies to "similar" entities are not fully represented in the individual's conceptual repertoire. Norms governing success or failure in application depend not only on what the individual (implicitly) knows or represents, but on the point and function of a usage within an environment. It also can depend on what joints mark the paradigms that are actually engaged with. The point and function of a usage, and the character of the paradigms, sometimes is not something that the individual has fully conceptualized.

Davis offers a good observation about the possibility of the individual's being mistaken about supposed paradigms for the reference of a term or concept. One might think that this point can be accomodated simply by formulating the semantical rules in a more general way. Thus, one might think, if one disjunctively specified all the "fall-back" positions that Putnam allows for, one would have a rule that the individual implicitly knew. I think that the point about error goes deeper than this response allows. Implicitly knowing a correct meta-rule is not necessary for using a term or concept with an extension or reference specified by the meta-rule.

Rules governing reference of concepts may not be represented and implicitly known by the individual because the relevant competence is embedded in unconceptualized perceptual capacities or in know-how that is not conceptualized. It is a typically individualist assumption that rules that fix reference (including indexical rules) are fully "implicitly" represented in the individual's conceptual or linguistic repertoire. The perceptual and conceptual contents of animals and young children are certainly not fixed by a semantical rule that the animal (implicitly) represents. Meta-rules are ontogenetically (hence psychologically) less basic than the terms or concepts whose referential patterns they specify.

Incomplete mastery of terms and concepts is another reflection of the fact that correct meta-rules may not be known or implicitly represented.[15] I agree with Davis, however, that incomplete mastery is not

---

[15] Although many cases of incomplete mastery depend on deference, not all do. Sometimes the most expert individuals will themselves have an incomplete mastery of

fundamental to my thought experiments. The thought experiments involving water, perception, and questioning of the experts do not use it at all.[16] Even the social-anti-individualist thought experiment that centers on arthritis can be altered so as to reach the same conclusion without relying on incomplete mastery in the sense discussed in my initial presentation of the thought experiment.[17]

Davis asks at the end of his paper whether experts and a division of linguistic labor are essential to anti-individualism. I believe that the answer is a firm "no". I believe that Putnam was right that the Greeks had terms for gold and water before they had any background knowledge that could distinguish for them between gold (water) and twin gold (twin water). I think that an analogous point applies to Greek concepts. I believe that perceptual contents and contents of many perceptual beliefs are pre-linguistic. The perceptual states and perceptual beliefs depend for their natures on relations to the environment. Moreover, I believe that what similarity standards project from the examples that the Greeks interacted with are dependent on the nature of the actual environment. Projection to a kind not completely fixed by the perceivable qualities of the kind depends partly on the way the actual environment and partly on the Greeks' having *some* conception that the examples *might* be of a kind that is not automatically determined by perceivable characteristics. I think that they need not have had our conception of a natural kind, much less an assumption that gold (water) *is* a natural kind. As I argued in "Intellectual Norms and Foundations of Mind", facts about the world can trump the views of experts in determining the natures of mental

---

their concepts. This is true of Dalton with respect to the concept of atom, and Newton with respect to the fundamental concepts of the calculus. Cf. my "Intellectual Norms and Foundations of Mind", *op. cit.* Cf. also my "Concepts, Conceptions, Reflective Understanding: Reply to Peacocke" in *Reflections and Replies: Essays on the Philosophy of Tyler Burge, op. cit.*

[16] This is evident from the thought experiments in "Other Bodies", *op. cit.*, in "Individualism and Psychology", *op. cit.* and "Cartesian Error and the Objectivity of Perception" *op. cit.*, and in "Intellectual Norms and Foundations of Mind", *op. cit.*

[17] For the initial presentation, see my "Individualism and the Mental" 4 (1979), pp. 73-121; reprinted in *The Nature of Mind* Rosenthal, ed., (New York, Oxford University Press, 1991); in *Language and Cognition*, Higginbotham ed. (London, Basil Blackwell, 1993); in *Basic Topics in Philosophy of Language*, Harnish ed. (Englewood Cliffs, NJ; Paramount Publishing, 1994); in *The Twin Earth Chronicles* Pessin and Goldberg eds., (New York, M.E.Sharpe, 1996 (partial reprinting, 18 pages); *Externalism and Self-Knowledge*, Ludlow and Martin eds. (Stanford, CSLI distributed by Cambridge University Press, 1998). For explanation of how it can be altered so as not to rely on the patient's failure to understand a quasi-definitional aspect of his concept, see "Wherein is Language Social?", *op. cit.*

states. They can also help determine those natures in the absence of experts.

Relations to objective reality are the fundamental source of anti-individualism. Linguistic relations through others are one sort of relation to objective reality. Moreover, linguistic practice in a group can specify boundaries within reality that concepts mediated by the language can be sensitive to. Social elements in anti-individualism are deep. They are deeply part of what makes us special as human beings. They are not, however, the only or ultimate source of the individuative dependence of our minds on a wider environment. There are sources--perceptual sources–that we share with animals that lack language and social practices altogether.

5 Reply to Martin Davies, "Externalism, Self-Knowledge and Transmission of Warrant"

Martin Davies paper contains a wealth of insightful observations on interesting topics. There are sharp remarks about the distinction between issues about warrant transmission and issues about closure. There are insightful warnings about not jumping too quickly from the case-based examples that I give to general principles. There is the fine point that one can beg a question without failing to transmit warrant from premise to conclusion. And there is much else. On the basic claims of the paper, however, I am sceptical. I think that Davies is on to something important about dialectic in philosophical argumentation. I am not convinced that the key matter is warrant transmission. I will try to lay out the main shape of my differences.

Davies claims that we need principles limiting the transmission of warrant from premises to conclusion in deductively valid arguments. He takes this claim to be required by "the problem of armchair knowledge". He writes,

> ...we have to accept that, sometimes, knowing that A and knowing that if A then B, then knowledgeably drawing the conclusion that B, does not constitute a route to knowledge that B. Sometimes, that is to say, the epistemic warrant or justification that we have for the premises of an argument is not transmitted to the conclusion, even though it is obvious that the premises entail the conclusion.

I believe that Davies has not yet produced a clear case that motivates his proposal to limit the transmission of warrant in simple, deductively valid arguments. Let me begin with the cases involving self-knowledge and externalism, or anti-individualism.

It is striking that in his initial formulation of the problem there is only a schematic representation of an "externalist dependence thesis". Yet in his introduction, he states that the puzzle that motivates his solution is already "clearly visible". I think that the puzzle cannot be clearly visible unless one produces a concrete case to illustrate it.[18]

In discussing the arthritis and water cases, Davies shows a good sense for the way in which the cases require holding constant very specific facts about the individuals involved. For example, one individual happens not to know that arthritis cannot occur in thighs, and another does not know the chemical composition of water. To produce a general externalist dependence thesis in either of these cases, one that does not depend on particular contingent facts and yields the general conditions under which one can have one of these concepts, is no simple matter. Such principles are likely to be highly disjunctive and very complex. I believe that they will not enable one to deduce from the armchair–together with the relevant sort of self-knowledge–anything about the environment that would clearly raise Davies' problem. At any rate, both the epistemology and the content of such principles requires much more investigation before one can conclude that they present anything like the "problem of armchair knowledge".

The particular externalist dependence principle that Davies works with is:

WaterDep Necessarily, for all x, if x is thinking that water is wet then x is (or has been) embedded in such-and-such ways in an environment that contains samples of water.

Despite its extreme schematic character, this principle–or any instance of it—is false. As I pointed out in "Other Bodies", water need not exist in an individual's environment in order for the individual to think that water is such and such.[19] An individual, in a world in which there was no water, but with sufficient knowledge of chemistry, could develop a concept of H20 by experimentally interacting with hydrogen and oxygen and theorizing how they would bond. If the individual could also imagine how H20 would behave in ordinary macro contexts—how it would flow in rivers, act in such and such ways when boiled or frozen, how it would look, taste, feel—and if the individual recognized that it would

---

[18] Later Davies admits that he "cannot show incorrect" the view that "there is no true externalist dependence thesis at all that gives rise to the problem of *armchair knowledge*". I think that this is a very serious admission. A counter-intuitive proposal should be motivated only as the best solution to an intuitively compelling puzzle or problem.

[19] "Other Bodies", *op. cit.*, last pages.

be possible to think of what is in fact macro-H20, with all those macro-properties, while discovering only later that it was H20, then the individual could have the concept of water. This shows that one cannot deduce that water exists from knowing that one thinks that water is wet and knowing principles governing conditions under which anyone can think that water is wet.

Of course, we know that water is a natural kind. This is empirical background knowledge. I have used such empirical background knowledge in forming theses about conditions under which it is possible to have the concept *water*. I have used the empirical background knowledge that compounds and elements exist. It is arguable that I have even assumed that water itself exists in some of the sketches I have given of conditions under which it is possible (or impossible) to have the concept *water*.

One could reflect and realize that one is not in the position of the scientist that had a theory and an imaginative capacity sufficient to have the concept of water in a world that in fact lacked any water. Could one then deduce from that realization, together with basic self-knowledge and a knowledge of anti-individualist theory, that water exists? Would this raise a problem of armchair knowledge? I think not. In the first place, the anti-individualist principles are too sketchy to be regarded as complete. There might be other ways to have the concept in the absence of any water in the world. In the second place, we have already made use of a lot of empirical knowledge. The realization that we lack a relevant theory presupposes that there is such a theory that someone has. Like the knowledge that water is a natural kind, this knowledge is empirical.

With the use of all this empirical knowledge and with the indefiniteness of the principles, I see no puzzle about an ability to derive empirical truths that one should not be able to know from the premises. Principles governing conditions on having the concept of water that we have so far discussed are framed in the light of considerable empirical knowledge about the nature of chemical compounds and the relation between chemistry and common sense knowledge of the macro world. Indeed, they have been framed in the light of empirical knowledge about what exists in the macro world.

If one were to try to specify conditions on having the concept *water* in such a way as *not* to assume on empirical grounds such matters as that the concept is a natural kind concept, the conditions would be much more complicated and abstract. A purely apriori principle governing such conditions would allow yet *more* ways in which one could have a concept even though it failed to apply to any existing entities. Thus it would not suffice to know that one did not have a theory of chemical composition, and that one had not learned of water from other people, to infer that the concept must have an application to existing entities.

Suitably generalized, these points show that the more obvious specific results about empirical existence (that water exists, for example) cannot be inferred from relevant self-knowledge and apriori (or purely armchair) anti-individualist principles governing conditions under which anyone can think relevant thoughts.[20]

Let me turn from anti-individualist principles to self-knowledge. Davies engages in some close reading and reasoning regarding my views about self-knowledge. I would like to clarify some of those views. I wrote,

> It is uncontroversial that the conditions for thinking a certain thought must be presupposed in the thinking....to *think* that water is a liquid, one need not *know* the complex conditions that must obtain if one is to think that thought....Such conditions need only be presupposed.[21]

I do *not* assimilate this notion of presupposition to a notion of assumption by the individual, as Davies conjectures. Such an assimilation would not leave it "uncontroversial" that the conditions must be presupposed. In order to think that water is wet, an individual need not have the concepts necessary to assume that the relevant conditions for thinking the thought are in place. A child can think that water is wet without having the concepts *condition, environment, causal relation between environment and individual subject, normal,* and so on. I did not intend presupposition to be a propositional attitude. It is an impersonal relation between the thinking and actual principles or conditions governing its possibility.

Such a presupposition plays no epistemic role in justifying (or warranting in Davies' sense) an individual's authoritative self-knowledge. I think authoritative self-knowledge is non-empirical, or apriori, in the strong sense that no sense experience need contribute any epistemic

---

[20] The same criticism applies to McKinsey's argument, which Davies discusses. A further criticism is that McKinsey assumes that all of anti-individualism is intended to be apriori. As I have indicated, I believe that many anti-individualist observations are informed by a great deal of empirical background knowledge. I think that certain general aspects of anti-individualism are apriori, however. I think that it is not obvious that anti-individualist principles governing very general categories, perhaps *space* and *physical object*, do not have existence implications. I think it possible to argue to the existence of instances of such categories from self-knowledge and anti-individualist principles. That is something that traditional rationalism aspired to do.

[21] "Individualism and Self-knowledge", *op. cit.,* 1988, p. 653.

force to the warrant (justification or entitlement) for an individual's authoritative self-knowledge.[22] To think a thought with the representational content that water is wet, or to think that one thinks that water is wet, it may be necessary to make inferences and even have beliefs about the empirical world. I think that such commitments need not figure in any way in the epistemology of warranted instances of authoritative self-knowledge that one is thinking that water is wet. Such inferences and assumptions figure at most into the enabling conditions necessary for thinking the thought.

The issues Davies raises about Moore's anti-sceptical argument seem to me very interesting. A detailed discussion of these matters is not in place here, of course. I want, however, to make a few comments.

The Moorean argument that Davies discusses is as follows:

(1) Here is one hand and here is another.

(2) If here is one hand and here is another, then an external world exists.

Therefore:

(3) An external world exists.

I agree with Stroud and Davies that this argument is an inadequate response to the sceptic. I think that there is a sense in which it begs the question. I am not convinced, however, that it fails because warrant is not transmitted through the argument. I think that the dialectical issue about whether a question has been begged should be distinguished from the issue over how the premises are warranted and whether their warrant is transmitted to the conclusion in such a way as to warrant belief in the conclusion. I think that the argument does do that, even though if one were to say nothing more, one would have not answered or even addressed the sceptic's doubts about wherein and whether the premises are warranted.

I think that this point is independent of the question of whether the conclusion *requires* any such argument from particular observation in order for one to be warranted (or entitled) in believing it. It may be that we are independently justified or entitled to believe the conclusion. It may be that (3) provides some sort of framework or holistic support for one or the other of the premises. It seems to me nevertheless that the premises provide one sort of support for the conclusion. And I think that

---

[22] Davies uses "warrant" as an apparent alternative to "justification"; he contrasts warrant with entitlement. I use "warrant" to apply to the genus of which justification and entitlement are sub-species.

their warrant (entitlement or justification)—at least one primary warrant that they have—does not derive from assuming the conclusion.

One is entitled to perceptual beliefs like (1) before one has any conception of a world, hence before one is entitled to any belief so generalized or abstract as a belief in an external world. One acquires general notions of space, externality, and world partly through conceptual maturation and through reflection on paradigms like hands. One realizes by reflection that hands are in a spatial world in a broad sense external to one's mind. Understanding the relation between particular spatial characteristics of hands and the presence of hands in space provides one ground for accepting (2): any hand is in space external to the mind of the individual with the hand. One could destroy or remove the hand without affecting the mind; one could destroy or affect the mind without affecting the hand. Transmission of warrant from (1) and (2) would yield one ground to believe (3). Yet none of these points so much as addresses the sceptic's doubt.

So I see no simple inference from the agreed-upon inadequacy of Moore's argument as an answer to the sceptic to a rejection of the idea that warrant (including entitlement) for premises is transmitted through a deductive argument to provide warrant (here, justification) for a conclusion. Being dialectically useless does not entail being lacking in warrant. Perhaps the sceptic is wrong to question the warrant for the premises, but needs to be shown why he or she is wrong.

I have independent doubts about Davies' limitation principles as accounts of failure of transmission of warrant. The First Limitation Principle (revised version) is:

> Epistemic warrant cannot be transmitted from the premises of a valid argument to its conclusion if, for one of the premises, the warrant for that premise counts as a warrant only against the background of certain assumptions, and acceptance of those assumptions cannot be rationally combined with doubt about the truth of the conclusion.

I think that this cannot be a reasonable principle for transmission of warrant. Suppose that the doubt of the conclusion is unwarranted, but suppose that the doubt could not be rationally combined with belief in the premises, or with belief in assumptions backing the premises. Then the principle says that epistemic warrant cannot be transmitted. It seems to me obvious that the unwarranted doubt should be epistemically irrelevant to whether the conclusion is warranted by the premises. Standing by the premises, one will remain epistemically warranted. And as far as anything that we have said here, the warrant can be transmitted.

In the case of the sceptic, simply giving the argument does in a sense beg the question against the doubter. To address the doubter one

needs to show why the purported warrant for the doubt does not constitute a warrant. One needs to explain why the warrants for the premises
stand. But to bear on the warrant or transmission of warrant, the doubt
must itself be warranted. If the doubt is warranted, then the warrant for
one of the premises is undermined or outweighed.

Davies Second Limitation Principle (revised version) is:

> Epistemic warrant cannot be transmitted from the premises of a valid
> argument to its conclusion if, for one of the premises, acceptance of the
> assumption that there is such a proposition for the knower to think as
> that premise cannot be rationally combined with doubt about the truth
> of the conclusion.

I think that this principle cannot be correct for the same kind of reason
that shows that the first principle cannot be correct. Suppose that someone doubted that a thinker exists, or that there are thoughts, or that there
are any events. Confront the doubts with the *cogito*. One thinks: I am
herewith thinking. Suppose that one infers that there is a thinker, a
thought content, and a thought event. One cannot rationally combine
acknowledgement of the existence of the premise, the thought that I am
herewith thinking, with any of the doubts. That hardly undermines the
self-evident premise or the self-evident inference from premise to conclusion. The doubt is shown by the reasoning itself to be unreasonable.[23] Thus, it seems to me that any limitation on transmission of war-

---

23   As the case has so far been described, it seems to me doubtful that the argument even begs the question against the doubt. This makes me think that the analysis
of begging the question attributed to Jackson by Davies is also incorrect. According to
Davies' attribution, according to that analysis, one begs the question when "anyone–or
anyone sane–who doubted the conclusion would have background beliefs relative to
which the evidence for the premises would be no evidence." Suppose that a dogmatist
who is clinically sane advances the doubts mentioned above (without warrant or even
purported argument). Suppose that the dogmatist would have to have the background
belief that since there are no thinkers, thought contents, or thought events, there can
be no evidence deriving from thinking, understanding, or warrant. Yet unless more is
said, I do not see that the appeal to the *cogito* begs the question. This is partly because
the doubter has not given any ground for his doubt. He has not raised an even prima
facie reasonable question. If the doubter were to give some elaborate account of why
science shows that there are no thoughts, then the dialectical situation would be different. I am inclined to think that no such elaborate account could undermine the
cogito. Even if appeal to science and the accompanying doubt were in the end unreasonable, it would seem to beg the question simply to enunciate the *cogito* in response.
One needs to address the prima facie grounds for doubt. Yet in the case of the dogmatist doubter, it seems to me that appeal to the *cogito* does *not* beg the question, since no
genuine, rationally backed question has been raised. It might even be that if the dogmatist were to consider the *cogito* carefully and dispassionately, he would be persuaded.

rant would have to take account of whether the doubt of the conclusion has some genuine epistemic force—whether the doubt is justified or entitled.

Revising the two principles to respond to this problem will, I think, deprive them of usefulness in adjudicating transmission of warrant. Doubt of the conclusion cannot affect evaluation of warrant involved in the argument independently of evaluating warrant for the doubt. If the doubt is unwarranted, then it cannot affect considerations of warrant involved (or transmitted) in the argument. If the doubt is warranted, then its being warranted must affect one's evaluation of the warrant of the premises. So evaluation of the argument will be suspended until the premises are re-evaluated. It is at least prima facie difficult to see how one could evaluate transmission of warrant along the lines Davies proposes independently of evaluation of warrant of the premises and conclusion. In carrying out these evaluations, I see no reasonable ground to avoid assuming that genuine warrant is transmitted through understood deductively sound arguments; and that genuine warrant for doubt of the conclusion is transmitted back (through modus tollens) into affecting the warrants for the premises. Such transmission is what arguments are for.

It seems to me that Davies' reflections bear more directly on understanding dialectic and the rational effectiveness of arguments in particular argumentative contexts, than on the general problem of transmission of warrant (in his sense or my sense of warrant–cf. my note 5). This is to say that the reflections are relevant to the deep problems of scepticism. I believe that scepticism is unreasonable and thus does not affect actual warrant. Showing it unreasonable is the deep problem.

I am not persuaded that there is a general problem of "armchair knowledge" that plausibly motivates the idea that warrant (in Davies' sense or mine) is not transmitted over simple deductive arguments. I am particularly unpersuaded that any such problem arises from reflecting on anti-individualism and authoritative self-knowledge. But there are profound problems that arise from such reflection. Some of the most profound problems in this area do have to do with how epistemology of self-knowledge and that of anti-individualism bear on identifying rational starting points. The questions of whether there are rational starting points, what they are (if there are any), and how to show them to be rationally good, are the primary questions raised by the sceptic's dialectic. I believe that properly reconceived, Davies' reflections can be seen as contributions to framing and answering these questions.

6 Reply to María J. Frápolli and Esther Romero, "Anti-individualism and Basic Self-knowledge"

I appreciate the patient and insightful exposition of my views in the paper by María Frápolli and Esther Romero. It is gratifying to be well-understood. The discussion of the relations between externalism about meaning and anti-individualism about mind, and the discussion of connections between meaning and concepts, bring out neglected elements in my work. Neglected not least by me. I have not developed some of those ideas, or even reflected upon them in a long time. I agree with the main point of the paper, although I see the point in a different light.

I would like to begin with some qualifications on the account of externalism about meaning and anti-individualism about mind. The stated contrast between my externalism and that of Kripke and Putnam is correct. I do not identify meaning (much less concepts) with referents or extensions, and I do not include referents or extensions as a component in meaning (or concepts). Meaning is intentional (or representational). Most referents and all extensions are not intentional or representational. On the other hand, it would be a mistake to think that the only thing that justifies counting my account of meaning externalist is the social nature of translational and lexical meanings.[24] For many non-indexical expressions, individuation of meaning is constrained by extension or reference: the meaning would be different if the reference were different. The explanation of the individuation of both social and idiolectic meaning takes the environment of entities that are in fact the referents as, in some cases, anterior to the meaning. In this respect my view is, within a different framework, congenial with the points of Kripke and Putnam.

One respect in which it would be a mistake to think that my account of meaning is externalist only inasmuch as it appeals to a social context is that I think an account of meaning must include meaning in idiolects. Meaning in idiolects is normally, perhaps in actual fact always, socially constrained. Even so, some idiolectic meanings are different from any social meanings. I believe that it is possible in principle for idiolectic meaning not to depend on relations to other people. Idiolectic meaning is individuated in an externalist manner. For meaning depends partly on relations between the user and the physical environment.[25]

---

[24] One of the authors' formulations suggests this mistake, though I am not sure that they make it.

[25] Cf. my "Wherein is Language Social?", op. cit.

Another respect in which it would be a mistake to think that my account of meaning is externalist only in its social dimension is that I think that certain meanings are learned primarily through association of words with perceptual experience. The social context is commonly present, but much early language learning derives from relatively simple association of words with perceived items–given, of course, an innate linguistic capacity.

A parallel qualification needs to be entered on the account of anti-individualism: "Burge's anti-individualism rests on the claim that we think using the concepts of the linguistic community we belong to...". I do believe that we often share concepts of a larger community and that an individual's thinking with the concepts he or she thinks with is often to be explicated partly in terms of the individual's relations to concepts communicated by others. Still, I do not think that all thinking is like this. There are idiosyncratic conceptual abilities. There is the possibility of intentionally blocking social dependency relations. There are perceptual concepts and other concepts that are not linguistically dependent at all. Yet much of this thought which is not individuated in terms of communal concepts is anti-individualistically individuated.

Even where there is social dependence, one can depend on the community for reference or extension without sharing a communal concept.[26] And as noted, many thoughts whose individuation is not socially dependent nevertheless have natures or individuation conditions that are necessarily associated with relations between the individual and a physical environment.[27] So my anti-individualism about the mental has other sources beyond sharing concepts through social interaction.

I would also like to enter a caution about one of my own former statements, quoted by Frapolli and Romero in their footnote 5. I do believe that concepts are frequently expressed in language. I do not think that the meaning (whether idiolectic or communal) of a word used in a sincere statement is in general, or always, the same as the concept thought by the speaker in using that statement. Often meaning expresses less than the speaker's concepts. This is most obviously true in cases of statements that express perceptual belief. Meanings in third-person attributions of belief bear an even looser relation to the concepts that the believer has. Frequently the purposes of such attributions and the content that depends on specifically linguistic use are not the same as purposes involved in the expression or attribution of the exact nature

---

[26] *Ibid*.
[27] Cf. "Individualism and Psychology", *op. cit.* and "Perceptual Entitlement", forthcoming.

of a relevantly associated thought. So individuation of meaning, both idiolectic and communal, is guided by principles somewhat different from the principles that guide individuation of mental content. This is so even though sometimes the representational content that is the meaning is the same content as the representational content that is the content of a relevant thought.

Let me turn to self-knowledge. As the authors note (footnote 13), direct authoritative self-knowledge includes what I call "basic self-knowledge" but comprises a much wider class of types of self-knowledge. Not only knowledge of one's pains, sensations, and some emotions, but knowledge of some of one's standing mental states--such as one's standing beliefs--is direct (non-inferential) and first-person authoritative. None of the types of "non-basic" self-knowledge in this wider class are self-verifying or infallible.

Pure *cogito* cases of basic self-knowledge are, I think, infallible. The infallibility is not only about the second-order thought, but about the first-order thought as well: *I am hereby thinking [in the sense of engaging in an act of thinking the content] that grass is green.* (This is relevant to the authors' footnote 14.) In view of the self-verifying character of the thought, I see no scope for error of any kind. Slightly less pure *cogito*-like cases of basic self-knowledge, such as *I hereby judge that grass is green*, are subject to more delicate considerations regarding the adjudication of infallibility. But I think that, with qualifications, a persuasive case can be made. I will not enter into these considerations here.

The authors are certainly right that the sort of authority involved in basic self-knowledge is not an authority (much less infallibility) over the boundaries of concepts or over distinguishing one concept from another. These latter are comparative, discursive, inferential cognitive activities. They are to be strictly distinguished from direct self-knowledge.

In attempting to elucidate the limits on basic self-knowledge, particularly knowledge involved in self-attributing mental content in basic self-knowledge, the authors introduce the paradigm: I think this: [writing requires concentration].[28] They then compare basic self-knowledge to a use of "this person is the murderer", where one backs the application of "this" with "whoever he or she may be", rather than with "Jones". They note that this comparison is a metaphor with shortcomings. They take

---

[28] I have argued against this sort of analysis, in my "On Davidson's 'Saying That'," Ernest LePore, editor, *Truth and Interpretation* (London, Basil Blackwell, 1986). I think the difficulties with it are not directly relevant to the points at hand here.

the metaphor to illumine the agreed upon fact that in basic self-knowledge we do not know "all the features of the content".

They seem to go further, however. Although I may misread them, they seem to suggest that we do not have "access" to the first order thought, and do not know what concept the linguistic community associates with the word "writing". Perhaps there are senses in which these remarks are correct. But they seem to me to be potentially very misleading.

In particular, in basic self-knowledge we have a canonical designation of the thought that is immediately associated with self-conscious thinking of the thought. One has the analog of a proper name for the representational content. And one has sufficient understanding of the content to think with it, not merely refer to it. The person with basic self-knowledge is not in the position of someone referring to words but not knowing what they mean or what concepts they express. Here the comparison to pointing at someone without knowing the person's name or gender seems very inapt. The way we think about the representational content that we self-attribute is the most fundamental way to think about it. It represents the content in terms of its essential nature or kind-name. There is no more basic or essential way to characterize the thought that writing requires concentration than as the thought that writing requires concentration. One uses those very concepts and designates them at the same time. What are lacking at least in basic self-knowledge itself are the associated relations which this mental content must bear to other contents and to other individuative conditions, in order to be the mental content that it is.

The authors correctly emphasize this lack. They state that we lack "an internal, introspective, and reliable path to all aspects of our beliefs about the world". They understate, however, the knowledge of the first-order mental content that is involved in basic self-knowledge. The key point here is that basic self-knowledge is non-inferential. So connections between what is known and other matters is not available to it alone.

Individualism does encourage the mistaken idea that all necessary individuating conditions associated with having concepts or mental representational content are contained within the concepts or mental content. It therefore encourages the mistaken idea that self-knowledge that provides knowledge of concepts or content will yield all necessary individuating conditions associated with concepts or mental content. These ideas contain two mistakes. First, anti-individualism shows that there are necessary individuating conditions that involve relations to matters beyond the mental content—indeed outside the mind and body. Second, authoritative self-knowledge must be strictly distinguished from reflective knowledge about the relations among concepts (or contents) and about the conditions that individuate having concepts (or contents).

It seems to me too much to claim, as the authors do, that basic self-knowledge has little philosophical interest. By itself it establishes the existence of particular thought contents, agents, events, and attitudes. It provides knowledge of the identity of the thought contents and the type of attitude. Alone, it can go no further. But reflection can go further. Some of this reflection can, I think, be apriori. Although one cannot expect a metaphysics from this base that is nearly as ambitious as Descartes', it seems to me that the methodology that he offers—of combining self-knowledge with reflection on the nature of the contents, agent, and states thus known—can yield results of substantial philosophical interest.

7 Reply to Antoni Gomila Benejam, "Thought Experiments and Semantic Competence"

Antoni Gomila Benejam's paper raises an extremely interesting and important issue—how is it possible that the thought experiments prove useful? More specifically, how are we to understand the semantic or conceptual competence that underlies our ability to recognize the application patterns of our concepts on reflection in the twin-earth thought experiments?

A traditional line is that to have the concept one must "implicitly" understand it. Explicit understanding emerges through reflection, which yields a clear and distinct definitional explication of it.

I have criticized this traditional line at almost every point. I believe that it is possible to have concepts without understanding them at all, even implicitly. Animals and young children have perceptual beliefs, hence concepts, but lack any understanding of the concepts. They have a minimal competence in the use of the concepts. Their concepts mark propositional, including inferential, abilities. Understanding requires a reflective or explicational ability, which includes an ability to objectify concepts, an ability which I think animals and young children lack.

Similarly, the cases of dependence on others that Putnam first brought to prominence and the cases of erroneous explicational understanding—such as the arthritis case—indicate that it is possible to have explicational abilities but not be able even on reflection to produce a correct explication.[29] So individuals have concepts without implicit understanding in these cases as well.

Someone who lacks some aspects of correct understanding cannot attain correct explicit understanding through mere reflection. Animals without any understanding, and people with a partially incorrect understanding, could not engage in the relevant thought experiments.

Moreover, where reflection does succeed in yielding better understanding, the success does not in general produce a definitional explication. This is because definitions play only a minor and occasional role in the understanding of concepts.

Even where a simple explication is found (such as chairs are artifacts made or meant for one person to sit upon), there is no internal guarantee that it is complete or correct. It rarely if ever provides a reductive replacement for the concept.

Finally, even experts may not have embedded in their conceptual abilities sufficient material to provide a correct explication, whether definitional or not. This is because of the fundamental point made by anti-individualism that a concept depends in various ways for its individuation on the way objective reality actually is. The similarity conditions that underlie our actual practices may not be knowable except through acquiring additional information.[30] In this respect, anti-individualism provides a genuinely different view of the potential of reflection to provide correct accounts of concepts.

Gomila notes that in my discussion of the linguistic aspect of these matters I distinguish between translational meaning and explicational meaning. He is correct in holding that what I say about these notions requires supplementation if we are to obtain a good account of semantic competence, and of the capacities of reflection through thought experiments to yield deeper understanding of our concepts and meanings.

He is incorrect in holding that I reduce semantic competence to translational meaning or to thoughts like *"arthritis" applies to arthritis*. Gomila quotes a passage from "Wherein is Language Social?" that is incompatible with such a reductive view. I think that there is nothing in what I write that indicates any such reduction.

I have always accepted that semantic competence, like conceptual competence, is a complex, multi-faceted matter. It frequently involves perceptual, recognitional, applicational abilities. It always involves

---

[29] Cf. Hilary Putnam, "Is Semantics Possible?", originally published 1970, reprinted in Putnam's *Philosophical Papers*, volume II (Cambridge, Cambridge University Press, 1975); and my "Individualism and the Mental", op. cit.

[30] On this, see my reply to Steven Davis.

inferential abilities–some deductive, some inductive. It sometimes involves explicational abilities and meta-semantical abilities. One cannot have a concept, or express a meaning, unless that ability is embedded in a nexus of further representational abilities. A concept and a word's translational meaning simply marks the basic representational ability. It certainly does not exhaust the range of abilities that have to accompany that ability in order for it to be what it is.

This view is also incompatible with the position, which Gomila holds that my writings suggest, that semantic/conceptual competence "amounts to" conformity in actual use with social practice. Conformity at most suggests competence. Moreover, I do not reduce this range of psychological or linguistic abilities to the "externalist" conditions that must be present for concept possession, as Gomila suggests I do. The representational abilities involve competencies in the individual that are partly individuated in terms of relations to the environment, but not reducible or replaceable by those relations. A theory of ideas or concepts is definitely not incompatible with my anti-individualism.

There are two reasons why my points in this area have been primarily negative. One is that the massive weight of the implicit-understanding tradition, though criticized by others, is very substantial. Getting free of the picture that I presented at the outset of this reply is no mean philosophical task. The second reason is that the positive story is inevitably much more complex than the traditional account indicates. It varies from one type of concept to another. So at present, I think that we are not in a position to provide a very rich and detailed account of the nexus of abilities that go into having a concept or expressing a meaning. The point of the thought experiments is, however, to begin to suggest large contours in certain maps of representational competence.

So what can be said in short compass about what makes the thought experiments possible? Concepts are not made what they are by understanding them. They are grounded in patterns of first-order usage. The usage has counterfactual implications. So it potentially extends to cases of application which never occur. Implicit in this potential is an ability to recognize the cases if they arise. With sufficient sophistication, commonly through language use, an individual may acquire the abilities to imagine counterfactual cases and to think up explications that are meant to cover all cases or simply to generalize about types of cases to which the concept would be applicable. These latter second-order abilities are epistemically posterior to the first order abilities, even though they may come to accompany the first-order conceptual abilities implicitly.

Much of the ability to test concepts on counterfactual cases depends on empirical knowledge. Knowing that water is a natural kind or that people can use the concept arthritis while misunderstanding it requires either knowledge of others or memory of one's own transition from misunderstanding to understanding. It may be that in some cases particular inferential connections are necessary to having some concepts. Sometimes with sufficient reflection one can come to understand apriori these constraints on minimal conceptual mastery. So understanding as opposed to having the concept of cat probably requires that one believe that if something is a cat it is, if anything, a physical being that occupies space. (I think a child can have a concept of cat before it has any general concept of space, and before it understands anything about the concept.) It may not require that one believe that a cat is, if anything, a mammal or perhaps even an animal.[31]

In mapping the competence associated with thought experiments, it is important, I think, to allow for different levels or types of competence. There is the minimal competence necessary to having the concept. There is the minimal competence necessary to attempting to understand the concept (or term). Such competence might be compatible with having a thoroughly incomplete or mistaken understanding—which might emerge in, among other ways, poor or uncertain explications. There is the competence sufficient to be socially acceptable. There is the competence of the experts in a given community. This might involve being able to provide short explications that no one in the community has improved on. It might also involve being able to persuade others about the application of the concept (or term) in difficult cases. Finally, there is the competence involved in having an ideal or complete understanding of the concept. As noted, this might go beyond what the experts have. It might depend on coming up with new knowledge about the patterns of usage and the environmental relations that fix the nature of the concept.

Post Daltonian atomic theory is an example of a move from an expert's competence (Dalton's) to a competence that encompasses a deeper knowledge of the environmental relations that fix the identity of states marked by the concept. Post Weierstrassian explication of the fundamental ideas of the calculus is an example of a move from an expert's competence (Newton's or Leibniz') to a competence that encompasses a deeper knowledge of the mathematical facts and usage that

---

[31] Cf. Hilary Putnam, "It Ain't Necessarily So", *The Journal of Philosophy* 59 (1962); reprinted in Putnam's *Philosophical Papers*, volume I (Cambridge, Cambridge University Press, 1975)

Newton and Leibniz were relying upon and that fixed *their* concepts as well as those of Weierstrass.[32]

I believe that anti-individualism helps explain why thought experiments are productive. Thought experiments center on cases. It is a range of cases, together with a pattern of usage that includes both a nexus of representational abilities (perceptions, inferences, and so on) and a pattern of relations to the environment or subject matter, that fix the representational content of terms or concepts. These content-fixers contrast with definition, or explication, or implicitly understood meta-rule. Definitions, explications, and meta-rules come later—when they come at all. They come to be understood as fitting the patterns of usage and the cases. We do not always carry such matters around in our minds, just by virtue of having the competence to employ a concept or term. That is why, finding the general principles that summarize conceptual applications is so much harder than recognizing whether a concept or term applies to a particular imagined case. It is also why the principles commonly turn out to be more complex and less obvious than they would have been if they were implicitly embedded in the concepts in such a way that we were being guided by them. Sometimes very general principles do guide. Usually such principles capture a usage and set of thinker-environmental relations that are antecedently in place.

As Descartes emphasized, reflection is very difficult to do well. It is hard to arrive at clear and distinct principles that are associated with our concepts. It requires good judgment. Still, we sometime manage to do it. A deeper account of the psychological and epistemic bases for our success through reflection on thought experiments is very much to be desired.

8 Reply to Carlos J. Moya, "Externalism, Inclusion, and Knowlege of Content"

Carlos Moya's incisive defense of the compatibility of externalism about mind and authoritative self-knowledge raises a number of interesting issues. He sets out the issues in an admirably clear and concise way. I agree with much of what he says. I think that he makes some valuable contributions in the development of compatibilism. His two points against the simple argument for incompatibilism are sharp and telling. He is certainly right that the simple principle that interprets ex-

---

32   This sort of point is developed in my "Intellectual Norms and Foundations of Mind", op. cit.; in "Frege on Sense and Linguistic Meaning" *op. cit.;* and in "Concepts, Conceptions, and Reflective Understanding: Reply to Peacocke"in *Reflections and Replies: Essays on the Philosophy of Tyler Burge, op. cit.*

ternalism in terms of typical causes for an individual is mistaken and too simple. Anti-individualism (or externalism) will not assign a concept to a person purely in view of what sorts of things cause the majority of a person's perceptions. There is room for a person's thinking about gold even though most of what he sees as gold is fool's gold. Moya's discussions of various subsidiary arguments seem to me plausible and right. I think that he is right to hold that deference to the actual community one happens to be in need not be unconditional, and right to emphasize that explicating how a person can take on a switched or twin concept is not as easy as it might first appear.

Moya's defense of compatibilism goes by way of accepting cousins of the transparency principle and accepting a relevant alternatives epistemology for self-knowledge, while arguing that switching or traveling cases cannot put one in the situation where one has two concepts without one's realizing that there are two. I think his ideas interesting, and the difficulty of these issues precludes quick definitive solutions–or in many cases, definitive refutations. I would like to express some reservations about some aspects of his defense of compatibilism.

The conceptual content of an individual's mental states depends on a variety of factors. One factor is the set of paradigms that figure in the individual's acquiring a conceptual content. This factor and others do make it more difficult than many suppose, or than I once supposed, for concepts to switch or change under changing environmental circumstances. Nevertheless, I do not see that these considerations can suffice to block the kind of situation in which an individual acquires a new concept, or undergoes a change in an old one, without being able to realize this from within.

Moya requires that "no new process of learning takes place" in his thought experiments. There seems, however, to be no principled obstacle to such a learning process. For example, the traveler could be told that he is traveling to a new community with a historically different language that has no ties to the old community. He could be instructed to look for small differences. He would be surprised to find that he could not find any differences. Still, there seems no bar to there being differences, or from his learning the meaning of the (twin-earth) words—assuming that he is open to learning the "new" language.

Even without such explicit openness to learning, the phenomenon of a shift in dominant source seems to be one of the features that affects linguistic change and conceptual change. There is no strict line that insures that learning, of a concept or with a word-form, is completed and no change can occur. Although shifts in meaning or content do not occur automatically just through a person's moving, it is clear, I think, that they can occur, even after one term is well learned. Such occurrences can fuel cases for the compatibility issue.

One factor in Moya's case that holds the individual's concept of diamond in place, even though he has moved into a situation in which zircon is the referent of the community's term, is the individual's specially valuing his possession as a diamond. This factor supplements the role of diamonds as paradigm cases in his particular beliefs about the object that he possesses. It does not follow that he fails to learn a new concept (applying to zircon) that might occur in other beliefs that are not so constrained by his past desires to own a diamond.

If a proper emphasis on the role of paradigm cases in learning will not suffice to block examples that provide challenges for compatibilism, we need to consider what motivated this emphasis. Moya cites two motivations. One is to retain the transparency principle. The other is to avoid "crude reliabilism" and to accord with a relevant-alternatives epistemology. Since Moya motivates the transparency principle by the relevant-alternatives epistemology, I shall discuss this latter first.

Moya claims that as it stands, presumably in my work, the inclusion model "draws too heavily on an externalist, reliabilist view of justification... for on this model, justification of self-ascriptions rests on the existence of a mechanism (which the subject need not have cognitive access to) ensuring that the content of first-order thoughts is ipso facto included in the self-ascriptions of those thoughts." Later he writes that his proposal can temper "the crude externalist reliabilism which underlies the inclusion model".

These attributions are simply incorrect. I do believe that depending on the type of knowledge, different sorts of reliability are necessary conditions on being warranted. In the present sort of case, I have never espoused or presupposed anything that is standardly called "reliabilism". In the relevant cases of self-attribution of a representational content, the warrant for getting-right the representational content rests on understanding and on having the capacity to designate the content in understanding it. These capacities guarantee reference, so they guarantee reliable reference. However, the understanding of the self-attribution funds the warrant, not the reliability alone.

Similarly, if we broaden our view to basic self-knowledge—the whole *cogito*-like self-attributions, not simply the part that attributes the content—it is not merely self-verification that underwrites warrant, but the understanding of the self-verification, or the self-evidence, of the self-attributions. *Basic* self-knowledge has internalist justification. Other, non-basic authoritative self-knowledge is warranted through entitlement, an externalist type of warrant. This warrant too depends partly on (minimally) understanding the self-attributed representational content in using it. It depends as well on other cognitive competencies. None of this epistemology is purely reliabilist, as I understand the term.

Productive discussion of the relevant-alternatives epistemology is too complex a matter for this occasion. I believe, however, that such epistemology is not applicable in these cases. In standard cases of relevant alternatives involving perceptual belief, we note that if there had been a relevant alternative object, indiscernible from the perceived object, the belief would have been mistaken. In the case of inclusion self-attributions, the supposed relevant alternatives do not yield mistakes. For if Peter had been judging *I am judging that twater quenches thirst* instead of *I am judging that water quenches thirst*, he would have been making no mistake. His different attribution would have remained true. So the supposed relevant alternative does not threaten the truth of the original thought.

The mistake that is supposed to threaten the original judgment lies in an entirely different sort of judgment–namely, the judgment that the two judgments are the same. This is not an alternative in the sense that relevant-alternatives epistemology standardly appeals to. One needs to explain, in view of the fact that the original judgment (*I am judging that...*) cannot err in what content has been understood, why the vulnerability of an entirely different sort of judgment to error should threaten the warrant or knowledge involved in the original judgment. I believe that it is the comparative judgment that is subject to relevant-alternatives epistemology. The original judgment seems to me no more subject than the judgment, with understanding, that $2+2 = 4$.

I believe that many may be tempted to think that they have produced cases of actual authoritative attributions that are subject to relevant alternatives objections because they do not hold steadily in mind that the authoritative self-attributions involve concurrent understanding of the self-attributed contents–understanding sufficient to think the contents and accurately–and to all appearances knowledgeably–self-attribute them. One could not have a more warranted grip on what the content is, although one could have a fuller understanding of the relation of the content to other contents, and of the conditions that make it the content that it is.

I do think it possible that an individual who had been informed that he had been switched many times over and that he had in his repertoire two distinct concepts might despair of attributing the concept to himself in certain contexts. But I think that if the individual does use one of the concepts in the self-attribution, there is no obstacle derived from the switching to his having self-knowledge. The warrant for the entitlement to self-attribute understood representational content does not derive from an ability to defeat relevant alternatives. It derives from the understanding itself. By hypothesis the individual has sufficient understanding to self-attribute in the canonical redeployed way thoughts with the relevant concepts.

This brings us to Moya's second motivation–the desire to retain the *transparency principle*. The transparency principle, as presented by Dummett and Moya, is really a pair of principles. The first holds that if an individual attaches a meaning to each of two words, he must know whether these meanings are the same. The second holds that an individual must be able to know in a direct, apriori way whether the contents of two thoughts of his are the same or not.

These principles can seem initially attractive. However, they do not seem to me well motivated from relevant-alternatives epistemology, as I have tried to show. They have natural motivations from a certain individualist standpoint: if relations that determined meaning or concepts were entirely contained in the meanings (concepts) themselves, with no dependence on relations to anything broader, it would be tempting to think that by understanding a meaning (concept), one would automatically be in a position to determine identity and difference relations to other meanings (concepts). We are assuming a rejection of individualism.

It seems to me that rather simple reflection should make one doubt the first transparency principle. I attach a meaning to both "physician" and "doctor". Whether they are synonyms depends on a large pattern of use—whether I use them interchangeably in all relevant contexts.[33] I think it obvious that I can be unsure whether the two terms are exact synonyms in my idiolect. This shows, I think, that the knowledge requirement in the first transparency principle is unreasonable. Dummett's truism is not true.

What of the capability-of-apriori-knowledge requirement, as applied to concepts in the second transparency principle? If one can think up a case or an inference that goes differently with respect to two meanings (or concepts), one can conclude that they have different meanings. If one cannot, it may be that one has not come upon a distinguishing case.

---

[33] What counts as a relevant context is itself an extremely complex matter. Must one know what counts as mere rhetorical colouring as opposed to a difference in meaning in order to attach meanings to the words?

Must one be *capable* of finding any difference by reflection alone? That seems to me to depend on whether the patterns and standards of use are transparent to reflection. Concepts mark abilities. They are not items for inner inspection, front and backside. Anti-individualism indicates that patterns and standards of use include matters not necessarily available to immediate inspection. There is the role of dependence on others. There is the role of dependence on the actual character of the environment. I think that one might be incapable by mere reflection of finding a difference between two concepts–or a difference in patterns and standards of use--if one does not know enough.

One can imagine a math novice not being capable, on mere reflection, of knowing that two slightly different concepts that he uses are different concepts, because he does not know precisely what exceptions govern special cases. It seems to me that empirical cases in which an old concept is accompanied by a new concept–whether this be a twin or an amalgam concept–supply such cases, though they seem to me to be rare. An ill-informed individual might use the concept of elm and the concept of beech interchangeably and not be able to tell that they are different concepts except by finding out that they apply to different things. I think that this situation may even arise in the case of experts.[34]

Since we have a fair amount of insight into our patterns of use, we are usually able to reflect and distinguish concepts when they are different. Since mastery of concepts involves mastery of inferences, and since concepts mark epistemic perspectives, we can determine that concepts are different when our inferential associations with them are different.

None of this adds up to the idea that when concepts are different we can always in principle determine the difference if we reflect well enough. Difference in concept is partly a matter of a role in a large pattern of use and standards. When one is reflecting on concepts as objects of reflective, discursive understanding, I see no general reason why sameness and difference should always be transparent to reflection. These matters deserve more discussion.

---

[34] This is one of the main upshots of "Intellectual Norms and Foundations of Mind", op. cit. and "Frege on Sense and Linguistic Meaning", *op. cit.*

9 Reply to Daniel Quesada, "Basic Self-Knowledge and Externalism"

Daniel Quesada argues that in certain circumstances there is a conflict between basic self-knowlege and externalism or anti-individualism. There is a misunderstanding that runs through the paper about my term "basic self-knowledge". Basic self-knowledge is the sort of self-knowledge that is illustrated by variations on the *cogito*. Thus all basic self-knowledge is present and occurrent. Examples of self-knowledge of standing attitudes and of self-knowledge that relies on memory are not cases of basic self-knowledge, in my sense. I characterized basic self-knowledge as not only direct and non-empirical but as authoritative and self-verifying. Many of the cases that Quesada discusses (Kinds 1 and 2 above) are authoritative, direct and non-empirical, but not self-verifying. As far as I can see, however, this misunderstanding does not affect the main points of the paper.

There are two main points. One derives from Macbeth's argument: (A1) I believe that *that dagger* (in front of me) is bloody; (A2) If x believes that *that dagger* (in front of him) is bloody, then the environment of x contains *that dagger* (that dagger in front of him); (A3) My environment contains *that dagger* (the dagger in front of me). Quesada thinks that Macbeth has reasoned validly to a false conclusion. He holds that the externalist cannot deny (A2) and must deny (A1). He holds that Macbeth does not understand a thought well enough to think one. He thinks that in the absence of a dagger for Macbeth to refer to, Macbeth lacks a perceptual-demonstrative concept. He appeals to Evans' view in holding that although Macbeth has attempted a thought, he has "failed to engage in one at all". So Macbeth's initial self-attribution (A1) is false. So Quesada concludes that self-knowledge can be undermined by externalist considerations in certain contexts.[35]

I believe that this Evans-like rejection of the view that Macbeth "engages" in a thought is deeply misguided. Psychological explanation

---

[35] In defending this view of (A1) Quesada notes that direct-reference theorists might deny that there are such things as perceptual-demonstrative concepts. He mistakenly cites me as a "very good representative of the view that the relation between thought and individual objects is fundamentally non-conceptual". I have consistently held that thought relates to individual objects only through concepts purportedly applying to the objects. It is just that in many cases, there are also irreducibly demonstrative-like applications that are representational or intentional elements in the thought but that are non-conceptual; and such cases, successful reference requires non-intentional (or non-representation) relations, commonly causal relations, between the demonstrative application and the object.

and epistemology, as well as common sense, require that Macbeth continues thinking thoughts despite his illusion of a dagger. I think it simply unacceptable to hold that Macbeth does not think any thought, full stop. The idea that he is thinking along and then fell out of thinking just because of a failure of demonstrative reference, accompanied by hallucination or perceptual illusion, is one that only a philosopher in the grip of a misguided theory could come upon.

Macbeth does fail to refer to anything. (A3) is false or truth-valueless, because (A1) is false or truth-valueless, inasmuch as *that dagger* is taken to produce a *de re* self-attribution, with successful reference to a dagger. Macbeth takes it that way, of course. Under normal construal, "*that dagger*" is used referentially in (A2). That is, if (A2)'s antecedent and consequent are to be true, then "*that dagger*" must have a referent. In such a case, if (A2) is true, it does not link well with (A1) to produce a good argument. For *that dagger* in (A1) lacks a referent. Insofar as *that dagger* in (A2) does not have a definite reference, its antecedent is false or truth-valueless. So either way, combination with (A1) (which is false or truth-valueless) cannot yield (A3). In what follows, I will discuss the matter on the assumption that *that dagger* can be used in Macbeth's thought even though it fails to have a referent (a re). It fails to have a referent even in contents that are *attributed* to Macbeth–attributed by us or by Macbeth.

In considering Macbeth's psychology and epistemology, one must consider Macbeth's point of view without assuming that he is infallible in the application of his demonstrative-governed thought-elements. I think it obvious that Macbeth thinks thoughts that purport to pick out individual objects but fail. In attributing such thoughts, we have to disengage the attribution from the presumption of successful demonstrative reference. So a correct self-attribution by Macbeth would be along the line:

(A1') I believe *that dagger is bloody* .

Macbeth thinks this second-level thought (A1') even in the absence of an actual referred-to dagger. Macbeth believes and applies the first-level propositional *representational* content *that dagger is bloody*. He applies it on the particular occasion with the mistaken presumption that there is a dagger in front of him. The representational thought content *that dagger is bloody* (tokened and applied in that context) is false or truth-valueless. Macbeth's first-level belief is false or truth-valueless (the thought-content *that dagger is bloody*, tokened and applied on that particular occasion). His second-level self-attribution of that content is, however, true. Macbeth's (A1') is true. The self-attribution is direct, non-empirical, authoritative and knowledgeable.[36]

Although (A1') is not an expression of *basic* self-knowledge, the argument could be recast using a *cogito*-like self-attribution involving a non-referring demonstrative-governed singular element in thought. Parallel conclusions could be drawn. For example, we can imagine Macbeth thinking: I am now hereby thinking that that dagger is bloody. I believe that understood so as not to presume with Macbeth that his singular element *that dagger* is referentially successful, Macbeth's self-attribution of representational content, with a token application of *that dagger*, is self-verifying and infallible, not merely authoritative. Of course, the thought that he self-attributes is false or truth-valueless.

(A1') is true. But the appropriate analog of (A2) is false:

(A2') If x believes *that dagger is bloody* (where there may or may not be a successful reference with x's application of *that dagger* putatively of a dagger in front of him), then the environment contains a dagger in front of x.

(A2') is obviously false. Anti-individualism or externalism is certainly not committed to the truth of anything like (A2'). It is not committed to the view that if a demonstrative-governed singular element in thought is to exist, it must succeed in referring. I have consistently rejected this view. So Macbeth cannot reason validly from his authoritative self-knowledge, expressed in (A1'), to the existence of a dagger in front of him.[37]

Anti-individualism is primarily concerned with the effects of environment-mind *patterns* of interaction and their effect on types of representational state. The representational state types are what they are because of a background of causal and representationally successful interactions between individuals (or cognitive systems) and the environment. The idea that this view carries over without qualification to token applications of demonstrative elements in particular contexts is mistaken. Here I shall not develop my views about demonstrative elements in thought. Suffice it to say that the relations between representa-

---

[36] Authority reaches only to the intentional or representational contents of attitudes (and the type of attitude), not to the *res* or referents of elements, even demonstrative elements, in those contents. Cf. "Individualism and Self-knowledge", *op. cit.*, note 8, where I write, "Mistakes about the *res* in de re judgements are not counterexamples to the claim that basic cogito-like judgements are self-verifying (hence infallible)." Macbeth's self-attribution (A1') is not basic self-knowledge, and is not self-verifying or infallible. But it is authoritative, and it does, I believe, count as self-*knowledge*.

[37] Cf. the beginning of "Other Bodies", *op. cit.* Cf. also "Belief De Re", *op. cit.*

tional state types, typed by concepts, and particular instances of representational states that involve token applications of demonstrative-like
elements in thought, are complex and subtle.

I am more sympathetic with Quesada's handling of his second main
point. Anti-individualism itself does not claim to be apriori–only to
state necessary truths. I believe that some aspects of anti-individualism
are apriori. Some are empirical. Anti-individualism is not committed to
the view that it is necessary (much less apriori) that in order to think
thoughts that specify water or mercury as such, there must be water or
mercury to interact with.[38] When we cite a person's interaction with
mercury, either through perception or through interlocution, as a natural
basis for the person's having a concept of mercury, we are assuming
empirical background knowledge that mercury in fact exists. A chemist
could have a mercury concept in a world in which mercury does not
exist, if there is enough else in the chemist's theory to ground the concept. For example, if the chemist had a mastery of where mercury
would fit into the periodic table, given that he had experimentally interacted with other elements, the chemist could have a concept that would
apply to mercury if there had been any in his world. Apriori arguments
for the existence of mercury (or water) are certainly to be regarded as
hopeless. Anti-individualism is not committed to them. On these
points, I appear to be in agreement with Quesada.

As I noted, I think that some elements of anti-individualism are
apriori. I think that apriori arguments for the existence of physical objects (where particular types of physical objects are not specified) cannot be ruled out as hopeless in advance. Such arguments were a fundamental ambition of anti-sceptical arguments in the rationalist tradition.
I think that such arguments are still worth developing. Of course, it is
also not immediately obvious, antecedent to their being given, that such
arguments will work. Since we do have empirical warrant for our belief
in physical objects, it is compatible with anti-individualism to hold, as
Quesada apparently does, that the only warrant for beliefs involving the
concept *physical object* is an empirical warrant. I think that we do have
such empirical warrant. Whether we have further warrant is a deep and
difficult question.

---

[38] Cf. "Other Bodies", *ibid*, last pages.

10 Reply to Manuel Liz, "Intentional States: Individuation, Explanation, and Supervenience"

Manuel Liz' paper comments negatively on the widely perceived importance of anti-individualism. He sees philosophy of mind as exaggerating the consequences that non-individualist individuation of mental states has for issues regarding supervenience. I prefer not to comment on philosophy of mind as a whole. I think, however, that some of Liz' sound points bear less on my views, and those of many others, than he suggests. This is because the only doctrine of individualist supervenience that he specifically formulates is very different from mine and that of many others. He alludes to other more standard formulations near the end of his paper. I do not see that his argumentation connects specifically to any of these more standard formulations.

Liz initially takes an individualist view of supervenience to be the following doctrine:

(S1) Something non-intentional must happen inside our bodies when we are thinking, and...different things must happen inside our bodies when we have different thoughts

This is the only specific formulation of an individualist supervenience doctrine in the paper. Liz calls this a "trivial" claim. I would agree that it is an extremely unambitious claim. (S1) simply denies that an individual can undergo a change in an occurrent thought that he or she thinks, without there being a non-intentional (or non-intentionally described) physical change in the individual.

I suppose that only the strongest, most separatist form of Cartesian dualism would deny (S1). I am inclined to accept (S1). I think it obvious that if one froze an individual and moved him to another environment, there could be no change in the individual's thoughts. New thought happenings would require new mental events, which I presume would require new underlying physical events. Since any new thought event type in an individual entails a new thought token, no new thought event *types* could emerge unless the individual were unfrozen and allowed to interact with the new environment. In order for changes to occur in the thought types that are available to the individual, the individual would perhaps have to interact with the new environment at great length and in very complex ways.

(S1) is not what is usually meant by individualistic supervenience. Supervenience is usually taken to bear on state (or property) types, not simply on token events. Moreover supervenience is usually not taken to bear merely on change in the history of the individual thinkers. It is usually taken to bear on possibilities in the abstract.

A stronger individualistic supervenience thesis that concerns state as well as event types, but continues to focus on change within a given individual's history (in a given possible world) is:

> (S2) Given the physical history of an individual with thoughts up to time t1, and given that there is some new mental state, representational property, or event in that individual at time t2, then that new state (etc.) is necessarily fixed by some change in the physical state (etc.) types in the body of the individual between t1 and t2. More generally, given the physical history of an individual's internal physical state and event types up to any given time, the sequence of representational mental state and event types up to that time cannot vary: it is fixed by that internal physical history.

A yet stronger individualistic supervenience thesis that concerns not change in a given individual's history, but possibility in the abstract is:

> (S3) Given a sequence of physical state and event types in an individual's body up to any given time, no individual (in any possible situation) with that sequence could have representational states or events that differ from those of that individual.

(S3), or some close variant, is usually what is meant by individualistic supervenience.

Liz initially proposes (S1). He seems mistakenly to take a denial of (S1) to play a large part in the discussion of anti-individualism. Or else he slides from that thesis to other stronger individualist supervenience theses, which are indeed rejected by anti-individualism. I have never discussed (S1), and have always focused criticism on (S3)–or occasionally (S2).

At any rate, I believe that (S1) is probably true. Hence I do not accept (R), which is the target of much of Liz' criticism:

> (R) The intentional states of a subject cannot be individualistically supervenient on her non-intentional history [where this is, at least initially, interpreted in terms of (S1)] because neither their individuation nor an adequate explanation of those intentional states can be individualistic.

In effect, (R) maintains that anti-individualism entails the rejection of (S1). (R) seems to me false because I accept anti-individualism, but also accept (S1). So I agree with Liz in rejecting (R). I am not sure whether *any* living anti-individualist accepts (R). I think that most of those that I have read have never discussed it. Perhaps someone who thought that anti-individualism involved maintaining that mental events are not in the mind or head would be moved to accept (R). Such a view does not define or even typify anti-individualism.

I have argued in various writings that (S3), in the general form that it is stated, is false. These arguments involve the basic twin-earth cases. I have also given reasons to believe that (S2) is false. These reasons derive from certain cases in which an individual moves to a different "twin" environment and stays there a long time, and engages with the environment in certain ways.

I have sometimes argued for anti-individualism from thought experiments that involve rejection of instances of (S3) that apply to particular mental states. What are the logical relations between anti-individualism and (S3)?

Anti-individualism is a view about the nature or individuation of mental states. It holds that the natures of certain representational mental state- and event types of individuals are necessarily dependent on relations between the individual (or his mental systems) and an environment beyond the boundaries of the individual's body.

Rejection of (S3) strongly supports anti-individualism. But there is no entailment. A Cartesian dualist could deny (S3) on the ground that the nature of mental states is completely independent of any relations to physical or environmental reality. The dualist could then consistently maintain individualism (at least as far as these considerations go). I am assuming here that the failures of (S3) are better explained by anti-individualism. I believe that this assumption can be argued for effectively. So rejection of (S3) supports anti-individualism but does not entail it.

Anti-individualism does not logically entail rejection of (S3). If the natures of physical states and events in an individual's body were just as dependent on an environmental history as the individual's mental states, then it might be that both (S3) and anti-individualism could be true. The very environmental relations that fix the nature of the mental types could also fix the nature of the individual's physical state types.[39]

There are other ways in which mental states in a particular domain might be very tightly connected with both the underlying physical states and the relations between the environment and the mental states. If these physical necessities were also metaphysical necessities–an issue on which I am sceptical but agnostic–, then anti-individualism could be true for those mental states. And the instance of (S3) that applies to those particular mental states could be true as well.

---

[39] For example, Davidson's view of the individuation of events, including physical events, would make failures of local supervenience (in the sense of (S3)) impossible but would be compatible with anti-individualism. Cf. Donald Davidson, "The Individuation of Events" in *Essays in Honor of Carl G. Hempel*, Rescher ed. (Dordrecht, D. Reidel Publishing Company, 1969); reprinted in Davidson's *Essays on Actions and Events* (Oxford, Clarendon Press, 1980). I do not accept this view of the individuation of events, but I do not regard it as logically false.

In some of my earlier writings, I did not distinguished with sufficient sharpness rejection of (S3) and anti-individualism, although I have always been aware of the distinction. I think that anti-individualism is the deeper doctrine. With respect to some types of representational states, particularly perceptual states and some perceptual beliefs, anti-individualism is best argued for independently of trying to establish the failure of a relevant instance of (S3).

Liz distinguishes between individualistic individuation and individualistic explanation. He cites quotations from my work to support the distinction. I regarded these quotations as expressing a single doctrine, not distinct doctrines. Liz quotes the following passage of mine as an expression of what is meant by an "individualist view of explanation":

> ...an individual's being in any given intentional state...can be explicated by reference to states and events of the individual that are specifiable without using intentional vocabulary and without presupposing anything about the individual subject's social or physical environments.

Here I meant by "can be explicated" *can be correctly explicated.* And I regarded explication as a statement of necessary conditions that bear on what it is to be in a given intentional or representational state. In Liz' attribution of quotations to me, he slips from my term "explication" to the very different term "explanation". Explanation is something psychology does. Explication is what one strives for in reflection on one's usage and in the thought experiments.

I want to enter two further reservations about Liz' exposition of my anti-individualism (which I take to be about natures or, equivalently, correct individuation). One has to do with the relation between my arguments for anti-individualism and issues about linguistic attribution. He correctly notes that some of my early arguments proceeded from (a) some remarks about the nature of *attribution* of mental states in that-clauses to (b) the nature of the mental states. I continue to believe that these arguments have some force. They were never the primary arguments, however. I would make them much less prominent now if I were to rewrite the articles.

The primary arguments have to do with the possibility of having concepts, or certain types of thoughts or perceptions, in various circumstances. The primary arguments do not make reference to linguistic attribution at all. These primary arguments can be found in all the early papers. The emphasis on language in the original papers was largely motivated by a desire to clarify my view in an intellectual context that tended to think of all philosophical issues through the lens of language use.

The second reservation is that the arguments I did give from linguistic attribution were not based on general principles but on judgments regarding particular cases. Liz attributes to me the claim that "different references in [oblique occurrences of terms embedded in that-clauses] always entail different mental contents [attributed via the that-clauses]". I have never made or believed this claim. I think that mentalistic attributions with that-clauses are carried out for many purposes other than to specify or indicate the contents of the relevant mental states. I have believed this since before I wrote "Individualism and the Mental", although my appreciation of how deeply ordinary attributions and description of mental contents can diverge has deepened over the years. So I agree with Liz' point that often we cannot go simply from differences of the references of terms embedded in that-clauses, and used obliquely, to the attribution of different mental contents. The cases he describes seem to me to be to the point. In fact, some of them are cases that I myself have pointed to in my work on switching between earth and twin-earth.

All the arguments from linguistic attribution involve judgment. All enter special factors in the cases that are described. These special factors were meant to head off the sorts of objections that Liz invokes against the oversimplified general principles that he criticizes. So although Liz' objections usually seem correct, they are not applicable to my thought experiments or to the way I argue from them. (See, for example, his footnote 5.)

Liz' diagnosis of my anti-individualism in terms of a reliability model of content- determination is out of keeping with my view of what fixes content. Content can be fixed by causes that do not at all reliably cause the use of a word or mental state. Unsuccessful references can outnumber successful references. Causal and referential reliability are indeed common. They are not the root ideas in anti-individualism. The explications of the role of individual-environment relations in determining the nature of mental states are more complex. This is a point that has been discussed elsewhere in my replies and in other essays in this volume.

While I agree with Liz' criticism of the view that there is some entirely general transition from attributions in that-clauses to the nature of mental content, I am not persuaded by his criticism of the step from mental contents to intentional states. It is, of course, true that mental states are type-individuated not only in terms of their mental (representational) content, but in terms of the type of attitude involved—belief, intention, fear, and so on. But he seems to deny that different mental contents entail different intentional states. In my sense of "mental content" (representational mental content), this entailment holds. I do not find the comparison to dispositions illuminating or apt. The allusion to a "robust relational" conception is too inspecific for me to evaluate.

In the last section of his paper, Liz seems to see his discussion as supporting the view that non-individualist "explanations" presuppose individualist "explanations". I think that here he may mean by "explanation" something different from what I mean by "explication". He appears to mean ordinary psychological explanation. I do not see that anything he says supports such a claim, so understood.

It is sometimes held that ordinary psychological explanations that clearly make use of mental states whose natures are non-individualistically determined, are compatible with other explanations that involve individualistic notions, sometimes characterized as attributing "narrow content". I used to be open to this idea, though I think that compatibility is not presupposition. The idea has come to seem to me increasingly empty of psychological or philosophical interest. Given supervenience of the mental on the whole physical world, there is some function from an individual's physical states and relations to the environment to his mental states. So there are a further set of functions composed of the original function and the individual's physical states. Each of these functions, given a relevant environmental relation, yields an ordinary non-individualist mental state. One might hope to identify or associate mental states that have narrow content with such functions. The existence of such a function for each individual does not insure that there is any psychologically explanatory notion here. Attempts to spell out such a notion have seemed to me more philosophers' games than articulation of a genuine framework for psychological explanation. I believe that psychology and common sense will continue to ignore such initiatives.

Insofar as Liz is concerned merely to hold that there are mental states and events that are broadly where an individual is, and that mental changes in an individual cannot occur without changes within the individual's body, I agree. That sort of "individualism" seems to me correct.

11 Reply to Stuart Silvers, "Individualism, Internalism, and Wide Supervenience"

Stuart Silvers raises interesting issues in his free-ranging discussion of my work and Rob Wilson's work. The discussion revolves around relations between the idea (1) that mental states and events are *internal* in the sense of being inside the individual's mind or inside the individual's brain or body, and the idea (2) that mental states have intrinsic or *essential* properties that do not supervene on the individual's brain or body.

Silvers, Wilson, and I all seem to agree in rejecting a direct inference from (1) to the negation of (2). We also seem to agree that no argument from local causation to individualism–or from local causation to the insistence on the supervenience of mental states types on physical state types within an individual's body--has succeeded. I believe that anti-individualism shows that these inferences are counter-valid.[40]

There are, however, difficult and interesting issues about these notions of internality and essence. Let me start with the notion of internality. At one point, Silvers associates me with Putnam's slogan that meanings (and perhaps by extrapolation, mental states) are not in the head. I do not accept Putnam's reasons for his slogan, and am not committed to any analog of it.[41] I think that meanings are abstract, and probably not anywhere. I think that mental states and events are located broadly where the individual who has them is. I think that there are epistemic perspectival reasons and action-theoretic reasons as well as causal-explanatory reasons for holding this, and for holding that there is some point, properly qualified, to taking mental states and events to be where the relevant individual is.[42] I believe further that a materialist who holds that mental state—and event—tokens are somehow made of brain events or states could consistently accept anti-individualism. A state or event can be necessarily individuated through relations to factors outside the individual without itself being outside the individual.

The reason why I have been reticent about asserting the negation of any analog of Putnam's slogan is that I think that such assertions are commonly taken to be ringing affirmations of materialism. I think that the notions of location and internality have a more qualified and nuanced application to mental states and events than they do to physical events. And I think that the neural properties that underlie at least higher level cognitive processes play relatively little role in psychologi-

---

[40] Cf. my "Individuation and Causation in Psychology,", *op. cit.,* and "Mind-Body Causation and Explanatory Practice," in *Mental Causation,* Heil and Mele eds.(Oxford, Oxford University Press, 1992).

[41] Cf. "Other Bodies", *op. cit.*

[42] A neglected reason that is relevant here is that most thoughts have demonstrative elements. Token applications of demonstrative elements in actual thoughts are commonly acts attributable to the individual, or else events in his perceptual subsystems. It is hard to see these acts or events as not located broadly where the individual is. This is especially so because many of these token applications in perceptual contents mark a perspective from a point of view within space.

cal explanation. Slogan mongering in this area—in either direction—tends to contribute to crudification of philosophy rather than to progress.

Silvers seems to be sceptical of the notion of an individual thinker. I do not share this scepticism. I think that epistemic, explanatory, action theoretic, and moral considerations all conspire to make such a notion deep and important. However, sometimes it appears that all that he means by denying that mental states are in the head is that mental state contents "are individuated by the satisfaction of external truth conditions". With this, I certainly agree. He further holds that the "mechanisms implicated in having and acquiring belief content" are "external to the physical boundaries of the individual whose belief it is". I agree with this also.[43]

The discussion of "wide computationalism" seems to me to need more specificity. I see no sound reason for thinking that a computational system that includes elements outside an individual need call into question the "integrity and autonomy" of individuals. Silvers presents no specific considerations that tell in this direction.

One could certainly have a broad computational system that includes elements outside the individual. I believe, however, that only individuals (thinkers or perceivers) and groups of them—and perhaps institutions which have individuals as their agents—can be attributed representational or intentional states. Those parts of the physical world that are independent of such entities do not represent anything. The computations might include other factors outside individual thinkers or perceivers that are not intentional or representational. Insofar as they operate on the contents of intentional or representational states, these states seem to be firmly associated with individuals in most ordinary psychological explanations. I do think, however, that there is scope for a "wide computationalism" that operates on the contents of mental states that include different individuals in a group, or contents shared by different individuals in a group. Most, enterprises of this sort have seemed to me to be speculative, or ideological, rather than fruitful. There are, however, already exceptions. The future may grant us a genuinely explanatory social psychology.[44]

---

[43] The criticism, and the attendant remarks about activity and passivity, that he attributes to Clark and Chalmers are based on a shallow misunderstanding of my view–a misunderstanding about "typical causes" that has been discussed in other replies and papers in this volume. I am not sure whether Silvers endorses this criticism and those remarks.

[44] A compelling, albeit simple, example of such an enterprise may be found in the excellent book Edwin Hutchins, *Cognition in the Wild* (Cambridge, Mass., MIT Press, 1995).

At the end of his paper, Silvers challenges a "non-individualist inference from the psychologically explanatory relevance of the wide supervenience base (historical and relational properties) to a taxonomic miscellany (or hodgepodge) of psychological kinds". He goes on to challenge an inference from taxonomies for the purpose of explanation to the conclusion that the taxonomized kinds are natural kinds. He is presumably particularly suspicious of the latter inference if the taxonomized kinds form a hodgepodge.

In the abstract, these challenges seem plausible. I believe that as applied to my non-individualist views, they are not forceful. To begin with the first: Anti-individualism is not committed to a hodgepodge of psychological kinds. One might think that it would be thus committed if one conflated the conditions in environment-individual relations that are necessary for the individual to be in an intentional or representational psychological state with the psychological kinds themselves. The environmental-individual relations are not only complex, various, and messy. They also tend to take the form of complex disjunctions. One can have a concept of mercury either through perceptual interaction with mercury and acquiring a few background beliefs about mercury, or through entering into dialog with others who have a concept of mercury and acquiring perhaps other background beliefs, or through theorizing in such a way as to locate mercury in a grid of relations with other elements, or perhaps in other ways. This disjunction is hardly very specific, and it certainly does not look like a scientific explanatory kind. In fact, the "historical and relational properties" are not the psychological kinds in terms of which psychological explanation, and epistemic evaluation, are carried out. The representational states in terms of which such explanation is carried out seem to me to form natural relations to one another. They yield a grid of propositional and representational relations that form a fine basis for explanation. They are not in any evident sense a hodgepodge. Until the challenge of the first inference is clarified, I am inclined to see it as inapplicable to my own anti-individualism.

The second inference does seem to me to be ill-advised if applied indiscriminately. This, for the reasons that Silvers gives. Examples of bad explanatory enterprises—astrology, for example—leap quickly to mind. It seems to me clear that ordinary psychological explanation in everyday life—and in perceptual, cognitive, and developmental psychology—cannot be reasonably compared to such deplorable misadventures. The propositional-attitude format for such explanation has been in place for many centuries. It forms the backbone of our understanding and knowledge of humankind. It has taken on explanatory specificity and even some depth and rigor in some areas of cognitive and perceptual psychology. This sort of explanatory practice is a good guide to genuine kinds. Whether one calls them natural, psychological, or simply real, I think that it is unreasonable to philosophize as if accepting their reality is still a matter of conjecture or misadventure.

Index

Meaning, Basic Self-Knowledge and Mind: Essays on Tyler Burge.
María J. Frápolli and Esther Romero (eds.).
Copyright © 2003, CSLI Publications.